THE HIDDEN DIMENSIONS OF OPERATION MURAMBATSVINA

THE HIDDEN DIMENSIONS OF OPERATION MURAMBATSVINA

EDITED BY
MAURICE VAMBE

WEAVER
W
-PRESS-

Weaver Press
P O Box A1922
Avondale
Harare
Zimbabwe
www.weaverpresszimbabwe.com

Published in South Africa
by the
Africa Institute of South Africa
P.O. Box 630
Pretoria, 0001

The publishers gratefully acknowledge
the financial assistance of the
Konrad Adenauer Foundation, Harare,
towards the publication of this book

ISBN 978 1 77922 071 4 (Weaver Press)
ISBN 978 0 79830 2166 (Africa Institute)

Printed and bound in South Africa by Fingerprint Co-operative

CONTENTS

Introduction
Rethinking Citizen & Subject in Zimbabwe

Maurice Taonezvi Vambe

The post-colonial state of Zimbabwe is in the throes of economic, political and cultural crisis. One of the symptoms of this crisis manifested itself between May and July 2005, when the government launched Operation Murambatsvina, described in official circles as a crackdown by government agents on vendors; innocent men and women doing their business. The crisis of legitimacy characterising the present political leadership has a far longer history than critics have been prepared to concede. The making of Operation Murambatsvina was initially embossed in the British colonial system in Rhodesia. Colonialism's methods of stripping Africans of their natural and material resources are well documented. Africans guided by the Zimbabwe African National Liberation Army (ZANLA) and Zimbabwe People's Revolutionary Army (ZIPRA) fought colonialism until 1980 when Zimbabwe became an independent country under the principle of majority rule, and one person one vote. However, ZANLA and ZIPRA did not 'provide space for dissenting voices to emerge from within the political movements' (Raftopoulos 2004, 1). Political scientist Eldred Masunungure quotes the then Prime Minister of the newly created Zimbabwe, Robert Mugabe, now President of the Republic of Zimbabwe, addressing the ZANU(PF) Congress held in 1984, saying that during struggle: 'This exercise [of crushing ZIPA and its Vashandi influence] was followed by a politicisation programme in the camps. We warned any person with a tendency to revolt that the ZANU axe would fall on their necks: *Tino tema nedemo* ['We will axe you'] was the clear message (2004:151).'

In 1984, when the prime minister was reported to have said that dissent would be dealt with severely, this message was not merely a metaphor. Between 1981 and 1986, the government sent the Fifth Brigade into parts of Matabeleland and Midlands provinces to pacify those perceived to have been sympathising with dissidents; as many as 20,000 lives were lost. The myth of Zimbabwe in the early 1980s being a successful developmental state overlooks the brutality of Gukurahundi. In the 1990s the government faced massive discontent from workers, students and academics who felt that its economic policies were hurting the people. The consistent response of the government was to suppress the critics: tear gas was used against university students and civil society leaders. According to Hammar and Raftopoulos (2003, 10) the watershed came in February 2000, when the government-sponsored constitution was rejected by a majority vote as people resented the 'unilateral changes made to the final draft by president Mugabe and ZANU(PF) inner circle' (p. 9).

This success of the 'No' vote by the majority of Zimbabweans during the 2000 constitutional referendum was the first politically open attempt at questioning ZANU(PF)'s quest for hegemony. The opposition Movement for Democratic Change (MDC) had been born a year earlier, and made a strong showing in the 2000 parliamentary elections. A battle-line had been drawn and the road to Operation Murambatsvina was mapped out. Raftopoulos (2003, 219) suggests that in order to make up lost ground, ZANU(PF) turned to an ill-conceived land grab, the intimidation of opposition members and arrest of innocent protesters, and presided over the disappearance of political foes: 'the authoritarianism of the ruling party [was] expressed in the assault on central and local government structures, as a precondition for the re-assertation of ZANU(PF) political dominance'.

After winning a controversial[1] election in March 2005, the government embarked on Operation Murambatsvina to clean up the country of vendors, flea-market traders and foreign-currency dealers, and to destroy illegally built structures.[2] The ferocity of the operation has continued to baffle many. Some say its swiftness was indicative of a government skilled in ruling through 'operations'.[3] Others say the decision to proceed without exploring dialogue with the people was itself an expression of power inflation[4] on the part of the authorities. Some suggest that the authorities are haunted by power daemons and that the government itself has become one.[5] And yet others argue that when a govern-

---

1   In March 2005 ZANU(PF) won parliamentary elections which were endorsed as free and fair by Southern African Development Community (SADC) and African Union (AU) observers. However, the opposition, Movement for Democratic Change (MDC) felt cheated and took the case to the Zimbabwean Court. Although MDC did not win, the political party had registered their dismay over the elections. The European Union (EU) also produced a report in which they argued that the elections were not free and fair. The point being that in a 'democratic' election there should be some recognisable 'threshold of acceptability' by those taking part in the elections. This fundamental principle was not fulfilled in the case of Zimbabwe, although ZANU(PF) won the elections. This is not to say that elections are democratic when ZANU(PF) loses. It is to say the elections were dogged with some irregularities that anybody who is patriotic and cares about Zimbabwe should acknowledge so that these are not repeated in future. Otherwise critics may run the danger of legitimising a political culture of impunity. That is not good for Zimbabwe.
2   See the speeches of the Mayor of Harare, Sekesai Makwavarara, in Tibaijuka, A. 2005. *Report of the fact finding mission to Zimbabwe to assess the scope and impact of Operation Murambatsvina by the UN Special Envoy on Human Settlements Issues in Zimbabwe.* New York: United Nations.
3   See Rupiya, M. 2005. 'Zimbabwe: Governance through military operations', *African Security Review* 14 (3): 117–18.
4   Arrighi, G. 2005. 'Hegemony unravelling: I', *New Left Review* II (32) (March–April): 23–80.
5   See Ngugi wa Thiong'o. 2006. *Wizard of the Crow: A novel.* New York: Pantheon Books.

2

ment begins to rule by military operations, this is a symptom of powerlessness; it is governance under stress.[6] Operation Murambatsvina forced the people of Zimbabwe to rethink the very idea of citizen and subject.[7] The concept of citizenship as enshrined in the Zimbabwean Constitution is limited to privileges attached to natality. Murambatsvina showed that citizenship is a social construct; that it is brittle and can be subject to revision, especially in contexts of political contestations. Murambatsvina was also an assault on liberal notions that separate citizen from subject. Citizens have rights, but they can be subjected to the rule of those in power. Citizens possess subjectivities to defer or resist subjection, or being turned into abject beings – human dirt, to use the language of Murambatsvina. During the course of disciplining a runaway democracy,[8] Operation Murambatsvina produced intense narratives of internal power dynamics that many people in Zimbabwe may have known about, but took for granted.

Murambatsvina targeted people in both rural and urban areas; ZANU(PF) supporters, MDC supporters and the non-aligned. This sent a strong message to many Zimbabweans, which is that in the course of protecting power, a chicken, a goat, a cow and even a human being can be sacrificed.[9] More was at stake than simply dividing the masses in terms of ZANU(PF) and the MDC. Murambatsvina marked the authoring of a new political *(im)morality*, where violence is instrumentally stepped-up to foil the manoeuvres of internal enemies. If the MDC could be described as the external enemy of ZANU(PF), through which ZANU(PF) is fighting a proxy war with Britain, the coloniser, whose kith and kin lost in the land war, the same MDC is simultaneously an internal enemy threatening to wrest power from a party that perceives itself as *Rain, Freedom* and *Zimbabwe*.[10]

For ZANU(PF), the worms of worry that presaged Operation Murambatsvina were also the internal fractions within ZANU(PF) itself. The 'Nhari and Badza' syndrome that had been enacted and ruthlessly suppressed was one of the probable reasons for the ruling party to adopt force through Operation

---

6   See Cohen, M.G. and S. Clarkson. 2004. *Governing under stress: Middle powers and the challenges of globalization*. London and New York: Zed Books.

7   See Mahmood, M. 1996. *Citizen and Subject: Contemporary Africa and the legacy of late colonialism*. Kampala: Fountain.

8   See Abrahamsen, R. 2000. *Disciplining democracy: Development discourse and good governance in Africa*. London and New York: Zed Books.

9   In *Arrow of God* (London: Heinemann, 1967), Chinua Achebe uses the metaphor of sacrifice showing that small problems demand small sacrifices, but big problems can even demand that human blood be shed. In Zimbabwe today it seems that the political stakes are so high that the authorities may have to shed blood to stay in power.

10 The irony of today's Zimbabwe leadership is captured in Charles Mungoshi's *Waiting for the Rain* (London, Heinemann:1975) in which Lucifer – whom the Mandengu family regard as the 'rain' to bring freedom to family (Zimbabwe) – actually regrets being born in the country and promises that if he ever leaves it, he will never come back again. The analogy is that people in Zimbabwe continue to show loyalty to a political party that ruined their businesses during Operation Murambatsvina. It is a case of misplaced trust in a government that no longer trusts itself.

Murambatsvina as a dramatisation of the philosophy of 'might is power'.[11] The 'war' of manoeuvre was fought in the backyard of the houses of the masses while the raging war of position was meant to take place in the minds of ZANU(PF) internal foes.[12] In the run-up to the 29 March elections of 2008, a new counterveiling force from ZANU(PF) is represented by Dr Simba Makoni, former Mugabe Minister of Finance, who is challenging President Robert Mugabe for the country's presidency. Dr Makoni has argued that the top leadership of ZANU(PF) – apparently referring to President Mugabe – must be defeated in the coming elections if Zimbabwe is to be pulled out of the political and economic intensive unit care where the country is now. A combination of these factors offers a more credible explanation than conventional postcolonial arguments that ascribe evil, vice and a tendency to excess and lack of proportion to leaders when they deal with their people, as if these qualities are irredeemable and inherent, and that their entire oppressive machinery cannot be dislodged.[13]

Understanding the phenomenon of Operation Murambatsvina has largely remained hidden, even when the physical acts of destroying people's properties were carried out in the early mornings and during broad daylight. This *hiddenness* of the dimensions of Operation Murambatsvina is apparent, conceptual and practical. The apparentness of the authorities' arguments that Operation Murambatsvina was meant to remove illegal structures, constitutes a mode of hiddenness precisely at the point where the argument is meant to appear as common sense, namely that dirt ought to be removed. After all, a person who harbours dirt is 'dirty'. An 'apparent' argument presented as the 'obvious' is exactly the diet that the people and the international community were fed by Zimbabwe's official media. And the argument made sense in some quarters, for Zimbabwe is not the first country to engage in slum clearance. But apparentness is a form of hiddenness because it diverts people's attention so that they spend time discussing what authorities define as obvious, apparent and logical.[14] Operation Murambatsvina was partially about the removal of dirt, but was mostly about the survival of those in politics; the politicians' own dirt and their failure to deliver on economic promises of decent housing could now be blamed on the victims.

But the hiddenness of the motives of Operation Murambatsvina is dramatised in the open and in a most practical way; if the people have failed to be responsible for the government's dirt, then the authorities should be seen removing it – but at a price. That price is the moral high ground that a government can assume when seen to be concerned not only with removing dirt from the back-

---

11. For a creative account of the Nhari and Badza rebellion during the Zimbabwe armed struggle, see Charles Samupindi's novel, *Pawns*. Harare: Baobab Books 1992.
12. For a detailed understanding of the concepts 'war of position' and 'war of manoeuvre' see Gramsci, A. 1971. *Selection from the prison notebooks*. New York: International Publishers.
13. Mbembe, A. 2001. *On the postcolony*. Berkerley: University of California Press.
14. It is possible to sustain the argument that Operation Murambatsvina was carried out to divert people from thinking about their immediate socio-economic problems. Through Murambatsvina, the government's economic problems were nationalised.

yards of people's houses, but also with dramatising that control by enacting a spectacle of excess. The spectacle of excess resides not so much only in the scope of the destruction, but also in the ordering of homeowners to carry it out themselves. It is realised further, in the squandering of petrol to feed bulldozers to pull down houses in a country suffering from an acute shortage of fuel; and in the deployment of police away from more worthy duties, such as catching thieves. The spectacle of excess was further dramatised in the state's actions of overriding municipal authorities with whom many small traders had a business relationship enforceable by existing by-laws.[15]

At a conceptual level, the hiddenness of the dimensions of Operation Murambatsvina is embedded in the histories of Murambatsvinas that have been carried out in Zimbabwe since colonisation.[16] Operation Murambatsvina also reflects the failed socio-economic and political policies that the government has, since 1980, attempted to hide from view; and its hidden dimensions also represent people's often casual appreciation of the workings of power.[17]

References

Hammar, A. and Raftopoulos, B. 2003. 'Zimbabwe's unfinished business: Rethinking land, state and nation', in Hammar, A., Raftopoulos, B. and Jensen, S. (eds) *Zimbabwe's Unfinished Business: Rethinking Land, State and Nation in the Context of Crisis.* Harare: Weaver Press.

Masunungure, E. 2004. 'Travails of opposition politics in Zimbabwe since independence', in Harold-Barry, D. (ed.) *'Zimbabwe: The past is the future'.* Harare: Weaver Press, pp. 147–92.

Raftopoulos, Brian. 2003. 'The state in crisis: Authoritarian nationalism, selective citizenship and distortions of democracy in Zimbabwe', in Hammar, A., Raftopoulos, B. and Jensen, S. (eds) *Zimbabwe's Unfinished Business: Rethinking Land, State and Nation in the Context of Crisis.* Harare: Weaver Press, pp. 217–41.

— 2004. 'Current politics in Zimbabwe: Confronting the Crisis', in Harold-Barry, D. (ed.) *Zimbabwe: The Past is the Future.* Harare: Weaver Press, pp. 1–18.

---

[15] Statutory Instrument 216 of 1994 allowed people to set up businesses in areas designated by the municipal councils in return for paying a fee. Operation Murambatsvina showed how the government usurped the authority of local government, and also undercut the latter's source of revenue. After rendering the local authorities weak, the government then promised to provide housing in order to be seen as benevolent.

[16] Since 1890, there have been various actions aimed at Africans flocking to the urban areas who were perceived by the colonial authorities as a source of potential trouble. The Government of Zimbabwe has invoked the same laws as those enacted by successive colonial governments.

[17] Although people were given the right to build businesses by the municipal councils under Statutory Instrument 216 of 1994, many did not regularise their plans and so were vulnerable when Murambatsvina descended. To such an extent, the people are also to blame for perpetuating the conditions that made the discourse of Murambatsvina thinkable; this is not a case of blaming the victim, rather of saying that the victim should think beyond the immediate 'politics of the belly'.

PART ONE

HISTORICISING MURAMBATSVINA

1

Historical Antecedents to Operation Murambatsvina

Alois Mlambo

This chapter seeks to contribute towards an understanding of the Murambatsvina phenomenon by, among other things, tracing Zimbabwe's economic experience since independence in 1980, from the period of economic prosperity in the first independence decade, through the lean years of the Economic Structural Adjustment Programme (ESAP), and the unfortunate effects of the country's involvement in the Democratic Republic of Congo (DRC) war and the decision to make large, unbudgeted financial awards to former combatants, to the economic fall-out of the land reform programme. It suggests that, after a promising start in which the country recorded impressive advances in the social sectors, the government was not able to sustain its programmes due to the progressively declining levels of economic performance, especially in the 1990s when there was a noticeable increase in urban poverty and unemployment.

Introduction

After years of bitter armed conflict, Zimbabwe became independent in 1980 full of promise and hope that the future would be one of economic prosperity, political freedom and a generally decent livelihood for all. An African-American magazine, *Essence* (Washington 1989), reported 'a feeling that positive change has only just begun and that even better days are ahead' in Zimbabwe. The magazine noted evidence of popular optimism, referring to 'men and women who once dreamed of living in decent housing – and who now do, or who know that decent housing is at least a possibility'.

The high hopes of 1980 contrast with the despondency and despair of the Zimbabwean people in the new millennium. Runaway inflation, escalating unemployment, declining household incomes, the informalisation of the economy, growing poverty – particularly in the urban areas – and severe housing shortages for the urban poor are stark indicators of just how much the nation's dreams had turned into a collective nightmare in a matter of decades. By 2003, it was being reported that Zimbabwe's housing shortage and economic crisis had 'robbed many urban Zimbabweans of the dream of ever owning their own house'. Indeed, the Ministry of Housing was quoted then as confirming the existence of a national housing backlog of no fewer than 1.5 million units. Harare, the capital, was said to have a waiting list of 300,000 and 'more than 10 informal settlements, where the poor have been forced to reside' (IRIN News, 2003).[1]

Aware of the harsh economic situation in the 1990s, the government relaxed some of the inherited colonial by-laws to permit people to engage more easily in informal business activities. Backyard businesses and flea-market stalls emerged. Shacks were also erected to provide housing for the many 'lodgers' in need of accommodation and to generate income for house owners in the high-density areas. This was meant to cushion those who had lost their jobs because of the shrinking national economy, or whose wages could no longer cater for their needs.

The 'sympathetic' relationship between government and the urbanites did not last. Operation Murambatsvina destroyed what accommodation the urban poor had been able to establish for themselves in the context of the failure of municipalities to provide adequate housing. Murambatsvina also ruined many sources of livelihood by razing flea-market stalls and informal workshops to the ground. By most accounts, it was carried out with a high degree of insensitivity to the rights and needs of those affected and with such ferocious speed that local people began to speak of 'Zimbabwe's tsunami'. When and why did the promise of independence turn into a national nightmare? What went wrong in the two decades of independence to lead to the Murambatsvina disaster?

The decade of promise, 1980–1990

At independence, Zimbabwe inherited a highly developed and diversified economy in which agricultural and mining were complemented by a well-developed manufacturing sector. This economy was, however, based on gross inequalities on the basis of race, characterised by a highly skewed distribution of income, wealth and social services in favour of the white minority and at the expense of the African majority who were largely marginalised and deprived (Saunders 1996).[2] The incoming government adopted a development strategy enunciated in a series of policy documents, including *Growth with equity: Transitional national development plan* and the *First five year national development plan* (Government of Zimbabwe 1982a; 1982b; 1986),[3] which tried to achieve the

---

1   IRIN, 'Zimbabwe: Housing backlog grows in tandem with economic crisis', 22 August 2003.
2   Saunders, R. 'Economic Structural Adjustment Programme (ESAP)'s Fables', *Southern Africa Report Archive*, Vol. 11, No. 4.
3   Government of Zimbabwe, *Growth With Equity: An Economic Policy Statement*. Harare: Ministry

socialist goal of redistribution of wealth while, at the same time, retaining colonial capitalist institutions and practices.

Much was achieved in the first years of independence, particularly with respect to improving the quality of life of the majority. Government invested heavily in education and health. Under the slogans of 'Education for All by 2000' and 'Health for All by 2000', notable achievements were registered in the 'expansion of the education system and improved access to both preventative and curative health services' (Davies 2004).[4] Between 1980 and 1990, the number of primary and secondary schools had increased by 80 per cent, and phenomenal growth was also registered in tertiary and professional education. Such achievements led the United Nations Educational, Scientific and Cultural Organisation (UNESCO) to commend Zimbabwe's educational system as a revolutionary system 'built on modern and enlightened principles of education that take into account the country's particular circumstances, opportunities and constraints' (UNESCO 1987).[5]

Health facilities were expanded through the construction of hospitals and clinics throughout the country and the promotion of primary health care. The World Bank commented on Zimbabwe's achievements in health as 'truly impressive', citing the increase in the country's life expectancy from 55 to 59 years, the highly successful child immunisation and contraception programmes and the notable decline in child and maternal mortality rates (World Bank 1992, x).[6]

This impressive achievement was made possible by the country's booming economy, especially in the first two years of independence, when the economy grew by 21 per cent in real terms, making the Zimbabwean economy the star performer in the region (Riddell 1984).[7] By 1982, however, the country was facing an economic downturn, partly due to the effects of a severe drought in that year which incapacitated agriculture, the backbone of the country's economy, and partly because of world recession that negatively affected exports. Furthermore, the massive levels of investment in the provision of social services were not matched by increased productivity and income generation. Levels of inflation escalated and balance-of-payments problems worsened. To address this situation, the government borrowed from the International Monetary Fund (IMF) in 1983 and found itself having to submit to that institution's conditionalities

(3 ctnd) of Finance, Economic Planning and Development, 1982; Government of Zimbabwe. 1982. *Transitional National Development Plan, 1982/83–1984/85.* Harare: Government Printer; Government of Zimbabwe. 1986. *First Five-year National Development Plan, 1986–1990.* Harare: Ministry of Finance, Economic Planning and Development.

4   Rob Davies, 'Memories of Underdevelopment: A Personal Interpretation of Zimbabwe's Economic Decline'. See http://www.sarpn.org.za/documents/d0001154/P1273-davies_zimbabwe_2004.pdf.

5   UNESCO. 1987. *Proceedings of the General Conference, Twenty Fourth Session, Paris, France.* Paris: UNESCO, October–November.

6   World Bank, 1992. *Financing Health Services.* Washington DC: World Bank, p. x.

7   Riddell, R. 'Zimbabwe: The Economy Four years After Independence', *African Affairs,* Vol. 83, No. 333 (October 1984), 463–76.

whose negative effects were such that the government ended the relationship the following year (Saunders 1996)[8].

Thereafter, economic performance improved, with real gross domestic product (GDP) growth averaging 5.3 per cent from 1985 to 1991 (Tekere 2001). But negative factors had an impact: the South African regime's sabotage of Zimbabwe's institutions and economy as part of that country's destabilisation policy (Mukonoweshuro 1992);[9] the high cost of maintaining armed forces in Mozambique to protect the country's oil pipeline and trade routes from the ravages of Mozambique's civil war (N. Mlambo 1991);[10] Zimbabwe's own fratricidal war of the 1980s, which saw government's Korean-trained Fifth Brigade massacring an estimated 20,000 people in Matabeleland, (CCJPZ/LRF 1997),[11] and mismanagement and corruption in public enterprises (A.S. Mlambo 1997).[12] The country found itself confronted with a stagnating per capita income, as population growth outstripped job creation and the country had to contend with 'under and unemployment, depressed state of investment, supply bottlenecks resulting from foreign exchange shortage and general deterioration in the standard of living of the people' (Kanyenze 199).[13]

The gains made in the 1980s in the social sectors were unsustainable because they were 'based primarily on redistribution rather than growth, and the redistribution was of income rather than assets' (Davies 2004).[14] Indeed, as early as 1985, the government (Government of Zimbabwe 1985, 22) itself had acknowledged that:

[t]he imbalance between material and non-material production, if continued, could have adverse effects on long-run growth performance of the economy and sustained development. The expansion of social services can only be sustained, in the medium and long term, through overall economic expansion at rates well above those attained in the previous five- to six-year period.[15]

In a bid to revamp the economy, government resorted to the IMF/World Bank-sponsored Economic Structural Adjustment Programme (ESAP) in 1990, a decision that was damaging to working people. Government was ignoring the evidence of the devastating effects of the ESAP in other developing countries. The ESAP resulted in 'permanent joblessness, hopelessness and economic

---

8   Saunders, R. 'Economic Structural Adjustment Programme'.
9   Mukonoweshuro, E. 1992. *Zimbabwe: Ten Years of Destabilisation, A Balance Sheet*. Stockholm: Bethany Books.
10   Mlambo, N. 1991. 'The Costs of Reopening Zimbabwe's Trade Routes Through Mozambique'. BA (Hons) Dissertation, Department of Economic History, University of Zimbabwe.
11   CCJP, Catholic Commission for Justice and Peace in Zimbabwe/Legal Resources Foundation. 1997. Breaking the Silence, Building True Peace: A Report on the Disturbances in Matebeleland and the Midlands, 1980 to 1988. Harare: CCJPZ/LRF.
12   Mlambo, A.S. 1997.*The Economic Structural Adjustment Programme:The Case of Zimbabwe*. Harare: University of Zimbabwe Publications, pp. 50-1.
13   Kanyenze, G. 1990. 'Trade liberalisation', in *Social Change and Development*, 3rd Quarter, pp. 12-13.
14   Davies, R. 2004. 'Memories of underdevelopment: A personal interpretation of Zimbabwe's economic decline, http://www.sarpn.org.za/documents/d0001154/P1273-davies.zimbabwe.pdf.
15   Government of Zimbabwe, 1985, 22.

insecurity' for the majority, and also in Zimbabwe mortgaging its economy to foreigners (ZCTU 2001: 8).[16]

The Era of Economic Reform, 1990–2000

The ESAP began with a trade liberalisation programme followed by the standard Structural Adjustment Programme (SAP), the targets of which were spelt out in *Zimbabwe: A framework for economic reform (1991–1995)*:

- reducing the central government budget deficit to 5 per cent of GDP by 1994–95
- achieving an annual growth rate of 5 per cent
- reducing inflation from 20 to 10 per cent by 1994
- monetary policy and financial sector reform; civil service reform to reduce the number of civil servants by 25 per cent and thus reduce the public wage bill
- domestic deregulation and investment promotion, to liberalise investment and deregulate prices
- protection of the poor and vulnerable groups through the social dimensions of adjustment programme (Government of Zimbabwe, 1990).[17]

The targets were to be achieved through:

- removal of price controls
- removal of exchange rate controls
- public sector reforms
- privatisation of public enterprises
- trade liberalisation
- removal of the foreign currency allocation system
- financial sector liberalisation (Ndhela 2003, 134–135).[18]

The impact of the ESAP on Zimbabwean society and the economy was deleterious. The inherent weaknesses of the reform package itself,[19] poor implementation by government and disruptions caused by exogenous factors were complicated by the record drought of 1992–93. As Saunders (1996) points out,

> ESAP's launch in the early 1990s hit the business sector and ordinary Zimbabweans very hard, and the impact ... was greatly exacerbated by the severe drought of the early 1990s. In 1992, after two consecutive poor rainy seasons, the economy contracted by at least 7.5 per cent, with all sectors in Zimbabwe's agriculture-

16 ZCTU, 'Strategy Document for the 1990 Congress', cited in Raftopoulos, B. and Sachikonye, L. (eds) 2001. *Striking Back: The Labour Movement and the Post-Colonial State in Zimbabwe, 1980–2000*. Harare: Weaver Press, p. 8.
17 Government of Zimbabwe. 1990. *Budget Statement, 1991–1996*. Harare: Government Printer, pp. 1–3.
18 Ndhela, D.B. 2003. 'Zimbabwe's Economy Since 1990' in Lee, M.C. and Colvard, K. (eds) *Unfinished Business: The Land Crisis in Southern Africa*. Pretoria: Africa Institute of South Africa, pp. 134–5.
19 For a detailed analysis and critique of the SAP package, see Mlambo, A.S. 1997. *The Economic Structural Adjustment Programme: The Case of Zimbabwe, 1990–1995*. Harare: University of Zimbabwe Publications.

based productive sector affected. At the same time, price control relaxation saw inflation explode and consumer demand shrink, by as much as 30 per cent.[20]

The manufacturing sector, rather than flourishing as expected, actually experienced deindustrialisation, as industries were forced either to downsize or to shut down completely. The textile industry, in particular, faced difficult times due to the influx of cheap imports. As a result, 'following the introduction of ESAP, the share of the textiles sub-sector in manufacturing output declined from 11.3 per cent in 1985 to 7.9 per cent by 1995', while the 'share of the manufacturing sector in GDP declined from a high of 27 per cent in 1992 to 19.2 per cent by 1995'. According to Kanyenze (2006, 8),[2] 'The index of the volume of production for the textiles sub-sector plunged from 100 in 1990 to 59.3 by 1995 (due mainly to trade liberalisation). The index for the clothing and footwear sub-sector fell from 100 in 1990 to 82.9 by 1995. The manufacturing sector dropped from an index of 100 in 1990 to 96 by 1995.'[21]

In October 1994, for instance, it was reported that 87 out of the 280 companies in the textile sector had closed down in 1990; and in the clothing sector 60 companies closed down between 1992 and 1994 (Reserve Bank of Zimbabwe).[22] By 1992, about 25,000 employees had been retrenched. Nearly 300,,000 school leavers were being thrown into the labour market annually at a time when only 10,000 or so new jobs were being created.

Some positive outcomes notwithstanding,[23] the ESAP generally failed to meet its targets and to increase economic growth and reduce poverty. In fact, both the economy and the majority of the people were worse off at the end of the reform programme than they had been before it. In the words of Richard Saunders (1996), whereas the ESAP was 'meant to herald a new era of modernised, competitive, export-led industrialisation', the reality was that Zimbabwe's high-performing economy of the 1980s was so damaged by the reform programme that, after five years of ESAP reforms, 'the country now appears firmly lodged in a quagmire of mounting debt and erratic growth.'[24]

The burden of the now non-performing economy fell on the poor. Studies of the Harare suburbs of Kambuzuma, Tafara and Dzivarasekwa in the 1990s

---

20 Saunders, R. 1996. 'Zimbabwe: ESAP's Fables II', *Southern Africa Report*, Vol. 11, No. 4 (July).
21 Kanyenze, G., 'The Textile and clothing Industry in Zimbabwe', in Jauch, H. and Traub-Merz, R. (eds) 2006. *The Future of the Textile and Clothing Industry in Sub-Saharan Africa*. Bonn: Friedrich-Ebert-Stiftung, p. 8. See also Tekere, M. 'Trade Liberalisation', p. 10.
22 Reserve Bank of Zimbabwe, *Quarterly Economic and Statistical* Review, Vol. 3, No. 6 (March); Vol. 3, No. 12 (December), pp. 7–8.
23 Such as the evident efficiency of some privatised parastatals like Dairiboard Zimbabwe Limited; Cotton Company of Zimbabwe Limited; and the Commercial Bank of Zimbabwe and the emergence of several Black-owned Banks because of financial reforms undertaken under the programme and the reduction of the public wage bill through public service reforms. See Dan B. Ndhela, 'The Zimbabwean Economy since 1990', 136-7.
24 Saunders, R. 1996. 'Zimbabwe: ESAP's Fables II', *Southern Africa Report*, Vol. 11, No. 4 (July).

revealed that many families were being forced to reduce their food intake in the light of mounting inflation (Balleis 1992; Matshalaga 1993a; 1993b).[25] By 1995, a Government of Zimbabwe Poverty Assessment Study was reporting that 62 per cent of the population was living below the Poverty Datum Line (Ministry of Public Service, Labour and Social Welfare 1996, 23),[26] while in 1996, the Zimbabwe Congress of Trade Unions estimated that workers were 38 per cent poorer than in 1980 (ZCTU 1993, 14).[27]

Public expenditure on health care declined by 3 per cent in 1994–95 and produced what came to be known as 'ESAP deaths'. These were deaths of low-income people who could not afford to pay for treatment or for medicines because of cost-recovery policies under the ESAP.[28] In education, most of the gains that the country had made in the 1980s were under threat during the ESAP. Cost recovery policies led to children dropping out of school because parents could not afford the fees.

With de-industrialisation and the shrinking economy came unemployment and the informalisation of the economy, as more and more workers lost their jobs in the formal economy and did whatever they could in the informal sector to survive. Informal economic activities that had existed even under the harsh legislation and enforcement regime of the colonial regime included the tin-smithing activities of the VaPostori groups, shebeens and tailoring. After 1980, with the relaxation of legal controls over the urban population, the informal sector expanded, with municipal authorities often encouraging such activities by setting up peoples' markets for the sale of vegetables, crafts and other items, and designating home industry sites, such as the well-known Siya-So or Durawall home industry in Mbare, and Gazaland in Highfield, where, in return for a small municipal levy, the self-employed could produce and sell their wares.

In the 1990s, the informal economy came into its own in Zimbabwe, mainly because of the effects of ESAP. 'Backyard industries' sprouted everywhere and more and more workers found their livelihood in this sector so that in the 1999–2000 fiscal year, the informal economy in Zimbabwe was estimated to be 59.4 per cent of GDP, the highest in Africa, whose average then was 42 per cent of GDP and exceeded only by the transitional economy of Georgia at 67.3 per cent (World Bank 2003).[29] In November 2000, the Confederation of Zim-

25 P. Balleis, 'The Social Costs of ESAP in Zimbabwe and the Ethical Dimension of a Free-Market based Economy', in Konrad-Adeneur-Stiftung and SAFER, 'On the Road to a Market-Based Economy', conference held in Harare, Zimbabwe, 3–5 November 1992; Matshalaga, N. 1993. *The Gender Dimensions of Urban Poverty: The Case of Dzivaresekwa*. Harare: Institute of Development Studies; N. Matshalaga, 1993. *The Gender Dimensions of Urban Poverty: The Case of Tafara*. Harare: Institute of Development Studies.

26 Ministry of Public Service, Labour and Social Welfare, *1995 Poverty Assessment Study Survey Preliminary Report*. April 1996, 23.

27 Zimbabwe Congress of Trade Unions. 1993. *Study of the Informal Sector in Zimbabwe*, p. 14.

28 Mumvuma, T. 'Understanding Reform: The Case of Zimbabwe. Third Draft'.

29 World Bank, 'The Informal Economy: Large and Growing in Most Developing Countries' (moderated by Simeon Djankov), Online Discussions. Archived June 2003.

babwean Industries (CZI) reported that approximately 1.7 million people were being supported by the informal sector (*Financial Gazette* (Harare) 2003).[30] By 2004, when unemployment was estimated at 70 per cent, the informal economy was providing approximately 40 per cent of the country's employment (Tibaijuka 2005, 24).[31]

The sector was producing everything from furniture and crafts to bricks and car parts, and providing employment in 'welding, carpentry, tin-smithing, shoe repair and small scale car repair' activities (Tekere 2001, 19–26).[32] Statutory Instrument 216 of 1994 (Regional Town and Country Planning (Use Groups) Regulations, 1994), specifically permitted the use of hitherto residential areas for specified non-residential activities, as authorities were forced to accept the importance of the informal sector (Tibaijuka 2005; Olaleye and Tungwarara 2005, 21).[33] Government appreciation of the growing role of this sector in the economy was evident in efforts to support the Informal Sector Training and Resource Network project operated by the Ministry of Higher Education and Technology in Masvingo, which started operating in 1995 and provided training for those wanting to start income-generating activities (*Financial Gazette* 2002).[34] The informalisation of the economy and the legal concessions from the government in terms of relaxing by-laws to facilitate easier entry into the sector, and production and distribution of goods and services inevitably brought with it the informalisation of operating and production infrastructure, as unauthorised vending stalls and open-air 'factories' sprang up everywhere, becoming a potential source of conflict with the authorities in the future.

Two fateful government decisions compounded the country's economic problems in the late 1990s. The first, in November 1997, was to award veterans of the liberation war, numbering some 70,000 or so men and women, a lump sum of Z$50,000 and a monthly pension of Z$5,000, as a way of mollifying them in the wake of sustained complaints that they had been sidelined by the government since independence. The immediate consequence was loss of investor confidence and the crashing of the Zimbabwean dollar on 14 November when it lost 74 per cent of its value to a United States (US) dollar. The second decision, taken in August 1998, was to send soldiers into the DRC to defend the Laurent Kabila regime that was under attack from various rebel groups. These expensive undertakings, neither of which had been budgeted for, undermined the country's economy further. The Reserve Bank reported in 1997 that, since 1991, annual economic growth had averaged 1.8 per cent, far less than govern-

---

30 *Financial Gazette*, Harare, Zimbabwe, 12 June 2002.
31 Tibaijuka, A.K. 2005. *Report of the Fact-Finding Mission to Zimbabwe to Assess the Scope and Impact of Operation Murambatsvina by the UN Special Envoy on Human Settlements Issues in Zimbabwe.* New York: UNHCS-Habitat, 2005, p. 24 (hereinafter 'the Tibaijuka Report').
32 Tekere, M. 'Trade Liberalisation', pp. 19–26.
33 Tibaijuka Report, p. 23; Olaleye, W.A. and Tungwarara, O. (eds) 2005. *An Analysis of the Demolitions in Zimbabwe.* Action Aid, p. 21.
34 *Financial Gazette*, Zimbabwe, 12 June 2002.

ment's envisaged 5 per cent, whereas the population had grown by 3 per cent. Living standards, particularly among the working poor, further deteriorated. The 1997 *Poverty Assessment Study Survey* revealed that 74 per cent (as compared to 65 four years earlier) of Zimbabweans were poor and 45 per cent of households were living below the food poverty line (Ministry of Public Service, Labour and Social Welfare 1997).[35]

The hardships faced by the poor majority as a result of the weak performance of the economy led to widespread workers' unrest in 1997. Most sectors, including security, catering, banking, construction and textiles were hit by strikes. Discontent with the status quo eventually led to the formation of the Movement for Democratic Change (MDC) by the Zimbabwe Congress of Trade Unions (ZCTU) and other groups in 1999 (Raftopoulos 2001),[36] setting in motion developments that were to culminate in the land invasions of 2000 and beyond, and Murambatsvina in 2005.

Hoping to arrest the deterioration of the economy, in 1998 the government introduced the Zimbabwe Programme for Economic and Social Transformation (ZIMPREST), which envisaged the creation of 44,000 jobs per annum and growth of 6 per cent per annum until 2000; it also sought to achieve a number of socio-political objectives including the promotion of good governance and the elimination of corruption (Mhone 2005).[37] Like ESAP before it, however, ZIMPREST failed to deliver on all its targets, let alone reduce poverty. It was followed in August 2001 by the Millennium Economic Recovery Programme (MERP), which sought to resolve the country's economic problems through acceleration of public sector reforms, stabilisation of prices, exchange rate stabilisation and the protection of vulnerable groups. Then came the National Economic Revival Programme (NERP) of February 2003, which focused mainly on providing humanitarian support to those affected by the drought that afflicted the country at the time. None of these reforms solved the country's economic problems and Zimbabwe experienced a veritable economic meltdown by the turn of the new millennium.

Towards the Precipice: The Making of a Crisis

In February 2000 a referendum was held on a government-sponsored draft national constitution, which included provisions to increase presidential powers as well as to allow the government to confiscate land without compensation.

---

35   Ministry of Public Service, Labour and Social Welfare. 1997. *Poverty Assessment Study Survey: Main Report,* Social Dimension Fund. Harare: Government of Zimbabwe.

36   Raftopoulos, B. 2001. 'The Labour Movement and the Emergence of Opposition Politics in Zimbabwe', in Raftopoulos, B. and Sachikonye, L. (eds), *Striking Back: The Labour Movement and the Post-Colonial State in Zimbabwe 1980–2000.* Harare: Weaver Press, pp. 1-24.

37   Mhone, G. 2005. 'Zimbabwe's Economic Policies 1980 to 2002', *DPMN Bulletin*, Vol. X, No. 2 (April).

Under the leadership of the National Constitutional Assembly (NCA), 54.7 per cent voted against the constitution. In the June 2000 parliamentary elections, the MDC won 57 seats, sweeping most urban centres, and sending shockwaves throughout the ruling party, which, from then on, grew increasingly suspicious and resentful of the urban electorate.

In reprisal, the government began an orchestrated vilification of the MDC as a puppet of the West, and a systematic attack on the white-dominated commercial agricultural sector. After denouncing whites as enemies of the state (CNN 2001),[38] it encouraged the invasion of white-owned farms and backed this up with the introduction of the fast-track land reform programme which targeted, initially, 2,076 white farms for compulsory acquisition by February 2001 (Government of Zimbabwe 2001, para 2.4).[39]

Farm invasions and the violence that accompanied them had far-reaching consequences, and made Zimbabwe a pariah state in the international community. The invasions crippled the economy by disrupting normal agricultural activity and eventually ruining the agricultural sector. Most of the people who were granted land under the programme were ill-equipped to make it productive, either because of lack of farming experience or lack of capital, production inputs and supporting services. The country that was once the breadbasket of southern Africa, responsible for the food security portfolio of the Southern African Development Community (SADC), was no longer able to feed itself (Human Rights Forum Zimbabwe),[40] let alone produce for export. The severe drought of 2001–02 only made matters worse.

Indeed, according to the CZI, by 2001, because of the unsettled agricultural situation, 450 engineering companies had been forced to adopt a shorter working week in order to reduce operational costs, and by December 2002, approximately 500 firms had closed down, resulting in the loss of over 13,000 jobs (*Business Day* 2002).[41]

Meanwhile, by November 2002, the Zimbabwe Tourism Authority (ZTA) was reporting that tourist arrivals from the United Kingdom and Ireland had dropped by 51 per cent and those from the United States and Canada by 42 per cent since 2001. Arrivals from Australia and New Zealand fell by 36 per cent in the same period. Even more significant was the fact that arrivals from Zimbabwe's neighbouring countries of South Africa, Botswana and Zambia had dropped by a colossal 78 per cent in the same period (*Business Day* 2002).[42]

The controversy surrounding the fast-track land reform resulted in the IMF and the World Bank, and economic partners such as the European Union (EU),

---

[38] 'Zimbabwe President Mugabe labels white farmers 'enemies', CNN, 18 April 2000.

[39] Government of Zimbabwe, 2001: para 2.4.

[40] 'Politically Motivated Violence in Zimbabwe, 2000–2001', see http://www.hrforumzim.com/evmp.

[41] *Financial Gazette* (Harare), 20 December 2002; and UN-OCHA, 'Zimbabwe: Industry Hurt by Land Reform'. See http://www.reliefweb.int (16 November 2002).

[42] 'Tourism Tumbles in Zimbabwe', *Business Day*, 22 November 2002.

withdrawing from the country, thus worsening the country's already precarious foreign currency situation. By the end of 2002, Zimbabwe was in the throes of an economic meltdown of unprecedented proportions, described by the United Nations Economic Commission for Africa (UNECA) as the 'worst economic crisis of its history', with the economy confronting a complicated combination of 'domestic and external debt, crippling foreign exchange shortages, poor weather conditions, negative real interest rates and escalating inflation' (Economic Commission for Africa 2002, 9).[43] It was estimated that over '200,000 jobs ha[d] been lost since the beginning of 2000, mostly in agriculture and manufacturing', that investment had shrunk by '80 per cent between January and May' 2002, and that 'over 60 per cent of the country's 12.5 million people' were living below the poverty line (CIIR 2002).[44] Other statistics told their own story. By 2004, inflation stood at 622.8 per cent (*IRIN News* 2004),[45] exports were a mere third of what they had been in 1977, the country's domestic and foreign debt was US$1.1 billion and US$1.1 billion, respectively (Mills 2005, 3),[46] and the currency had lost 99 per cent of its value since 2001. This was, by all accounts, the worst peacetime decline of an economy (Robertson 2005).[47] Such economic problems meant that government could not fulfil its earlier promises, including that of providing housing for all, which in any case had long lagged behind demand since independence.

Urban housing provision in the postcolonial era

Soon after independence, the government had promised that it would strive to ensure housing for all by 2000 and, to this end, spelt out its commitment in the Transitional National Development Plan 1982–83 to 1984–85 (Government of Zimbabwe 1982, 1).[48] It would achieve this goal by introducing a home ownership scheme (freehold tenure), implementing an aided self-help approach; establishing building brigades, promoting the formation of building co-opera-

---

43 Economic Commission for Africa, 'Zimbabwe – A Crumbling Economy (Abstract)', in ECA. 2002. *Economic Report on Africa 2002: Tracking Performance and Progress*. Addis Ababa: ECA, p. 9.

44 CIIR. 2002. 'Economy and Voters Lose Out: Post-Election Blues in Zimbabwe', http://www. ciir.org/ciir.asp?section=news&page=story&id=90. 22 November.

45 IRIN News. February 2004.

46 Mills, G. 2005. 'Agitator, Facilitator or Benefactor? Assessing South Africa's Zimbabwe Policy'. Testimony given to the House Committee on International Relations, Sub-Committee on Africa, Global Human Rights and International Operations, Washington DC. April, p. 3.

47 Robertson, J. 2005. 'Cost-benefit analysis of the past 25 years', http://www.zimbabwesituation. com/may8_2005.html#link3 2005.

48 Government of Zimbabwe. 1982. *Transitional National Development Plan 1982/3–1984/5*. Harare: Government Printer, p. 1.

49 Chikwanha, A.B.H. 2005. 'The Politics of Housing Delivery: a Comparative Study of Administrative Behaviour in South Africa and Zimbabwe'. PhD thesis, Department of Administration and Organisational Theory, University of Bergen, Norway, June, p. 89.

tives, introducing rent control regulations and harnessing the private sector in efforts to provide affordable low-income housing (Chikwanha 2005, 89).[49] The government did indeed provide accommodation, either by setting up new suburbs such as Kuwadzana, Warren Park and Hatcliffe in Harare, or by expanding existing high-density suburbs. However, it was never able to meet the demand for urban housing throughout the period preceding Operation Murambatsvina.

According to a 1986 study by the Ministry of Public Construction and National Housing, 54,000 housing units per annum were needed to meet demand in the country's urban areas (Chenga 1993, 46),[50] yet, as the then Director of Harare's Department of Housing and Community Services, Alban Musekiwa wrote in 1983, 'in the seven years prior to Independence, 2,703 housing units, on average, were constructed annually while during the period 1980–1987 the annual average was 2,463, despite the greatly increased demand for housing estimated at 13,400 per annum'.[51] Among the constraints cited were a 'shortage of professional manpower such as land surveyors and physical planners', a shortage of building materials as local companies failed to cope with growing demand in the face of a post-colonial building boom, and a lack of adequate funding (Chenga 1993, 50).[52] By the late 1990s, there were over 200,000 people on the Harare Municipal housing waiting list alone, compared to 10,000 in the 1980s. Conceding the fact that it would not be able to meet its target of Housing for All by 2000, the government moved the target date to 2020 (*Financial Gazette,* 1997).[53]

In the face of the perennial shortage of housing, urban dwellers responded in a variety of ways. Some established temporary informal dwellings made of plastic sheeting and corrugated metal sheets and any durable material they could lay their hands on in unoccupied spaces around the cities. Those who owned houses in the high-density suburbs took advantage of the housing shortage by building unauthorised extensions to their houses, usually in the form of wooden shacks at the back of their houses, for letting out. Such backyard shacks became so commonplace that, according to L. Zinyama, in Harare alone there were no fewer than '9,870 such illegal residential structures in the high-density suburbs by mid-1987'.[54] As early as 1993, therefore, the high-density suburbs of Harare, at least, were already carrying a much larger population than was designed for them. As Zinyama also pointed out, because of the prevalence of illegal backyard structures, 'low income residential areas in Harare today are excessively over-

50 Chenga, M. 1993. 'Provision of Housing in Zimbabwe: A National View', in Zinyama, L. *et al.* (eds) *Harare: The Growth and Problems of the City.* Harare: UZP, p. 46. Musindo Chenga was then Permanent Secretary in the Ministry of Public Construction and National Housing.

51 Musekiwa, A. 'Low-Income Housing Development in Harare: A Historical Perspective', in Zinyama L. *et al.* (eds) *Harare: The Growth and Problems of the City.* Harare: UZP, p. 58.

52 Chenga, M. 'Provision of Housing in Zimbabwe', in Zinyama, L. *et al.* (eds) p. 50.

53 *Financial Gazette,* 15 August 1997.

54 Zinyama, L. 'The Evolution of the Spatial Structure of Greater Harare' in L. Zinyama, L. *et al.* (eds) p. 25.

55 Ibid.

crowded', with 'densities of fifteen persons or more per dwelling unit' being quite common.[55]

As the economy went into a tailspin after 2000, urban unemployment levels and populations also increased as many farm workers of non-Zimbabwean descent who were driven off the land by the violent farm seizures drifted into the urban centres, not having anywhere to go, as they had no rural homes in the Communal Areas. Such people were still regarded as aliens, notwithstanding the fact that most of them knew no other country apart from Zimbabwe. They had no option but to drift to the towns to try and earn a living as best they as could in the burgeoning informal sector, thus adding to the already considerable pressure on municipal amenities and services.

Therefore, by May 2005 when government launched Operation Murambatsvina, the dream of owning a house in the urban areas that many cherished at independence had turned into a nightmare, while, on its part, government had long abandoned its rhetoric of providing housing for all mainly because, even had the political will existed, the economy was in such shambles that there were no resources to do so. In any case, because urban dwellers had become politically suspect in the eyes of the ruling ZANU(PF) elite, being seen as supporters of the opposition, there was no longer any enthusiasm within government for promoting their interests. Murambatsvina can be seen in part, therefore, as an attempt by the government to punish the urban poor for having turned their backs on the ruling party, and also to dilute MDC support in the cities by forcing large numbers of people into the rural areas where they could be better controlled and monitored.

Conclusion

This chapter has sought to provide the historical background to Murambatsvina, emphasising the failure of the government to live up to its earlier promise of providing health, education and housing for all by 2000 due to a number of factors, among which the poor performance of the national economy must rank very highly, especially in the aftermath of ESAP, which left the Zimbabwean economy worse off than before. The economy was dealt yet another severe blow by the farm invasions of 2000 and beyond, which made Zimbabwe a pariah state shunned by the West, led to capital and skills flight, the closure of local industries, growing unemployment and uncontrollable inflation levels that reduced a once vibrant country regarded as the region's breadbasket into a basket case. The rise of a strong political opposition movement in 1999 followed by its strong showing in the subsequent national elections so incensed and threatened the ruling party that it reacted in ways that eventually proved destructive to its citizens. Murambatsvina is clear evidence of this.

Notes

a. For a detailed analysis and critique of the SAP package, see Mlambo, A.S. 1997, *The Economic Structural Adjustment Programme: The Case of Zimbabwe, 1990–1995*. Harare: University of Zimbabwe Publications.
b. See also Tekere, M. 'Trade Liberalisation', p. 10.
c. Such as the evident efficiency of some privatised parastatals like Dairiboard Zimbabwe Limited; Cotton Company of Zimbabwe Limited; and the Commercial Bank of Zimbabwe and the emergence of several black-owned banks because of financial reforms undertaken under the programme and the reduction of the public wage bill through public service reforms. See Ndhela, D.B. 2003 pp. 136–7.
d. Hereinafter 'the Tibaijuka Report'.
e. Musindo Chenga was then Permanent Secretary in the Ministry of Public Construction and National Housing.

References

Balleis, P. 1992. 'The social costs of ESAP in Zimbabwe and the ethical dimension of a free-market based economy', in 'On the Road to a Market-based Economy Conference' held in Harare, Zimbabwe, 3–5 November. Konrad-Adeneur-Stiftung and SAFER.

Business Day. 2002. 'Tourism tumbles in Zimbabwe', 22 November.

CNN. 2000. Zimbabwe President Mugabe labels white farmers 'enemies', 18 April.

Catholic Commission for Justice and Peace in Zimbabwe & Legal Resources Foundation. 1997. *Breaking the Silence, Building True Peace: A Report on the Disturbances in Matebeleland and the Midlands, 1980 to 1988*. Harare: CCJPZ/LRF.

CIIR. 2002. Economy and voters lose out: Post-election blues in Zimbabwe. See http://www.ciir.org/ciir.asp?section=news&page=story&id=90 (22 November).

Chikwanha, A.B.H. 2005. 'The politics of housing delivery: A comparative study of administrative behaviour in South Africa and Zimbabwe'. Unpublished thesis submitted for PhD, Department of Administration and Organisational Theory, University of Bergen, Norway.

Chenga, M. 1993. 'Provision of housing in Zimbabwe: A national view', in Zinyama, L. *et al.* (eds) *Harare: The growth and problems of the city*. Harare: UZP.

Davies, R. 2004. Memories of underdevelopment: A personal interpretation of Zimbabwe's economic decline, http://www.sarpn.org.za/documents/d0001154/P1273-davies.zimbabwe.2004.pdf

Economic Commission for Africa. 2002. Zimbabwe: A crumbling economy (Abstract). In ECA, Economic report on Africa 2002: Tracking performance and progress, ed. <<??, 9. Addis Ababa: ECA.

Government of Zimbabwe. 1982a. *Transitional National Development Plan 1982/3–1984/5*. Harare: Government Printer.

— 1982b. *Growth with Equity: An Economic Policy Statement*. Harare: Ministry of Finance, Economic Planning and Development.

— 1986. *First Five-year National Development Plan, 1986–1990*. Harare: Ministry of Finance. Economic Planning and Development.

— 1990. *Budget Statement, 1991–1996*. Harare: Government Printer.

Human Rights Forum Zimbabwe. n.d. 'Politically motivated violence in Zimbabwe, 2000–2001'. http://www.hrforumzim.com/evmp.

IRIN News. 2003. 'Zimbabwe: Housing backlog grows in tandem with economic crisis', 22 August.

— 2004. February.

Kanyenze, G. 1990. *Trade liberalisation*. *Social Change and Development* (3rd Quarter): pp. 12–13.

Kanyenze, G. 2006. 'The textile and clothing industry in Zimbabwe', in Jauch, H. and Rudolph Traub-Merz, H. (eds) *The Future of the Textile and Clothing Industry in Sub-Saharan Africa*. Bonn: Friedrich-Ebert-Stiftung.

Lee, M.C. and Colvard, K (eds) *Unfinished Business: The Land Crisis in Southern Africa*. Pretoria: Africa Institute of South Africa.

Matshalaga, N. 1993a. *The Gender Dimensions of Urban Poverty: The Case of Dzivaresekwa*. Harare: Institute of Development Studies.

— 1993b. *The Gender Dimensions of Urban Poverty: The Case of Tafara*. Harare: Institute of Development Studies.

Mhone, G. 'Zimbabwe's economic policies 1980 to 2002', *DPMN Bulletin* X(2) (April).

Mills, G. 2005. 'Agitator, facilitator or benefactor? Assessing South Africa's Zimbabwe policy'. Testimony given to the House Committee on International Relations, Sub-Committee on Africa, Global Human Rights and International Operations, Washington DC. April.

Ministry of Public Service, Labour and Social Welfare. 1996. 1995 *Poverty Assessment Study Survey Preliminary Report*. April.

— 1997. *Poverty Assessment Study Survey: Main Report*. Social Dimension Fund. Harare: Government of Zimbabwe.

Mlambo, A.S. 1997. *The Economic Structural Adjustment Programme: The Case of Zimbabwe 1990–1995*. Harare: University of Zimbabwe Publications.

Mlambo, N. 1991. 'The costs of reopening Zimbabwe's trade routes through Mozambique'. Unpublished BA (Hons) Dissertation. Department of Economic History, University of Zimbabwe.

Mukonoweshuro, E. 1992. *Zimbabwe: Ten Years of Destabilisation: A Balance Sheet*. Stockholm: Bethany Books.

Mumvuma, T. 'Understanding Reform: The Case of Zimbabwe'. Unpublished ms.

Musekiwa, A. 1993. 'Low-income Housing Development in Harare: A Historical Perspective', in Zinyama, L. et al. (eds) *Harare: The Growth and Problems of the City*. Harare: University of Zimbabwe Press.

Ndhela, D.B. 2003. 'Zimbabwe's economy since 1990', in Lee, M.C. and Colvard, K (eds) *Unfinished Business: The Land Crisis in Southern Africa*. Pretoria: Africa Institute of South Africa.

Olaleye, W.A. and Tungwarara, O. (eds) 2005. *An analysis of the demolitions in Zimbabwe*. Action Aid.

Raftopoulos, B. 2001. 'The Labour Movement and the emergence of opposition politics in Zimbabwe', in Raftopoulos, B. and Sachikonye, L. (eds) *Striking Back: The Labour Movement and the post-colonial state in Zimbabwe 1980–2000*. Harare: Weaver Press.

Raftopoulos, B. and Sachikonye, L. (eds) 2001. *Striking Back: The Labour Movement and the post-colonial state in Zimbabwe 1980–2000*. Harare: Weaver Press.

Reserve Bank of Zimbabwe. *Quarterly Economic and Statistical Review*, 3(6) (March).

— *Quarterly Economic and Statistical Review*, 3(12) (December).

Riddell, R. 1984. 'Zimbabwe: The economy four years after independence', *African Affairs* 83 (333) (October).

Robertson, J. 2005. 'Cost-benefit analysis of the past 25 years'. http://www.zimbabwesituation.com/may8_2005.html#link3.

Saunders, R. 1996. 'Zimbabwe: ESAP's Fables II' in *Southern Africa Report Archive* 11 (4) (July).

Tekere, M. 2001. 'Trade Liberalisation Under Structural Economic Adjustment – Impact on Social Welfare in Zimbabwe'. Paper for the Poverty Reduction Forum (PRF) Structural Adjustment Programme Review Initiative (SAPRI) (April).

Tibaijuka, A.K. 2005. *Report of the Fact-Finding Mission to Zimbabwe to Assess the Scope and Impact of Operation Murambatsvina by the UN Special Envoy on Human Settlements Issues in Zimbabwe.* New York: UNHCS Habitat.

UNESCO. 1987. Proceedings of the General Conference, Twenty-Fourth Session, Paris, France. Paris: UNESCO, October–November.

United Nations OCHA. 2002. 'Zimbabwe: Industry hurt by land reform'. http://www.reliefweb.int, 16 November.

World Bank 1992. *Financing Health Services.* Washington DC: World Bank.

— 2003. 'The informal economy: Large and growing in most developing countries', moderated by Simeon Djankov. Online Discussions. Archived June.

Washington, E.B. 1989. 'Zimbabwe: Building a Nation', in *Essence*, October:

Zinyama, L. et al. (eds) *Harare: The Growth and Problems of the City.* Harare: University of Zimbabwe Press.

Zinyama, L. 'The Evolution of the Spatial Structure of Greater Harare', in Zinyama, L. et al. (eds) *Harare: The Growth and Problems of the City.* Harare: University of Zimbabwe Press.

Zimbabwe Congress of Trade Unions. 1993. *Study of the Informal Sector in Zimbabwe.*

— 2001. 'Strategy document for the 1990 Congress', in Raftopoulos, B. and Sachikonye, L. (eds) 2001. *Striking Back: The Labour Movement and the Post-Colonial State in Zimbabwe, 1980–2000.* Harare: Weaver Press.

2

Coercion, Consent, Context
Operation Murambatsvina & ZANU(PF)'s
Illusory Quest for Hegemony

David Moore

If Operation Murambatsvina is seen within the context of a long history of ZANU(PF)'s failed efforts to establish its rule as hegemonic – that is, more through consent than coercion and threats thereof – then it is understandable. Rather than being perceived as a sudden and almost inexplicable eruption of violence and terror on behalf of a ruling party shocked at its recent loss of legitimacy and inability to deal with economic crisis, Operation Murambatsvina should be seen as an almost logical extension of the techniques of a party that has consistently failed to rule Zimbabwe through consent rather than force or its possibility. Indeed, closer inspection and historical analysis of the ruling party itself suggests that the leading elements within it rarely reach even a position of 'minimal hegemony' (i.e., agreement within members or factions of a ruling group). This lack of consensus spreads throughout the party and into society in manifestations of violence. Operation Murambatsvina is part of a long continuum that this chapter interrogates.

Just a little after the middle of 2004, as Zimbabweans were gearing up for the parliamentary elections scheduled for early the next year, an internationally respected research organisation released the results of its public opinion survey. It told readers that ZANU(PF)'s effective 'political propaganda' – in particular a 'comprehensive campaign to revive the nationalist fervour of the liberation war' since 2000 – was the 'most important factor' explaining why 'political support for the incumbent has apparently increased' (Chikwana et al. 2004: vii; cf. Moore 2005a).[1] To be sure, the survey indicated less than enthusiastic support: it said Zimbabweans 'overwhelmingly reject[ed] political violence', were 'sick and tired of the deadlock between the country's two main political parties', and felt that 'problems in this country can only be solved if the MDC and ZANU(PF) sit down and talk with one another' (Chikwana et al. 2004, vii). Thus it suggested that because people had acquiesced to ZANU(PF) rule and otherwise lost their

---

1   This report has also been published, in almost exact replication, as Bratton et al., 2005.

will to engage in political change, there was no need for the violence to continue. Both the opposition MDC and its (once) coercive competitor would have every reason to negotiate a transition (Chikwana et al. 2004, 30).

In the same month, the Zimbabwe Human Rights NGO Forum (2004, 2-3) chronicled events indicating that struggles for power within ZANU(PF) itself, let alone between it and its challengers from within the MDC, were far from the public opinion surveyors' ideal of calm negotiation. Didymus Mutasa, ZANU(PF) Member of Parliament for Makoni North, Minister of Special Affairs in the President's Office Responsible for the Anti-Corruption and Anti-Monopolies Programme,[2] and one-time enthusiast of the Christian Socialist Cold Comfort Farm, and his 'A-team' of 42 youths were reported to have undertaken acts of coercion against James Kaunye, who hoped to challenge Mutasa in the ZANU(PF) primaries. Kaunye was stripped naked, assaulted, revived by pouring water over him and taken to the Rusape hospital with head wounds. The 'A-Team' – accompanied by Mutasa, says the report – went on to ravage bus stops, supporters' homes, and a petrol service station. They broke two victims' legs, shot a dog, pummelled a woman's back with a spade, stabbed the ZANU(PF) district chairperson's buttocks with a screwdriver, and stole cash from a house. Then they 'retired to Minister Mutasa's house where they were said to be based'. Most of them were later arrested and eventually 16 were sentenced to three years' imprisonment. Mutasa paid bail of Z$300,000 for each. He evaded questioning at the time, although the case continued in various manifestations and was well publicised for more than two years.[3]

In the same month, inter-party violence – the sort more expected than intra-party conflict – continued. In Epworth, one of Harare's poorest townships, a young MDC supporter was rounded up by ZANU(PF) youth and 'war veterans' whilst distributing his party's leaflets. He said he was attacked with baton sticks and sjamboks for 30 minutes, and then taken to their base and beaten until he lost consciousness. He next found himself in a police station, where police officers attacked him while the 'war vets' watched. The police returned him to the 'war vets' who took him back to their headquarters, forced him to 'fight' 11 ZANU(PF) youth and then handcuffed him while the youth took their vengeance on him. Other police officers arrived, took the whole group to the central police station, released the ZANU(PF) youth, beat him during the night and

---

[2]   At the time of writing Mutasa was Minister for State Security.

[3]   The ramifications of this incident spread up through the ZANU(PF) hierarchy as war veteran and retired Major Kaunye accused Justice Minister Patrick Chinamasa of attempting to stop him from taking Mutasa to trial. Kaunye also stated that Mutasa had offered to build him a weir and finance a dairy herd if he would stop the legal process. As of February 2007, the Attorney-General's office had withdrawn charges against Chinamasa, but the head of the Central Intelligence Organisation in Manicaland and three others were still facing charges based on their attempts to stop Kaunye's efforts. These cases are widely seen as part of the succession issue in Manicaland: see, inter alia, BBC 2006; Daily News Online 2004a (in which Mutasa is quoted as saying he was 'set to become ZANU(PF)'s vice president behind Cde Emmerson Mnangagwa at the party's December congress'); Manyukwe 2006; 2007; Nkatazo 2006.

asked him to reveal the names of some of his MDC colleagues. On refusal they beat him again, charged him under the Public Order and Security Act (POSA), and released him on Z$250,000 bail (Human Rights NGO Forum 2004, 3-4. The forum's report had ten pages of stories similar to these. For the first eight months of 2004 it listed: 51 abductions and kidnappings, 288 assaults, three murders, eight attempted murders, two rapes, 58 displacements, 449 incidents of political discrimination or victimisation, 471 infringements of the freedom of assembly or expression, 28 unlawful detentions and 61 unlawful arrests. All of this was calculated in the same month that Afrobarometer released its survey saying 'propaganda' was beginning to work, and that ZANU(PF) was winning the hearts and minds of Zimbabweans, albeit grudgingly. How could these two realities coexist? One was based in the day-to-day empirical world of beating and brutality, as the violence pervading the Zimbabwean reality sloshed in and out of both parties,[4] to be counted and recorded assiduously by the protagonists of the new human rights order ZANU(PF) was trying so hard to stop. Yet the other – propounded by people equally 'liberal' and scorned by the ruling party as the 'puppets' of evil foreigners, and likewise obsessed with quantifying the horrific and baffling circumstances surrounding them, as if concretising them thus would make them understandable – seemed to be based on an illusion. This chimera is linked to a hope that *interpretations* and *opinions* could be added up, and if they could be sifted through a screen, separating coercion and consent, their calculations could validate a liberal belief that coercion can never work for very long. The supine superiority of social 'science' and the authority of statistics could convince them thus. Ironically, however, such a belief made fools out of the subjects of science's surveys – or perhaps, people willing, out of sheer exhaustion, to have the wool pulled over their eyes (or to tell the surveyors what they thought they wanted to hear). The less-opinionated accountants of abuse did not make any such assumptions. Nor, it turned out, did ZANU(PF).

The Afrobarometer report came and went, as opinion surveys do, to rest on websites and in an academic journal. The election of March 2005 arrived and departed too (Bond and Moore 2005). By the first of April those who had been willing to suspend their disbelief that the ruling party would ever pay any attention to the notion of 'free and fair' – surely, given the examples in 2000 and 2002, a hard task, so hard indeed that the MDC 'suspended' its participation in the election process for a few months – had learnt again that by hook or crook, the wily masters would never give up power to their pretenders. Just a few weeks later, as if to hammer home that lesson, Operation Murambatsvina ensued (Tibaijuka 2005; Kamete 2006; Potts 2006). Hundreds of thousands were hit – only a very few of them active members of any oppositional forces – and they still hurt at the time of writing (Solidarity Peace Trust, 2006b). This, surely, would teach Zimbabweans and international survey scientists alike that ZANU(PF) would not rest with propaganda alone. Fear would be the operative

---

4   For an examination of the MDC's internal fracturing and violence, see Raftopoulos 2006a.

concept once again. Of course, a year or so later the same surveyors could come in again and find a sullen acceptance of ZANU(PF) dominance; but would that be due to 'propaganda' or the constant memories of the consistent and calculated (but incalculable) meting out of coercion?

It is not the purpose of this chapter to recount the horrors of Operation Murambatsvina or the follies of Operation Garikai/Hlalani Kuhle, accurately summed up by the Solidarity Peace Trust as 'a scandal of dismal delivery and ZANU(PF) patronage' – and international agency negligence (Solidarity Peace Trust 2006b: 26, 68).[5] Its goal is not to predict that these campaigns – along with Operation Taguta/Sisuthi, in which the army is taking over agriculture (Solidarity Peace Trust 2006a) – are harbingers of a state completely dominated by the military. Nor is it to ascertain the immediate reasoning for this most explicit demonstration of ZANU(PF)'s remorseless power, although it would seem that 'punishment' of poor urban people for voting for the MDC and a Pol Pot-like desire to put urban people back into a 'year zero' rural homeland (wherein they are easier to watch in any case) merged together with a pre-emptive move against suspicions of a Ukraine-style 'Orange Revolution' and a belief said to be emanating from the Reserve Bank that 'cleaning up' informal markets of all sorts might magically transform the foreign exchange problem, and the state would have enough money to pay its debts to the International Monetary Fund, make as much sense as any other guesses (Sachikonye 2006, 19-20).[6]

The intent of the following words is to continue the discontent with the sort of research and analysis represented by Afrobarometer, and to expand it with criticism of the way in which analysts of Zimbabwe tend to separate consent and coercion while they search for the means by which ZANU(PF) rules. They try too hard to find an all-embracing hegemony, bringing all Zimbabweans into it with nationalist fervour or developmental pragmatism or a combination of them both in a 'peasant option' (Ranger 1985). Or, failing that, the ruling party becomes violent and intimidating, with a discourse demonising all opposition, reigning with cruelty and subterfuge (Kriger 2003; 2005). Or, in a slight variation on this theme, it may not be that the party is permanently on one side of the hegemonic/dominating divide, but that crisis of one sort or another turns it to one option or the other: if ZANU(PF) is hitting out hard in all directions,

5   Even the United Nations Secretary-General Kofi Annan was unable to make a visit to Zimbabwe.
6   The Ukrainian parallel was revealed to the state press by the Ghanaian journalist and Mugabe praise-singer, New African editor Baffour Ankomah (Sachikonye 2006: 19). On the IMF side, see Bond 2005. To be sure, the MDC, the Zimbabwe Congress of Trade Unions, the National Constitutional Assembly and other civil society groups were under some pressure to pursue street action soon after the election. (Some zealous, if naïve, activists believed that if such activity instigated a repressive state response, the 'international community' would intervene). These possibilities undoubtedly would have encouraged some elements of the state security apparatus, eager to believe international agents were behind such actions and thus that the demonstrators were traitorous, to act precipitously – knowing the minimal chances of meaningful international reaction. If anything, Operation Murambatsvina should disabuse activists of the idea that help resides in other quarters. The International Crisis Group's Zimbabwe: An opposition strategy (2006) indicates that brave international advice is plentiful and cheap (cf. Moore 2001b).

it must be due to some externally induced – or even, through policy failure, internally caused – hiccup on the path of 'normal' and consensual rule. As Brian Raftopoulos (2006b, 212) puts it, 'the ravages of neo-liberalism combined with the loss of ruling party legitimacy and the emergence of a formidable opposition' have turned ZANU(PF) into something new and nasty.

The question this chapter will raise is: what if it is not just these 'ravages' that have made ZANU(PF) malicious (even though Operation Murambatsvina has brought its malevolence to the fore in an almost unprecedented way); what if 'crisis' cannot quite explain the constant recurrence of viciousness? But it also queries the cracks in its coercion as well as its consensus gathering; it wonders why attempts to craft degrees of consent[7] are not only wrapped up in a shallow anti-imperialism, pan-Africanism, gay-bashing and foreigner-expelling, but in the sorts of policies and *politesse* that once allowed people such as Victor de Waal (1990, vi) to write that 'moral principle ... political realism ... exceptional quality of statesmanship ... clear perception [and] sacrifice' would steer Robert Mugabe (and his party) beyond the precipices of Stalinist holocausts or Chinese cultural revolutions. Why, as so many commentators and scholars ask, is there, still, a significant degree of support for Zimbabwe's rulers? In spite of the above disparagement of Afrobarometer's measure of things, one has to concede that there is a lack of revolutionary anti-ZANU(PF) fervour in Zimbabwe and it is not all because of fear, the MDC's or civil society's inability to rally the troops, or an innate Zimbabwean passivity. Yet neither can it be said that there is enough popular support for a nearly universal desire to bend with 'fascist' winds blowing from State House: these tendencies notwithstanding, it is premature to say that Zimbabwe is fascist, simply because there is very little evidence of its mass base.[8] Perhaps it is the historical variations among the binaries of coercion and consent, and the constant and intricate mixture of the two concepts – which means, of course, that they are not binaries at all but ebbs and flows between a nirvana of happy hegemony and a dystopian crisis-derived dominance, in a 'chaotically pluralistic, yet ... internal[ly] coherent ... distinctive regime of violence' (Mbembe 1992: 3)[9] emerging with different emphases in new contexts – that make up Zimbabwe's particularities, and the spaces in which they can be contested.

Vacillating Between Hegemony and Domination: A Short History

Within the above framework, it would be generous to say that the Zimbabwean ruling group has been able to exercise the 'moral and political leadership' to

---

[7]   Rather than, as David Blair (2002) punned, on 'degrees in violence'.

[8]   Cf. Scarnecchia (2006). Although he does not suggest there is active popular support for fascism in Zimbabwe he sees many other parallels: fortunately, fascism does not appear to be hegemonic.

[9]   There is, too, a specific regime of accumulation here (ignored by Mbembe), in which ruling class members and associates benefit extraordinarily even during long-term economic meltdown.

gain it the active consent of Zimbabwe's contending classes and groups, be they 'subaltern' (Vambe 2005) or only slightly less than 'ruling', for more than a few years. This group is a fragmented entity in itself, torn asunder by frictions based on differences ranging from ethnicity (Chinembiri 2005; Maroleng 2005)[10] to ideology (Moore 1991; 1995),[11] factions rooted in generation and gender,[12] and fictions imagined in versions of history (Bhebe 2004)[13] and patriotism (Ranger 2004), in which only some people (or maybe only one!) have been able to rule coherently some of the time: it is only rarely that a 'minimal hegemony' (Femia 1981), in which the members of an elite itself can agree how to rule, has been achieved in Zimbabwe.

Very generously, one might argue that aside from a brief post-1980 'honeymoon' for a couple of years, ZANU(PF) only came *close* to the revered status of 'hegemony' from 1987, after the unity pact signed with the Zimbabwean African People's Union (ZAPU), to 1997, when the embattled political faction of the ruling party was forced to enter into the concord with the war veterans: the one that plunged it to the depths of its fiscal crisis.[14] Yet even this premise is very faulty. It could be argued that the first elections results were ethnically split, and that even Shona areas were rife with coercion (Kriger 2005, 4-5). Given the prelude to the Unity Accord, it could hardly be called a consensual agreement: it was born of the coercion and fear of the Gukurahundi campaign, which many claim was a genocidal attempt waged against the Ndebele people. Estimates of those killed in that still murky military operation range from 3,000 to 20,000 (Saunders 1996; Moyo 2002; Eppel 2005; Rupiya 2005, 117). Recent documents claim that 400,000 people 'were deliberately brought to the brink of starvation by 5 Brigade', the name of the North Korean-trained soldiers who carried out the reign of terror in Matabeleland and the Midlands (Solidarity Peace Trust 2006a, 5). Rather than ZAPU coming to the rulers'

---

10 These analysts examine intra-Shona tensions; there are, of course, those between Shona and Ndebele within the party, too.

11 Perhaps now, discussions of 'technocrats' versus 'ideologues', along with 'critical cosmopolitans' versus 'agrarian patriots' (Moore 2004b) are akin to the ideological disputes of old.

12 In Moore (1991; 1995) generation rivals ideology in importance. In many respects a new generation of political activists invented the National Constitutional Assembly and took much responsibility for the inauguration of the MDC. Intra-ZANU(PF) struggles involve generation and gender, too, as the current vice-president Joice Mujuru's appointment and the struggles around it illustrate in both regards. Succession issues take on a particular salience if norms for the transfer of power from one generation to another are not established.

13 Bhebe's biography of the late Vice-President Simon Muzenda has inspired lawsuits about its disparaging of some liberation strugglers, and is a good indication of 'history as hegemony' (Moore 2005b).

14 It is said that retired Air Force head Josiah Tungamirai and other leaders were kidnapped by the veterans in order to bolster their pension negotiation strategy in August 1997. When the Z$50,000 one-off payment and the Z$2,000 per month pensions to the 'war veterans' were announced – along with the promise to take real action on the land issue, and ensure that 20 per cent of that land would go to the veterans – the Zimbabwean dollar lost 75 per cent of its value. Soon after that the war in the Democratic Republic of the Congo was joined, in defence of Laurent Kabila's sovereignty and in hopes of mineral concessions. On the political economy of Zimbabwe-DRC relations see Nest (2001).

table motivated by thoughts of national unity or the lure of partaking in the spoils of government, the reality of a defeat and surrender grounded in violence must be conceded. Once the hinge of unity is sundered, the post-1987 era looks fragile too. The 1987 constitutional changes, including the creation of an executive presidency, heralded an incipient 'Bonapartism'.[15] During the next year, the 'Willowgate' scandal, in which many Cabinet ministers were found selling their subsidised cars to their friends (sometimes instant friends), was exposed – and hundreds of citizens rushed to watch their leaders wither in the courts (Nyarota 2006, 150-71). Also, when one unpacks the Gukurahundi moment even further (i.e. to the thought that ZANU(PF) might have been 'hegemonic' east of the Matabelelands and Midlands, and, by the way, seen as hegemonic allies by those among its former colonisers happy to see the essence of their old Rhodesia trundle along, secure in the knowledge that it was not in the hands of the Soviets, and that their 'kith and kin' did not bear the brunt of Five Brigades) the cracks shown by Operation Chinyavada indicate the precariousness of ruling party legitimacy within its supposed Shona heartlands – unless one brackets the gender issue to the side of a politics usually run by males for males. During Chinyavada, over 3,000 (some say 6,000) women whose apparent similarity to prostitutes threatened the pristine and puritanical perceptions of ZANU(PF)'s reputation were arrested in advance of a Non-Aligned Movement meeting in late 1983, some being dumped at Mushumbi pools (Hansard 1983, 1135; Rupiya 2005, 117; Mushonga 2006). This, too, undermines any pretensions or notions of intra-Shona hegemony. As if to warn of a future foretold in the form of Murambatsvina, Operation Chinyavada was also called 'Operation Clean-up' (Makanje, Shaba and Win 2004, 11-13).[16]

15   The notion of Bonapartism refers to Karl Marx's (1852) idea of how a 'dictator' gains power because stalemated class struggle leaves power in a vacuum and/or those who once fought for liberal democracy support a 'great man' rather than see their power slip to who they think are their subordinates, ill-deserving of democracy. See Moore (2001a; 2003) for attempts to expand this notion to Zimbabwe.

16   Thanks to Tamuka Chirimambowa for research in *Hansard*, in which the reference to the Mushambi pools is made. Evidence suggests Operation Chinyavada may have been subsumed under Gukurahundi: apparently the leader of the United African National Council, Abel Muzorewa, was accused of sending 5,000 recruits to South Africa for training in anticipation of a coup, and arrested briefly (Mukaro and Mugari 2006), under the aegis of Operation Chinyavada. Perhaps, for a government feeling under siege, prostitutes and apartheid agents are similar threats. Notably, the 1983 Chinyavada inspired the creation of a vigorous woman's rights group, the Women's Action Group. Significantly, too, the group beating up Kaunye in Rusape (note 2 above) was called Chinyavada as well as the 'A-Team'. The term – meaning 'scorpion' or 'angel of death' – is often used today. For example, a Bulawayo student leader says his torturers called themselves chinyavada (Blessing 2006). Further indicating the link with ZANU(PF), one writer states that the ruling party has its 'own chinyavada' (Mutyambizi-Dewa 2006) in contradistinction to the Central Intelligence Organisation, ostensibly concerned with matters of 'state' rather than 'party'. A Kwekwe MDC member of parliament states that Emmerson Mnungagwa (a potential president in Mugabe's wake, and considered to be one of the prime movers of Gukurahundi) is often called Chinyavada (Chebundo 2003).

If one goes back further, into the history of the liberation war, there is also little unity of a hegemonic sort. The list of tensions is a long one: the split eventuating in ZANU emerging out of ZAPU; the March 11 Movement (Tshabangu 1979); the Front for the Liberation of Zimbabwe (Frolizi, or, as some of its detractors called it, the Front for the Liaison of Zezuru Intellectuals); the Nhari Rebellion – and centrally, the Chitepo Assassination (White 2003) – the Zimbabwe Peoples' Army and Vashandi moment (wiped out with particular Machiavellian cold-heartedness and ideological hypocrisy by the man these young radicals helped into power[17]); the Hamadziripi-Gumbo 'coup' in 1978; and the mysterious death of Josiah Tongogara the day after he advised Robert Mugabe to go into the 1980 elections together with ZAPU, with which ZANU was ostensibly allied in the Patriotic Front. The closer one looks at the history of Zimbabwe, the more one wonders how anyone could 'imagine' a 'community' based on the nationalism exemplified by its political brokers (Anderson 1983). It is hardly a wonder that Robert Mugabe thinks he is the only human being who can hold the fragments together, nor that enough people around him think so too, thus holding him at his vantage point and allowing him to pull the threads the way he wants (Moore 2005c).

Jumping from the pre-state forms of hegemonic struggle to those thereafter, one sees the Zimbabwe Unity Movement, founded by former ZANU(PF) stalwarts Edgar Tekere and Patrick Kombayi, arising just after the Willowgate fiasco.[18] Tekere, who after the Chitepo assassination in early 1975 threw ZANU into chaos, accompanied Mugabe on his mythical trip from Salisbury to Mozambique (and then to house arrest in Quelimane, because the new Mozambican president Samora Machel did not think they were constitutionally affirmed leaders), claims Mugabe dismissed him from the party for being too critical of the party's corrupt tendencies. Just after he had walked out of State House, he says, he went to a shop and saw the Bulawayo *Chronicle*'s headlines about the corrupt car dealers in the Cabinet (Tekere 2004). Kombayi, provisioner for ZANU in Zambian exile and logistics organiser later in Mozambique, had been mayor of Gweru. He and Tekere were approached by 'the Americans and the British' to form an opposition party (Kombayi 2004).[19] When asked if this was not fitting in with an 'imperialist' agenda, Kombayi responded that 'we agreed [with them], we had something in common: I had seen the disasters of one-party states in Zambia, Tanzania, and Mozambique and I did not want to see one here.

---

17   Wilfred Mhanda's discussion of the Vashandi moment in Nyarota (2006, 104-9) is an important historical intervention. For sometimes inaccurate, but interesting nonetheless, reflections on the Nhari revolt, the Chitepo assassination, and the ZIPA conjuncture, see Chung (2006, 124-88).

18   Ironically, ZUM used the notion of Murambatsvina to signify its intention to remove ZANU(PF)'s corruption.

19   Tekere confirmed assistance by a Cape Town activist and financier, who was deported when his activities were discovered by ZANU(PF). Tekere (2007) mentions the man's name and acknowledges his – and many others' – personal financial support but does not indicate he funded ZUM directly.

We agreed with the so-called imperialists on that' (Kombayi 2004). ZANU(PF) zealots who see an imperialist under – or behind – every opposition party might have thought as much. Their experience riding this particular tiger would have forewarned them of such eventualities when their own hegemony began to unravel. The party's history is criss-crossed with cheques from foreign bank accounts.[20] Kombayi's attempted assassination by one of the then vice-president's right-hand men indicated how well the ruling party knew the effectiveness of such alliances (Saunders 2000, 44; Guma 2005; Nyarota 2006, 133, 332, 334). It does not take much to unravel hegemony hanging by a thread, especially when the party losing it seems intent on hastening the process.

Even one attempted murder in order to quieten an opponent is a clear signal that hegemony has gone. Perhaps, though, the 1993 expulsion of hundreds of 'squatters' from Ndabaningi Sithole's 'Churu Farm', who, with the lack of government-approved alternatives took up his offer for cheap housing and thus joined a pact that would be seen in political terms by ZANU(PF), indicated a prophetic waning of hegemony (Auret 1994).[21] It accompanied the start of the pressures instigated by structural adjustment, which hastened the ZCTU's loosening of the links between workers and party state, undoubtedly also hurried by the example of Kenneth Kaunda's unseating to the north (beginning the oxymoronic process of trade unions leading movements towards economic as well as political liberalism). The ZCTU's divorce was epitomised by the deep 1996 strike of the Public Service Workers – and 230 more the next year (Moyo and Yeros 2005, 186). ZANU(PF)'s bell was beginning to toll shrilly. It took the war veterans from one side of '(un)civil society' to ring it louder: yet when the Central Intelligence Organisation accompanied them up the aisle to ZANU(PF)'s new marriage altar, it was hard to know whether the state was leading this 'social movement' or vice versa.[22] The other marriage, of the NGO–Human Rights–Legal Fraternity to the unions, in the NCA and then the MDC (later embraced by some white commercial farmers), was also a conjugation of temporarily attracting opposites. Nevertheless, the face-off between two potentially conflictive, but provisionally united, ensembles of hegemonic intent began in earnest with millennial haste in early 2000, including the constitutional referendum (the question of more land resettlement, but accompanied by more power for an executive president, was answered in the negative), the land invasions, and the first election with a really challenging opposition, all in the context of an accelerating economic meltdown that only real fears for property rights can trigger.

---

20 See Moore (2005b, 158) for archival evidence of Sarah Mugabe's secretarial scholarship in London, granted by the Ariel Foundation, a CIA front run by Denis Grennan. Grennan was later a foreign policy advisor to the Labour government on affairs Zimbabwean.

21 Thanks to Tamuka Chirimambowa for bringing this documented parallel to Operation Murambatsvina to light.

22 Moyo and Yeros (2005, 187-200) assert the 'social movement' side of the equation, but also note that the war veterans were 'firmly embedded in the state apparatus ... indeed ... in charge of security, including the president's office' (p. 187), thus tending to negate claims of spontaneity, besides eliding the forces within the state. Cf. Moore (2004b, 418-20).

The road to Operation Murambatsvina was thus opened. The paving is not finished yet. So far, it is the clearest example of the failed hegemonic project, given its immediate impact – 650-700,000 livelihoods and homes lost; 2.4 million people directly and indirectly affected (Tibaijuka 2005; Potts 2006) – and its instantaneous global broadcasting. Gukurahundi's genocidal attributes and higher immediate death toll may make it worse, of course, but, horrifically, its slow release into the public realm, its ethnic dimensions, and ZANU(PF)'s ability to use Cold War and racial politics to its international advantage, meant that it did not indicate a loss of overall hegemony so vividly. Murambatsvina and Gukurahundi are probably tied, though, for the long-term animosity towards ZANU(PF) they had to have generated. Yet in the short and medium term, there is no end in sight for the kind of power ZANU(PF) embodies.

It is clear, then, that ZANU(PF) in power held very little in the way of hegemony, and slipped into dominance all too quickly. ZANU(PF) has almost never been able to 'lead society in a direction that not only serves the dominant group's interests but is also perceived by subordinate groups as serving a more general interest', and to obtain what Giovanni Arrighi (2005, 32) calls the 'power inflation' ensuing from that pleasant condition. With this failure to attain hegemony, domination has been the order of the day. A combination of various degrees of coercion, along with a waxing and waning of levels of sullen acquiescence with (more hopefully) challenging opposition and even, perhaps, 'counter-hegemonic struggles', reigns – in a context in which the system delivers, much but not all of the time, to just enough people in and around these circles of coercive power. Within this order, however, it remains to be seen *how much* coercion has to be meted out in order to maintain and increase the ruling party's power (and accumulation strategies). Inside these parameters, the overall harm to Zimbabwe must be calculated. In short, does ZANU(PF)'s failure to attain hegemony infringe on 'systemic' functioning and legitimacy?

In other words, which comes first: lack of hegemony or inability to rule? When do the two add up to create system-wide instability, crisis, and chaos? In the early nineties, Zimbabweans were less poor than most Africans, a 'civil war' (with 300 'dissidents' at most, but inflated in the minds of ZANU(PF) leaders to include the whole of ZAPU in Matabeleland and the Midlands) had been ended, and the unity of the contending political parties could have engendered a developmental state. Perhaps structural adjustment destroyed that possibility. Maybe the emerging Zimbabwe Unity Movement (ZUM) unsettled the rulers so badly that they lost the ability to make policy pure and simple, and in the context of succession uncertainties, ZANU(PF)'s man at the centre battened the hatches. It could also be that the saying brought into the public realm by once critical political scientist, then election manager and propaganda minister for the 2000–2004 version of the ZANU(PF) regime, Jonathan Moyo – 'the land is the economy and the economy is the land' – is at the root of Zimbabwe's long crisis, and until the structural contradictions brought into being when capitalism arrived in Zimbabwe's space and failed to transform it fully are solved with an acceptable and productive tenure system, hegemony will be but an unevenly articulated dream [23]

To say this is not to be reductionist,[24] because the transformations of modes of production are simultaneously economic, social, cultural, ideological and ultimately political, bringing in all the clashes of structure and agency that struggles for accumulation and hegemony produce. That Operation Murambatsvina demonstrated the merging of the 'urban' and the 'rural' dimensions of this transformational dilemma better than any other manifestation of Zimbabwe's crisis so far illustrates the depth and the difficulty – and the intellectual vacuum that violence so easily fills – of this country's transitional, but almost frozen, moment. The only thing that can be said with assurance about getting out of the impasse is that to start the logjam breaking will take a force willing to test its hegemonic power democratically. That will get people thinking again, without fear, without propaganda and without the 'clean-up' of enemies so imaginary that they can only be called 'trash'.

Acknowledgements

Thanks to Tamuka Chirimambowa for research assistance and Tinashe Chimedza for engaging email discussions on these issues.

---

[23] See Maguranyanga and Moyo (2006) for a plea for rather conventional and straightforward tenure forms to be implemented on the new, and old, agricultural terrain. To say their proposals are conventional, however, is not to say they are easy. They chart the creation of a new mode of production which is not even half-way implemented yet. See also Sachikonye's excellent article on land (2005). Essential background on the 'agrarian question' is Bernstein (2004). More generally on 'primitive accumulation', see Moore (2004a).

[24] As Brian Raftopoulos (2006b, 17 and passim), contends of the 'political economy' approach to Zimbabwe. The task is to incorporate democracy – analytically and practically – in the structures, so 'structuralists' cannot avoid it.

References

Anderson, B. 1983. *Imagined Communities: Reflections on the Origins and Spread of Nationalism.* London: Verso.

Arrighi, G. 2005. 'Hegemony unravelling – I', *New Left Review* II (32) (March–April): 23–80.

Auret, M. 1994. *Churu Farm: A Chronicle of Despair.* Harare: The Catholic Commission for Justice and Peace in Zimbabwe.

BBC World Service. 2006. 'Zimbabwe justice minister tried'. August 8. http://news.bbc.co.uk/go/pr/fr/-/1/hi/world/africa/5257360.stm (accessed 3 March 2007).

Bhebe, N. 2004. *Simon Vengayi Muzenda: The Struggle For and Liberation of Zimbabwe.* Gweru: Mambo Press.

Blair, D. 2002. *Degrees in Violence: Robert Mugabe and the Struggle for Power in Zimbabwe.* London: Continuum.

Blessing, V. 2006. 'Police torture Bulawayo poly student leader'. *Zimbabwe Daily Online* (December 3). http://zimdaily.com/news/117/ARTICLE/1166/13.html (accessed 4 March 2007).

Bond, P. 2005. 'Zimbabwe's hide and seek with the IMF: Imperialism, nationalism, and the South African proxy', *Review of African Political Economy* 106 (December): 609–19.

Bond, P. and Moore, D. 2005. 'Zimbabwe: Elections, despondency and civil society's responsibility'. *Pambazuka News* 201 (April 7). www.pambazuka.org/index.php?id=27627 (accessed 12 April 2005).

Bratton, M., Chikwana, A. and Sithole, T. 2005. 'Propaganda and public opinion in Zimbabwe', in *Journal of Contemporary African Studies* 23 (1) (January): 77–108.

Catholic Commission for Justice and Peace and the Legal Resources Foundation. 1997.

Chebundo, B. 2003. 'A story of the political violence experienced by Blessing Chebundo, Member of Parliament, Kwekwe, Movement for Democratic Change, Zimbabwe', *Kubatana.* October. www.kubatana.net/docs/hr/chebundo_pol_viol_031008.doc (accessed 4 March 2007).

Chikwana, A., T. Sithole and M. Bratton. 2004. 'The Power of Propaganda: Public Opinion in Zimbabwe'. Afrobarometer Working Paper No. 42, Cape Town: Michigan State University, Institute for Democratic Alternatives, Centre for Democratic Development (August).

Chinembiri, J. 2005. 'Mugabe to tighten Zezuru clan power: With an election victory behind him, president now sets sights on bolstering his clan'. *Africa Reports: Zimbabwe Elections,* 25. London: Institute for War and Peace Reporting, 4 April.

Chung, F. 2006. *Re-living the Second Chimurenga: Memories from Zimbabwe's Liberation Struggle.* Harare and Uppsala: Weaver Press and the Nordic Africa Institute.

Daily News Online. 2004a. Mutasa implicated in terror campaign. Zimbabwe Information Centre. August 18. http://www.zic.com.au/updates/2004/31august2004.htm (accessed 4 March 2007).

— 2004b. 'Net closes in on Mutasa'. Zimbabwe Information Centre. 21 September. http://www.zic.com.au/updates/2004/21september2004.htm. (accessed 4 March 2007).

de Waal, V. 1990. *The Politics of Reconciliation: Zimbabwe's First Decade.* London: Hurst and Company.

Eppel, S. 2004. 'Gukurahundi', the Need for Truth and Reparation', in Raftopolous, B. and Savage, T. (eds) *Zimbabwe: Injustice and Political Reconciliation.* Cape Town: Institute for Justice and Reconciliation, pp. 43-62.

Guma, L. 2005. 'I was robbed', says Kombayi'. *The Zimbabwean.* 5 September. http://www.thezimbabwean.co.uk/2-september-2005/patrick-kombayi.html

(accessed 4 March 2007).

Hansard. 1983. Parliament of Zimbabwe. 29 November.

Human Rights NGO Forum. 2004. *Political Violence Report*. Harare. August.

International Crisis Group. 2006. 'Zimbabwe: An Opposition Strategy', *Africa Report* No. 117 (August). Brussels: ICG.

Kamete, A. 2006. 'The return of the jettisoned: ZANU(PF)'s crack at 're-urbanising' in Harare', *Journal of Southern African Studies* 32 (2) (June): 255–71.

Kombayi, P. 2004. Interview, Gweru. September.

Kriger, N. 2003. *Guerrilla veterans in Post-war Zimbabwe: Symbolic and Violent Politics, 1980–1987*. Cambridge: Cambridge University Press.

Kriger, N. 2005. 'ZANU(PF) Strategies in General Elections, 1980–2000: Discourse and coercion', *African Affairs* 104 (414) (January): 1–34.

Manyukwe, C. 2007. 'Chinamasa off the hook'. *Financial Gazette*, 15 February. http://all africa.com/stories/200702151057.html (accessed 3 March 2007).

Manyukwe, C. 2006. 'Chinamasa not off the hook yet'. *Zimbabwe Independent*, 15 September. http://www.thezimbabweindependent.com/viewinfo.cfm?id=7244 &siteid=1&archive=1 (accessed 3 March 2007).

Makanje, R., Revai, L., Shaba, M. and Win, E. 2004. 'Linking rights and participation: Zimbabwe Country Study', at Linking Rights and Participation. November. Brighton and Washington: Participation Group, Institute of Development Studies and Just Associates.

Maroleng, C. 2005. 'Zimbabwe's Zezuru Sum game: The basis for the security dilemma in which the political elite finds itself in', *Africa Security Review* 14 (3) (September): 86–8.

Marx, K. 1963 [1852]. *The 18th Brumaire of Louis Bonaparte*. New York: International Publishers.

Mbembe, A. 1992. 'Provisional notes on the postcolony', *Africa* 62 (1) (January): 1–26.

Maguranyanga, B. and Moyo, S. 2006. *Land Tenure in Post Ftlrp Zimbabwe: Key Strategic Policy Development Issues*. Harare: African Institute for Agrarian Studies (April).

Mutyambizi-Dewa, J. 2006. 'Bemoaning the misguided use of state apparatus'. Association of Zimbabwean Journalists. October 20. http://www.zimbabwejournalists. com/story.php?art_id=1194&cat=4 (accessed 2 March 2007).

Moore, D. 1991. 'The ideological formation of the Zimbabwean ruling class', *Journal of Southern African Studies* 17 (3) (September): 472–95.

— 1995. 'Democracy, violence and identity in the Zimbabwean War of National Liberation: Reflections from the realms of dissent', *Canadian Journal of African Studies* 29 (3) (December): 375–402

— 2001a. 'Democracy is coming to Zimbabwe', *Australian Journal of Political Science* 36 (1) (March): 163–69.

— 2001b. Searching for the iron fist and velvet glove in the Democratic Republic of the Congo. Canadian Journal of African Studies 35 (3) (December): 547–60.

— 2003. 'Zimbabwe: Twists on the tale of primitive accumulation', in Smith, M. (ed.) *Globalizing Africa*. Trenton: Africa World Press.

— 2004a. 'The Second Age of the Third World: From Primitive Accumulation to Public Goods?' *Third World Quarterly* 25 (1) (February): 87–109.

— 2004b. 'Marxism and Marxist intellectuals in schizophrenic Zimbabwe: How many rights for Zimbabwe's Left? A comment', *Historical Materialism* 12 (4) (December): 405–25.

— 2005a. 'A reply to "The power of propaganda": Public opinion in Zimbabwe 2004', *Journal of Contemporary African Studies* 23 (1) (January): 109–19.

— 2005b. 'ZANU(PF) and the ghosts of foreign funding', *Review of African Political*

Economy 103 (March): 156–62.

— 2005c. 'History and Hegemony: A Political Biography in Zimbabwe'. South African Association of Political Studies Colloquium, University of KwaZulu-Natal, Pietermaritzburg, 22–23 September.

— 2005d. '"When I am a century old": Why Robert Mugabe won't go', in R. Southall, R. and Melber, H. (eds) *Legacies of Power: Leadership Change and Former Presidents in Africa*. Cape Town and Uppsala: Human Sciences Research Council and Nordic Africa Institute.

Moyo, G. 2002. 'Gukurahundi mooted in 1979: document', *Zimbabwe Standard*, 8 October.

Moyo, S. and Yeros, P. 2005. 'Land Occupations and Land Reform in Zimbabwe: Towards the National Democratic Revolution', in Moyo, S. and Yeros, P. (eds) *Reclaiming the Land: The Resurgence of Rural Movements in Africa, Asia and Latin America*. London and Cape Town: Zed Books and David Philip.

Mukaro, A. and Mugari. S. 2006. 'CIO bungling exposed in arms cache: Plan to make arms 'discoveries' in different parts of the country', *Zimbabwe Independent*, 17 March. http://www.zwnews.com/print.cfm?ArticleID=14033 (accessed 4 March 2007).

Mushonga, N. 2006. 'Don't use 'culture' to oppress women'. *Zimbabwe Standard*, 22 April. http://www.kubatana.net/html/archive/opin/060422nm.asp (accessed 4 March 2007).

Nest, M. 2001. 'Ambitions, profits and loss: Zimbabwean economic involvement in the Democratic Republic of the Congo', *African Affairs* 100 (400): 469–90.

Nyarota, G. 2006. *Against the Grain: Memoirs of a Zimbabwean Newsman*. Cape Town: Zebra Press.

Nkatazo, L. 2006. 'Chinamasa trial postponed after no-show'. Newzimbabwe.com. 11 March. http://www.newzimbabwe.com/pages/quit14.14274.html (accessed 3 March 2007).

Potts, D. 2006. 'Restoring order'? Operation Murambatsvina and the Urban Crisis in Zimbabwe', *Journal of Southern African Studies* 32 (2) (June): 273–91.

Raftopoulos, B. 2006a. 'Reflections on opposition politics in Zimbabwe: The politics of the Movement for Democratic Change (MDC)', in B. Raftopoulos, B. and Alexander, K. (eds) *Reflections on Democratic Politics in Zimbabwe*.Cape Town: Institute of Justice and Reconciliation, pp. 7–29.

— 2006b, 'The Zimbabwean Crisis and the Challenges for the Left', *Journal of Southern African Studies* 32 (2) (June): 203–19.

Ranger, T. 1985. *Peasant Consciousness and Guerrilla War in Zimbabwe*. London and Harare: James Currey and Zimbabwe Publishing House.

— 2004. 'Nationalist Historiography, Patriotic History and the History of the Nation: The Struggle Over the Past in Zimbabwe', *Journal of Southern African Studies* 30 (2) (June): 215–34.

Rupiya, M. 2005. 'Zimbabwe: Governance through Military Operations', *African Security Review*, 14, 3: 117-18.

Sachikonye, L. 2005. 'The Land is the Economy: Revisiting the Land Question', *African Security Review* 14 (3): 31–44.

— 2006. 'The impact of Operation Murambatsvina/Clean up on the working people in Zimbabwe'. Report for the Labour and Economic Development Research Institute of Zimbabwe, Harare. March: 19–20.

Saunders, R. 2000. *Never the Same Again: Zimbabwe's Growth Towards Democracy, 1980–2000*. Harare: ESP.

Scarnecchia, T. 2006. 'The 'Fascist Cycle' in Zimbabwe, 2000–2005', *Journal of Southern African Studies* 32 (2) (June): 222–37.

Solidarity Peace Trust. 2006a. *Operation Taguta/Sisuthi: Command Agriculture in Zimbabwe; Its impact on Rural Communities in Matabeleland.* Port Shepstone: Solidarity Peace Trust. April.

— 2006b. *Meltdown: Murambatsvina One Year On.* Port Shepstone: Solidarity Peace Trust. August.

Tekere, E. 2004. Interview, Mutare. August.

— 2007. The people who saved me from poverty, Newzimbabwe.com. 26 February. http://www.newzimbabwe.com/pages/tekere8.15030.html. Excerpts from A Lifetime of Struggle, Harare: Southern African Political Economy Series.

Tibaijuka, A. 2005. *Report of the Fact-Finding Mission to Zimbabwe to Assess the Scope and Impact of Operation Murambatsvina by the UN Special Envoy on Human Settlements Issues in Zimbabwe.* New York: United Nations.

Tshabangu, O. 1979. *The Revolution in the Revolution: The March 11 Movement.* Hull: Paper Tiger.

Vambe, M. 2005. 'Can the critic listen? Representing subaltern subjectivities', in *Why Don't You Carve Other Animals,* paper presented at Yvonne Vera Conference, University of KwaZulu-Natal, Pietermaritzburg, 8 September.

White, L. 2003. *The Assassination of Herbert Chitepo: Text and politics in Zimbabwe.* Bloomington, Harare and Cape Town: Indiana University Press, Weaver Press and Double Storey.

3

Discourses of Dirt and Disease in Operation Murambatsvina

Ashleigh Harris

Anna Kajumulo Tibaijuka's (2005) report for the United Nations (UN) provides a list of reasons for Operation Murambatsvina, which include, broadly, the notions that it was driven by an economic and social impulse or that it was politically motivated and/or retributive. Since the operation negatively affected ZANU(PF) supporters and detractors alike, there is no easy way to establish simple party politics as the cause. The government of Zimbabwe argued that Murambatsvina was aimed at 'arresting disorderly or chaotic urbanization, including its health consequences; stopping illegal, parallel market transactions; and reversing environmental damage caused by inappropriate urban agricultural practices.' (Tibaijuka 2005, 20).

This chapter focuses on the history of the 'discourse of dirt' in the Zimbabwean colonial and post-colonial contexts, and considers the discursive matrix in which Murambatsvina occurred. Murambatsvina is also read as symptomatic of various governmental anxieties about loss of control of the urban population, irrespective of political affiliation. A further concern, is the reasons for *naming* the operation 'clean up the filth'. These questions will address how 'dirt' became moralised in the discourse surrounding Murambatsvina, and how this moralisation came to justify the operation in ZANU(PF)'s view. Furthermore, this discursive construction around 'dirt' might symptomatically lead to another set of morally determined discourses in the Zimbabwean administration, which have to do with disease and illness, particularly HIV/AIDS. Thus, Operation Murambatsvina was also driven by thinking about dirt and cleanliness with their roots in colonial, post-colonial, and nationalist constructions of cleanliness and dirt, purity and impurity, health and disease, and morality and immorality.

Racial 'dirt' in the colonial imaginary

This moralising and politicisation of dirt is not a new phenomenon in Zimbabwe. Timothy Burke (1996, 20) argues that 'for most whites living or travelling in Zimbabwe after 1890, the African world was a world of universal dirt and filth, while their own social world was its opposite, cleansed and pure' (Burke ibid: 20). This racialised binary of cleanliness/dirt perpetuated racist ideology, and also justified policies that divided geography along racial lines, and ensured the preservation of imperial power. As Burke notes (1996, 35-36):

> The leading specialists of the new disciplines of tropical medicine at the end of the nineteenth century often argued that sanitation and hygiene were crucial for making the tropics safe for Europeans. In so doing, they frequently contended that 'dirty' races and their practices were one of the primary sources of contagion. This tendency to regard the proximity of Africans as a primary source of contagion has been referred to by Maynard Swanson as the 'sanitation syndrome.' Swanson writes 'Overcrowding, slums, public health and safety ... were in the colonial context perceived largely in terms of colour differences. Conversely, urban race relations came to be widely conceived and dealt with in the imagery of infection and epidemic disease. This 'sanitation syndrome' can be traced as a major strand in the creation of urban apartheid.

Racialisation of dirt, and illness, played a significant role in justifying the creation of segregated African 'locations' in colonial Zimbabwe (p. 36). The extension of *bodily* dirt to a broader state of *moral* dirt was clearly perpetuated in colonial mission schools in which 'most textbooks and course outlines began with an explicit linkage between cleanliness and godliness' (p. 39). Burke further notes that:

> [m]issionaries and their allies often preferred to define dirt as an elemental component of immorality, a distilled, vague, and generalized essence of profane living. The 'Catechism' warned students against both 'dirt of the mind' and 'dirt of the body', giving the following definitions of each: 'dirt of the mind' was 'thinking bad thoughts or not thinking at all' and 'dirt of the body' was 'to live in a dirty way and to have dirty habits'. In another text, pupils were told that 'dirt ... is anything that makes something unclean' and that disease, especially venereal disease, 'comes as a punishment for doing things that are prohibited.'

Here, dirt and disease are connected to exclusionary practices that separate the 'dirty' and the 'sick' from the 'clean' and the 'healthy', and provide the justification for such segregation. In *Illness as Metaphor and AIDS and Its Metaphors* Susan Sontag (1991, 60) outlines the process of the moralisation of disease when she argues that:

> [f]irst, the subjects of deepest dread (corruption, decay, pollution, anomie, weakness) are identified with the disease. The disease itself becomes a metaphor. Then, in the name of the disease (that is, using it as a metaphor), that horror is imposed on

other things. The disease becomes adjectival. Something is said to be disease-like, meaning that it is disgusting or ugly. Once the disease metaphorically comes to signify corruption, decay, and pollution, it becomes inflected with moral meaning.[1]

Moralising of disease leads to condemning of the ill. The ill, themselves, get understood, by virtue of their connection to the moral causes of disease as immoral and the illness becomes read as just punishment for what is considered to be the moral degeneracy of the sick. As Sontag argues, 'the disease metaphor in modern political discourse assumes a punitive notion: of the disease not as a punishment but as a sign of evil, something to be punished' (p. 81).

Metaphors around illness abound in specific relation to venereal disease, because it is already embedded in the highly moralised discourses of sex and sexuality. In colonial Zimbabwe, fears of the dirtying of the pure (read: white Europeans) were often attached to fears of venereal disease. Burke (p. 20) notes how 'many early Native Commissioners represented their African charges as generically "syphilitic", and believed this "syphilis" could be spread to whites through shaking hands, physical proximity, or handling hut taxes'. This fantasy of the 'moral dirt' of the colonised black subject infecting the 'innocent' white administrator is taken further in Sontag's (1991, 112) argument that: 'Infectious diseases to which sexual fault is attached always inspire fears of easy contagion and bizarre fantasies of transmission by non-venereal means in public places.' In other words, projecting infection on to a racialised black body and culture was meant be a 'systematic [way to] use hygiene as the underlying logic of certain colonial institutions concerned with ruling and disciplining Africans' (Burke 1996, 34).

Entanglement of the colonial past in Operation Murambatsvina

Operation Murambatsvina must then first and foremost be understood in the context of an entanglement with the colonial past in Zimbabwe. This entanglement, as Achille Mbembe (2001, 15) demonstrates, 'is in reality a combination of several temporalities', which resists the easy distinction of a time before and after colonisation. Mbembe argues, instead, that we 'repudiate not only linear models but the ignorance that they maintain and the extremism to which they have repeatedly given rise' (p. 17) and focus, instead, on the *time of entanglement*, of which Mbembe writes:

[T]his time of African existence is neither a linear time nor a simple sequence in which each moment effaces, annuls, and replaces those that preceded it, to

---

1   As Sontag (1991, 60) notes, of the etymology of the word *pestilence*: "from pestilence (bubonic plague) came 'pestilent,' whose figurative meaning, according to the *Oxford English Dictionary*, is 'injurious to religion, morals, or public peace – 1513'; and 'pestilential,' meaning 'morally baneful or pernicious – 1531.'"

the point where a single age exists within society. This time is not a series but an *interlocking* of presents, pasts, and futures that retain their depths of other presents, pasts, and futures, each age bearing, altering, and maintaining the previous ones. (p. 16)

In 'Displacement and disease: Epidemics and ideas about malaria in Matabeleland, Zimbabwe 1945-1996', JoAnn McGregor and Terence Ranger (2000, 204), contemplate the colonial 'pattern ... of removing African populations from healthy areas to infected zones' focusing specifically on the 'late 1940s and early 1950s, [which saw] ... large-scale forced resettlement of peoples from the southwestern Zimbabwean plateau in the malarial forests of northern Matabeleland' (p. 207). The organisation of colonial territory along lines of infection is expertly documented by their reference to John Ford's (1971, 208) demonstration that 'white Rhodesians were content to leave great areas of the colony as what he calls *Grenzwildnis* – tsetse zones which coincided neatly with African reserves'.

These colonial practices of exclusion and eviction are comparable, in method and discursive justification, to those of Operation Murambatsvina. For example, there is a striking similarity between ZANU(PF)'s instruction that evictees 'return to their *homes* in Zimbabwe's rural areas' (Bratton and Masunungure 2006, 2, emphasis added), and the Rhodesian government's argument that 'Africans were only temporary inhabitants of the highlands and that they could adapt once again to the malarial forests from which they had originated' (McGregor and Ranger 2000, 217). Moreover, as was the case on 17 May 2005, these colonial 'evictions were carried out by armed police in dawn swoops'.

The eviction of Africans from the malaria-free plateaux into the malarial zones of the country creates a binary of plateau–forest that might be understood as the pre-text for the urban–rural binary that played such a significant role in Operation Murambatsvina. Indeed, colonial history and the protection of white Europeans from malaria in Rhodesia resulted in the major urban areas of the country being developed in non-malarial areas, and so, geographically, these binaries overlap in significant ways.

In the colonial era, the Rhodesian government's justification of these evictions carefully constructed African bodies as a threat of contamination and infection. D. M. Blair, the then director of preventative services, writing to the World Health Organisation regional malaria consultant for Africa, Prof. Cambournac, stated on 30 August 1950, that 'it is these communities with their large numbers of African children who provide the reservoir of infection which spreads to the neighbouring European mining and farming areas' (cited in McGregor and Ranger 2000, 210). The point at which illness departs from the individual body and becomes metonymically infused in the broader environment (the African children are seen as an *a priori* 'reservoir for infection') is the point at which the official Rhodesian discourse starts to justify its removal of Africans from 'European', and by implication 'pure' and 'healthy', areas. It is another, vivid, example of Swanson's 'sanitation syndrome'.

Unfortunately, the ideology of racial purity in African nationalism is also informed by a vocabulary moralising discourses of dirt. The discourses of Operation Murambatsvina might be read, then, as a palimpsest, superimposed onto colonial and Africentric discourses of cleanliness and dirt, and as such, neither unexpected nor new but, rather, eerily predictable in their entanglement with the violent and exclusionary discourses of nationalist politics in Zimbabwe.

Racial purity in African Nationalism

The historical trajectory of discourses of dirt is not, of course, restricted to how it was used within the colonial era. In the nineteenth century, the Ndebele used 'the Shona word *tsvina* (dirt) to describe their antagonists as *chiTsvina*, 'dirty people" (Burke 1996, 25-6). The discursive constructions of a binary of African purity against colonial dirt is one that can be traced in a variety of ZANU(PF)'s, and Robert Mugabe's, vilifying statements about the contemporary Western world. Lene Christiansen (2005, 204) points out that Mugabe's 'Third Chimurenga' – defined 'as a final decolonisation' – is meant to imply a struggle to return Zimbabwe to a 'pure' past, unsullied by the history of colonisation. The danger of such Africentric notions of a pure, precolonial past is that it easily demarcates absolute lines between the pure and the impure. Mugabe places amongst the impure: the West; any political opposition to his rule;[2] whites;[3] and homosexuals,[4] arguing, in each of these cases, that these 'impurities' are *unAfrican*. However, as Paul Gilroy (1993, 188) argues, Africentricism '[a]ppeals to the notion of purity as the basis of racial solidarity ... sets tradition and modernity against each other as simple polar alternatives as starkly differentiated and oppositional as the signs black and white'. The reality is that in Africentric ideologies, African 'traditions' are made wrongly

2   Philip Gourevitch, reporting for *The New Yorker*, writes that Mugabe 'told the ZANU-P.F. central committee in July of 2000 [that] Tsvangirai's party represented 'the resurgence of white power' and 'the revulsive ideology of return to white settler rule'.' http://www.newyorker.com/fact/content/?020603fa_FACT1.
3   Mugabe has claimed, 'Africa is for Africans. [Our] land is ours by birth, ours by right,' and, 'We call on all blacks to stand together to isolate these whites.' Zimbabwe President: Fight Whites, *Associated Press*, 14 December 2000. http://www.zimbabwesituation.com/dec15.html#link3.
4   At a Heroes' Day Rally in Harare in 1995 Mugabe infamously stated of homosexuality: 'If dogs and pigs don't do it, why must human beings? Can human beings be human beings if they do worse than pigs?' During a parliamentary debate designed to show support for Mugabe's attacks, one MP, Aeneas Chigwedere, suggested that gays and lesbians be quarantined so they could not 'infect' the rest of the nation (Zaverdinos, Nico, 'Mugabe Hounds Gays: Zimbabwe's President acts unnaturally' http://www.newint.org/issue281/update.htm). In Mugabe's statement, it is interesting that gays should be seen as 'worse' than the animals considered to be the dirtiest, thereby associating homosexuality with filth, and that in Chigwedere's statement, homosexuality is seen as an infectious disease, justifying quarantine. The dynamic between homosexuality and a morally absolute notion of 'Africanness' is discussed in E. P. Antonio, 'Homosexuality and African culture', in P. Germond and S. de Gruchy (eds), 1997. *Aliens in the household of God: Homosexuality and the Christian faith in South Africa*. Cape Town: David Philip.

to exist in a 'pure' space, prior to the sullying history of colonisation. A more pervasive and persuasive discourse of purity and dirt has played a critical role in the creation of the Zimbabwean post-liberation nation state: that is, the discourse of Africentricism.

Of Plague and Purgation: Diseased body/body politic and the discourse of dirt in official statements about Operation Murambatsvina

The conflation of the discourse of dirt, disease and Operation Murambatsvina abounds in statements made by the authorities who supported and carried out the operation. In a speech officially launching the operation, the chairperson of the Harare Commission, Comrade Sekesai Makwavarara (*The Herald* 28 May 2005) stated that the operation sought to enforce by-laws to stop all forms of illegal activities:

> These violations of the by-laws in areas of vending, traffic control, illegal structures, touting/abuse of commuters by rank marshals, street-life/prostitution, vandalism of property infrastructure, stock theft, illegal cultivation, among others have led to the deterioration of standards thus negatively affecting the image of the City.... Harare was renowned for its cleanliness, decency, peace, tranquil environment for business and leisure, therefore we would like to assure all residents that all these illegal activities will be a thing of the past.

In this first official statement about the operation, 'cleanliness' becomes immediately attached to both 'illegal activity' and 'decency'. This metonymic link (which will be the subject of much of my analysis) is continued later in the speech where Cde Makwavarara states that Operation Murambatsvina was 'intended to bring sanity back to the City of Harare' (*The Herald* 28 May 2005). The 'unclean' are already associated, in one short speech, to the illegal, the indecent, and the insane. Dr Chombo, the Minister of Local Government, Public Works and Urban Development, made similar statements in the 28 June parliamentary debate on Operation Murambatsvina, stating that the cities and towns of Zimbabwe had been 'essentially rendered ... lawless, disorderly and completely devoid of public decency and civility.' He went on to insist that, 'there will be stern measures [taken] to rid the City of illegal structures and unlicensed trading premises ... some of which had essentially been transformed into havens for thieves and criminals, touts, illegal immigrants, illegal foreign currency dealers, drugs traffickers, street dwellers and such other vice-perpetrating elements that had effectively contributed to [a] growing moral decadence' (MMPZ 2006).

A similar moralisation of disease as dirty emerges in the official state response to the cholera outbreak of January 2006 in Harare. The Media Monitoring Project of Zimbabwe states that the official responses to the outbreak 'narrowly fingered vendors, particularly those in Mbare, as the source of the pestilence' and reports that '*The Herald* (9 January) concealed revelations of more cholera infections in Harare in a story hailing government's purge of the urban poor under Murambatsvina as having helped prevent the spread of the disease.' Furthermore, 'local government officials [claimed] victory over the outbreak, alleging that it would have been '*a major catastrophe*' had government not embarked on its 'clean-up' exercise last year.' ZTV quoted one official, Simbarashe Madungwe saying: 'We thank God for Operation Murambatsvina ... [without which we] could not have been able to contain the disease' (ZMMPZ 2006). The 'purge' of the city is justified and the 'dirty' vendors of Mbare (one of Harare's townships worst hit by the operation) are blamed for the outbreak. Read against the prior statement by the Minister of Health, this represents Harare, along with all cities in the nation, as infused with a miasma of dirt and disease. Sontag (1991, 127), again, argues: 'Specific diseases, such as cholera, as well as the state of being generally prone to illness, were thought to be caused by an 'infected' (or 'foul') atmosphere, effusions spontaneously generated from something unclean ... [This] disease-carrying atmosphere came to be identified with urban rather than rural squalor.'

HIV/AIDS: The silent illness

What, then, constituted the 'reservoir for infection' in Operation Murambatsvina? A number of possibilities have been discussed elsewhere: that the 'infection' is poverty, political opposition, the threat of mass action against the government, etc. Yet, there has been an alarming omission in these discussions of the domain of infection; real illness. Given that 'an estimated 24.6 per cent of adult Zimbabweans are infected with HIV/AIDS' (Tibaijuka, 2005, 39), this is disquieting. Tibaijuka's report considers the problem of HIV/AIDS only by way of indicating how many HIV/AIDS sufferers would have been directly affected by Operation Murambatsvina (ibid.). The report considers the consequences of Murambatsvina on HIV/AIDS sufferers, but does not see the disease itself as one of the possible motivations for the evictions or, at least, as part of the government's discursive justification of the evictions.

We can read HIV/AIDS as the unspoken threat that discursively represents the miasma of social decay in urban Zimbabwe. The banishment of the urban poor, a loosely defined category, but the one with the highest HIV-infection rate in Zimbabwe, is the most effective populace to evict in the attempt to purge the city of its (metaphorical, but discursively concrete) miasma of AIDS. It is not only the pauper, but the HIV-positive pauper, whose body becomes the site onto which the government's anxieties about loss of urban control is projected.

This argument is strengthened if we consider it alongside various contemporary discourses around HIV/AIDS in Zimbabwe, particularly the proposed policy presented by ex-Brigadier General David Chiweza. Chiweza is the founder of the organisation CAST (Citizens' AIDS Survival Trust), which bases its approach to HIV/AIDS on his unpublished book *HIV and Aids: The Final Stand*, now archived in the National Archives of Zimbabwe. In this book, the title of which is disconcertingly reminiscent of the Nazi's 'final solution', Chiweza argues for

[t]he 'Embryo Effect Strategy' – which is a [sic] central to CAST ideology [and] is aimed at creating an Aids-free generation ... The Embryo Effect Strategy operates as a pre-emptive measure specifically targeting the low HIV risk group of between 10 and 13 years. This strategy advocates for a complete cut off between the HIV-free generation and the rest. Strict laws should be put in place to make sure that those who cross this line should be severely punished. For the 'Aids-free' generation, after this cut off date, it should be made mandatory whenever one wants to take an important step in his or her life to produce HIV-negative results. CAST has been lobbying for a law that makes HIV-testing mandatory, which will encompass the meting out of punishment to those who willfully pass on the virus to others. Under the law, if embraced, those tested would get certificates to show that they had been tested and should produce the certificates before they could secure employment.[5]

This discourse of quarantining AIDS sufferers (who become, following the logic of the acronym of Chiweza's organisation, 'outcasts') is supported by Paul Chimedza (*The Sunday Mirror* 22 October 2006), a medical doctor and weekly columnist who argues for a 'SARS act on HIV/AIDS, by way of quarantine.' Chiweza, who is the chairperson of the HIV/AIDS commission for the Evangelical Fellowship of Zimbabwe (EFZ) has also been instrumental in the formulation of that organisation's HIV/AIDS policy, launched in February 2006. Chiweza's ideas would be less troubling were it not for the Public Health and Child Welfare Minister's approval of them. The minister, David Parirenyatwa, welcomed the EFZ's policy, claiming that it goes 'a long way in strengthening existing efforts. I am happy that the church has taken this initiative in complementing government efforts in the fight against HIV/AIDS' (*People's Daily online* 2006). That the policy 'complements' the 'existing efforts' of the Zimbabwean government indicates that Chiweza's radical approach is not entirely out of line with ZANU(PF)'s. Chiweza also sees his own ideas as complementary to national policies and programmes. He writes, on CAST's website, that the organisation 'commends the Ministry of Health and Child Welfare ... [for its] successful initiatives in the fight against the pandemic. Recent statistics have shown that there has been a general improvement in sexual behaviour in the population at large'.[6] This moralising is certainly in line with Parirenyatwa's comment, that 'the clean up exercise is bringing back better moral standards in

---

5   *Sunday Mirror*, 22 October 2006.
6   The highest levels of HIV infections are found in urban areas. http://www.wcc-coe.org/wcc/what/mission/ehaia-html/sa-zimbabwe-e.html. Indeed, according to the same report, the current percentage of HIV infections in both Harare and Bulawayo, Zimbabwe's two largest cities, is around 35 per cent.

the country and reducing the transmission of sexual transmitted diseases especially HIV and AIDS in this country'.[7]

Moreover, if one considers the time-line of the development of Chiweza's theory, from 1995, when he founded CAST, to the present, it is unlikely that this discourse of exclusion exists at a complete remove from that presented in Operation Murambatsvina itself. Just as Murambatsvina sought to purify the cities of Zimbabwe through evicting and purging the social and moral 'dirt' of those cities, so too must the HIV/AIDS sufferer be separated from the rest of society. All the physically and morally 'ill', according to ZANU(PF), must be quarantined: the HIV-positive along with homosexuals, as suggested by Member of Parliament Aeneas Chigwedere, and perhaps all threats to the physical and moral 'health' of the body politic and the city. This division and quartering of the social body enables the government to ensure its continued control of the populace, whilst simultaneously justifying these banishments and expulsions through the othering, and moralising, discourses of dirt and infection. Following various metaphorical constructions of illnesses, from leprosy, tubercolosis and cholera, to cancer and HIV/AIDS, I believe that HIV/AIDS is playing an important role in the organisation of ZANU(PF)'s discourse of urban 'dirt'. This is by no means overt, or even (necessarily) intentional. Sontag (1991, 180) connects the militarising of the language about cancer to the ways in which the metaphorically 'diseased' in the body politic are dealt with by the state. She argues that this militaristic discourse 'not only provides a persuasive justification for authoritarian rule but implicitly suggests the necessity of state-sponsored repression and violence (the equivalent of surgical removal or chemical control of the offending or 'unhealthy' parts of the body politic)'. It is valuable to read the contemporary discourse about HIV/AIDS in Zimbabwe along similar lines; and as one does this, observing the language of quarantine and purging, one understands some of the complexities of the relationship between this discourse and the eviction of the metaphorically 'dirty and diseased' that was Operation Murambatsvina. These metaphors play an active role in the political spatialisation of cities and nations. As Sontag, observing the relationship between city slums and tuberculosis, notes:

> the importance of tuberculosis and the alleged or real threat of it in the slum-clearing and 'model tenement' movements of the late nineteenth and early twentieth centuries, the feeling being that slum housing 'bred' TB. The shift from TB to cancer in planning and housing rhetoric had taken place by the 1950s. 'Blight' (a virtual synonym for slum) is seen as a cancer that spreads insidiously, and the use of the term 'invasion' to describe when the non-white and poor move into a middle-class neighbourhood is as much a metaphor borrowed from cancer as from the military: the two discourses overlap. (p. 75)

The power of such discourse is redoubled, in the present argument, by the fact

---

[7]   I am indebted to Robert Muponde for drawing my attention to Chiweza's policy.

that, given the spatialisation of HIV/AIDS in Zimbabwe, a large proportion of those evicted in Operation Murambatsvina were not only metaphorically and morally 'diseased' in the eyes of the state, but were actual sufferers of HIV/AIDS.

Conclusion: a rejection of 'purifying' and 'purging'

In the official discursive construction of Operation Murambatsvina, dirt became metonymically and metaphorically linked to disease and infection, and this nexus of metaphorical connections was moralised so as to justify discursively the evictions as an act of 'purifying' the cities. Moreover, the discursive justification of the forced removal of peoples, of human purging, has inhumane precedents in the segregation of races in colonial Rhodesia. This chapter acknowledges the ways in which the current administration of Zimbabwe is deeply entangled with the violent, racist colonial past. Current discourses around HIV/AIDS in Zimbabwe are in danger of constructing HIV/AIDS sufferers as the epitome of the 'moral dirt' so reviled in Murambatsvina. The consequences of such revulsion are likely to be cataclysmic in a country with one of the highest HIV-infection rates in the world. One hardly needs reminding that the Nazi term for the massive extermination of the populations targeted by Hitler was *die Reinigung*: the cleansing.

Bibliography

Antonio, E.P. 1997. 'Homosexuality and African culture' in P. Germond and S. de Gruchy (eds) *Aliens in the household of God: Homosexuality and the Christian faith in South Africa*. Cape Town: David Philip.

Blair, D.M. 1950. *Malarial control: Southern Rhodesia*. National Archives of Zimbabwe, Harare S.2413/400/78/8.

Bratton, M. and E. Masunungure. 2006. *Popular reactions to state repression: Operation Murambatsvina in Zimbabwe*. Afrobarometer: Working paper No. 59. Michigan State University, The Institute for Democracy in South Africa, and the Centre for Democratic Development, Ghana.

Burke, T. 1996. *Lifebuoy men, Lux women: Commodification, consumption, and cleanliness in modern Zimbabwe*. London: Leicester University Press.

CAST. http://www.castzimbabwe.co.zw/CAST_News_1.htm.

'Catechism of Health' July–September 1926. *Rhodesian Native Quarterly* 1:1.

Chidavaenzi, P. 2006. CAST: Casting a new light on HIV, Aids fight. 22 October. *The Sunday Mirror*. http://www.zimmirror.co.zw/sundaymirror/view_news.cfm?story id=18473&categoryid=14&issueid=649&issuedate=2006-10-22%2012:11:00.0&issue_type=current.

Christiansen, L. 2005. 'Yvonne Vera: Rewriting discourses of history and identity in Zimbabwe' in Muponde, R. and R. Primorac (eds), *Versions of Zimbabwe: New approaches to literature and culture*. Harare: Weaver Press.

Ford, J. 1971. *The role of the Trypanosomiases in African ecology*. Oxford: Oxford University Press.

Gilroy, P. 1993. *The Black Atlantic: Modernity and double consciousness*. London: Verso.

Hansard. 2005. 'Zimbabwe parliamentary debate on Operation Murambatsvina'. Vol. 32, No. 6, Parliament of Zimbabwe, 28 June. http://www.kubatana.net/html/archive/demgg/050628parlzim2.asp?sector=URBDEV&year=0&range_start=1#chombo.

Kubatana.   http://www.kubatana.net/html/archive/demgg/050628parlzim1.asp?sector=URBDEV&year=0&range_start=1#muguti.

Makwavarara, S. 2005. Speech delivered at the official launch of Operation Murambatsvina at the Town House on 19 May 2005.

Mbembe, A. 2001. *On the postcolony*. Berkeley, CA: University of California Press.

McGregor, J. and T. Ranger. 2000. 'Displacement and disease: Epidemics and ideas about malaria in Matabeleland, Zimbabwe 1945–1996', *Past and Present* 167: 203–37.

Morgenster Mission. 1950. *Hygiene: Standard IV*. Fort Victoria: Morgenster Mission Press.

Gourevitch, P. *The New Yorker*. http://www.newyorker.com/fact/content/?020603fa_FACT1.

People's Daily online, 'Church Group Launches AIDS policy in Zimbabwe', 15 February 2006. http://english.people.com.cn/200602/15/eng20060215_242792.html.

Sontag, S. 1991. *Illness as metaphor and AIDS and its metaphors*. London: Penguin.

Swanson, M. 1977. 'The Sanitation Syndrome: Bubonic plague and urban native policy in the Cape Colony, 1900–1909', *Journal of African History*, 18: 3.

Tibaijuka, A. K. 2005. Report of the Fact-Finding Mission to Zimbabwe to assess the Scope and Impact of Operation Murambatsvina by the UN Special Envoy on Human Settlements Issues in Zimbabwe.' http://www.kubatana.net/docs/urbdev/un_tibaijuka_murambatsvina_050718.pdf.

Zaverdinos, N. Mugabe hounds gays: Zimbabwe's president acts unnaturally. http://www.newint.org/issue281/update.htm

PART TWO

THE HIDDEN IMPACTS OF OPERATION MURAMBATSVINA

4

Displacement and livelihoods: the longer term impacts of Operation Murambatsvina

Deborah Potts

'It is common cause that the definition of an indigenous person is one who has a rural home allocated to him by virtue of being indigenous'

– *Phineas Chihota, Deputy Minister of Industry and International Trade, in Parliament,* Discarding the filth: Operation Murambatsvina

'[T]he vast majority of evicted residents [of Hatcliffe Extension] have not been offered any alternative place to settle and *have been told to go back to the rural areas they originally come from*'

– Habitat International (emphasis added).

Introduction
Operation Murambatsvina
and rural–urban linkages in Africa

The immediate impacts of Operation Murambatsvina were unprecedented by African standards in terms of the scale of destruction and livelihoods. One of the stated aims of the campaign was to displace urban residents 'back' to rural areas. As evident from the quotations above, a major objective of Operation Murambatsvina was to displace, forcibly, to rural areas those urban people whose houses had been demolished. The government's own statistics indicated that some 570,000 people (Tibaijuka 2005, 32), or 133,534 households, were potentially subject to such displacement, this being the estimate of the population housed in the 92,460 dwelling units demolished throughout the country (Ministry of Local Government, Public Works and Urban Development cited in Tibaijuka 2005, 85).

There is one explicit and one implicit assumption underlying the government's argument that the displaced should 'return' to rural areas. Explicitly, it assumes that they *all* originated from rural areas – since they were being told to 'return'. Implicitly, it assumes the displaced could find sufficient livelihood opportunities in rural areas to subsist. Neither of these was true, as will be shown below. Furthermore, and crucially, the forced displacements were a flagrant breach of human rights on a massive scale. The government's arguments and related rhetoric, however, were founded (however manipulatively) on the reality of continued linkages between rural and urban areas in Zimbabwe, and elsewhere in sub-Saharan Africa, which are briefly surveyed below.

Rural–urban linkages in contemporary sub-Saharan Africa and Zimbabwe

Rural–urban linkages, as both cultural and economic factors in sub-Saharan Africa, are of great significance. There is evidence from a wide range of countries (including Zimbabwe) that these links have been revitalised by the increasing poverty and more vulnerable livelihoods that have become typical of the poor who dominate city populations. The ubiquitous downturn in the livelihoods of low- and middle-income urban populations relates to global economic forces such as the outcomes of the 1970s' oil crises and subsequent structural adjustment policies (Rakodi 1997; Becker et al. 1994; Bryceson and Potts 2006). These declines have led to many adaptations including changes in the links many urban households maintained with rural families (Potts 1995, 2006a).

Links between rural and urban areas are not peculiar to Africa (Tacoli 2006; 1998) but are probably most important and vital there. It remains common for people living in urban areas to have a strong affiliation with a particular rural area that, if asked, they may identify as their 'home'. Such *cultural* links may be strongly felt and are widely acknowledged throughout Africa. Beyond this there is an active *economic* link that is also of great significance for a component of the urban population, whereby some people maintain an actual plot of land, or other productive assets (e.g. cattle), in a rural area or the expectation of obtaining these in the future. This is predicated to a significant extent on the continuation of indigenous tenurial systems on much of the land so that many men (or, in matrilineal systems, women) have birthrights to arable and/ or grazing land. In Zimbabwe, these sorts of linkages and patterns of circular migration between rural and urban areas were enforced throughout the colonial period for many male workers, as permanent residence in towns was institutionally restricted. Surveys undertaken after independence found that, contrary to initial expectations, post-colonial rural–urban migrants to Harare were generally retaining these linkages, especially if they had some rural land. Economic factors relating to people's need for security in the future, as they aged, or if they should become unemployed or ill, dominated their explanations for keeping rural production going, and keeping their active interests in the rural economy (Potts and Mutambirwa 1991).

The economic significance of rural linkages for post-colonial urban migrants increased, rather than decreased, after the 1980s according to the evidence of these surveys. Migrants surveyed in Harare in 1994 and in 2001 were feeling increasingly *economically* insecure in town, and less likely to anticipate that their stay in town would be permanent, or even long term (Potts 2006b). By 2001 only 13 per cent of the migrant respondents planned to stay in Harare for good, compared to around a third of those interviewed in the 1980s. Of the *rural-born* migrants, 67 per cent expected eventually to return to the communal areas. The primary reason was clearly the weakening urban economy and lack of formal sector jobs.

Heterogeneous urban populations in Zimbabwe

There are two countervailing forces in contemporary African urban populations in relation to the significance of linkages to rural areas. On the one hand, declines in real urban incomes and formal sector job opportunities have often reduced the rural–urban income gap and mean that, for urban residents who have rural assets and who have been able to maintain their social links with a rural area, rural livelihood options are seen as important economic security and are being utilised more (e.g. Ferguson 1999). On the other hand, as time passes, an increasing proportion of most African cities' populations are born in town, and population growth is now mainly accounted for by natural increase within the city (i.e., births over deaths), rather than by net in-migration from the countryside (Potts 2006a; 2005). The urban-born are much less likely to have viable economic links to a rural area, even if many retain a socio-cultural link of affection to the birthplace of their parents or grandparents. Rather obviously, they may also lack the necessary agricultural and other skills to be able to subsist in a rural area. A cultural link is not the same as, and no substitute for, an existing urban livelihood. Given the blanket assumption of viable rural links inherent in Operation Murambatsvina's attempts to force the resultant internally displaced people (IDPs) into rural areas, it is useful to assess the available evidence for the relative size of urban population components in Zimbabwe.

In 1982, 33 per cent of Harare's population, and 35 per cent of Bulawayo's, were born within their respective provinces. By 2002 the population born in each province was almost exactly one half (CSO 2004). A further percentage will have been born in other towns. The 2002 census shows that 1.5 per cent of the urban population of Harare Province was born in Bulawayo, and 4.7 per cent of Bulawayo's population was born in Harare province. Further evidence comes from the Harare migrant surveys, already mentioned in the introduction to this chapter. These found that an increasing proportion of in-migrants to Harare is urban-born (Table 4.1, overleaf). In 2001, 22 per cent of recent

Table 4.1: Birthplace and previous residence of recent migrants to Harare
1985, 1994 and 2001

Year of survey	Previous residence			Place of birth			
	Another town	Communal land	Commercial farming area	Another town	Zimbabwe rural	Malawi/ Mozambique	Other
1985	20	77	2	6	88	4	2
1994	33	67	<1	10	88	1	1
2001	29	70	<1	22	77	<1	<1

Source: Migrant surveys conducted by Potts and Mutambirwa

Table 4.2: Landholdings of migrants to Harare
1985, 1988 and 2001

Year of survey	% with land	Average landholding (acres)	Modal landholding (acres)
1985	40	4.6	2
1994	53	4.3	2
2001	23	3.6	2

Note: Data on landholdings calculated for those with land only.

migrants interviewed had been born in another town. Today, therefore, probably about 60 per cent of Harare's populations is urban-born.

These surveys have also found that recent migrants are less likely to have land, and that those who do, have less (Table 4.2, above). Only about a quarter claimed to have land by 2001. This may be due both to land shortage and that the propensity of rural residents *with land* to migrate to town was falling. Also, as argued in Potts (2006b), there has probably been a natural upturn in out-migration from Harare by people for whom this was economically viable. Thus migrant streams from rural areas would contain a higher proportion of landless people and the pool of recent migrants in town would increasingly be characterised by those for whom rural economic alternatives were difficult or infeasible.

This evidence suggests how grossly simplistic and misleading the government's justification was for forcing IDPs caused by Operation Murambatsvina to 'return' to 'their' rural areas. In summary, first, over half Zimbabwe's current urban residents are urban-born and thus their rural links are weakened. Second, by 2001 even many recent rural–urban migrants did not have the basic asset of rural land to fall back on, and it can be safely assumed that this would be even truer of the urban-born.

Two further differentiating factors influence the nature of rural linkages: gender and foreign descent. Both are emphasised in the numerous reports on Operation Murambatsvina. Women's claims to land in the communal areas *in their own right* are far weaker than men's in patrilineal systems; they mainly access land via male kin, especially husbands. While it is not impossible for divorced or widowed women to obtain land, in a land-short environment their position is vulnerable, low priority and contingent on social capital. Indeed, many divorced, widowed or separated women have migrated to town *because* they have been squeezed off the land and their social links in rural areas have become dysfunctional. The permanence in town of migrant female household heads is, perforce, significantly greater than migrant men's therefore (Schlyter 1990). Foreign descent is also likely to preclude local rural linkages, for obvious reasons. Zimbabwe's long colonial history of recruitment of foreign labour, particularly from Malawi and Mozambique, has left a legacy of descendants from those immigrants. Most are nowadays Zimbabwe-born, but they will rarely have economic links into the communal areas, unless they have married into a local rural community. This issue figured large during the fast-track land reform post-2000, as significant numbers of commercial farm workers were of foreign descent, and many lost their jobs and, being conveniently cast as 'non-Zimbabwean', were excluded from the land resettlement process (Sachikonye 2003). Some ended up in and around towns and, already marginalised in Zimbabwean society, were more likely to live in the peri-urban communities and informal housing stock that were the very targets of Operation Murambatsvina.[1] If people in these groups were forced into rural areas during Operation Murambatsvina, it is inevitable that they will have had to return to town as their livelihood options there would have generally been non-existent.

Where have Operation Murambatsvina internally displaced persons gone?

The government's concerted efforts to force Operation Murambatsvina IDPs to move to rural areas included general exhortations to do so, and force. IDPs who remained visible, on the streets, or camping out in the ruins of their old dwellings, were taken in groups to 'holding camps' in Harare. The main such camp was Caledonia Farm, on the outskirts of Harare towards Ruwa, near Tafara high-density area. It rapidly achieved an infamous reputation as a place of extreme deprivation and terrible environmental conditions. In Bulawayo many IDPs took shelter in churches for a few weeks but even this was then forbidden by the government, and they were removed. People were 'processed' in these camps, or after abduction from the churches (SPT 2006), with the authorities asking them where they could go to in rural areas. Many were put on trucks and

---

1   Interview with trade union informant, 3 August 2006. I interviewed 11 different organisations in Zimbabwe, representing various NGOs, church-based organisations, trade unions and civil society groups plus people who had lost their housing under Operation Murambatsvina. In most cases, those I interviewed agreed that I could identify them and/or their organisations. However, it has been decided to conceal their identities for ethical reasons. All the interviews were conducted in Harare.

taken from the towns. Later reports from Harare generally indicated that people were offloaded in the vicinity of a communal area but were not taken, with whatever goods they had managed to rescue from the demolitions, to specific villages. Even if they were near the 'right' communal area where they actually had connections, most therefore faced a long journey by foot or whatever means they could devise.

There were other IDPs who left towns 'voluntarily'. Evidently, this was not a real choice – their movement was essentially forced but they decided that, on balance, given the circumstances, they would try to establish a residence and livelihood elsewhere. Often this *would* be in a rural area, but not necessarily. Reports indicated that out-migrants' destinations included other towns and international destinations, such as South Africa and Botswana (SPT 2006). In many cases reported by non-governmental organisations (NGOs), 'voluntary' out-migration involved a shift in family composition. Thus one adult might stay in town, or join the Diaspora, to try and maintain a cash income, and others, primarily wives and children, would leave for the rural areas. Later surveys heard that households who used to live on certain urban plots had made this 'choice'. In some cases, church-based groups did offer some assistance to out-migrants, although they were often keenly aware of the dilemmas involved (pers. comm.).[2] In Victoria Falls, 4,000 people were returned on a voluntary basis by churches (SPT 2006). They could be seen as thereby supporting the government's inhumane action but were nonetheless persuaded that they should respond to specific requests from IDPs to help them move. As one priest in Mbare said (Mbare Report 2005): 'This week we start to transport people to their rural homes. Only those who really want to go. Some people say we should not do this, we were doing the dirty work for government. I think we have to do what the people ask us to do.'

Although there is no specific evidence to this effect, logic would suggest that this 'voluntary' and unrecorded group would primarily comprise those who fell into the minority component of the urban population discussed above – that is, those who had some rural assets, or some expectation of accessing such, and active kinship links in a specific communal area. In fact, their characteristics would have been those that the government was rhetorically, and erroneously, ascribing to the entire urban populace. An essential *caveat* made by the priest quoted above relates to the need to differentiate between the victims of the campaign in this respect: 'Those who have no longer strong roots at home should not attempt to go.'

The precise numbers of IDPs who, at least initially, moved out of the towns because of Operation Murambatsvina, will never be known. Partial records were kept by some organisations involved in humanitarian assistance, for example by churches in Bulawayo (pers. comm.),[3] and the government evidently recorded

---

[2] Interviews with church-based informants, 30 July 2006, 2 August 2006.
[3] Interview with church-based informants, 2 August 2006, and NGO informant, 28 July 2006.

data on those in the 'holding camps'. However all those who bypassed institutional assistance (or coercion) would have been unrecorded. Some indications emerged nonetheless at the time: a large Harare-based survey in the high density areas found 40 per cent of respondents were from family units disrupted by the campaign, *mainly* because a wife and/or children had gone to rural areas (Action Aid/CHRA 2005). A later, similar survey of Harare, Bulawayo and Mutare found essentially the same pattern, although in this case it was reported that some of them had gone to other suburbs (Action Aid et al. 2005). Such surveys miss households who left in their entirety, however, so this would underestimate the impact. Human Rights Watch (2005, 32) estimated in September 2005 that of the 700,000 or so estimated to be displaced by Operation Murambatsvina, 114,000 (20%) had gone to rural areas.

Initial urban–rural displacement was significant, this evidence suggests, although the majority of IDPs stayed in town. The longer-term numbers displaced to rural areas were fewer, however, as there is plenty of evidence from the various reports and surveys conducted some time after the immediate campaign that, of those who were either literally forced to rural areas, or went 'voluntarily', many subsequently returned. One survey conducted in Bulawayo in January 2006 by the SPT followed up 143 households who had been living in backyard structures, now demolished, on a sample of plots in two high-density areas. In only 2 per cent of these cases had *entire* households left Bulawayo for a rural area. In a further 4 per cent, families moved to rural areas but left their breadwinner in Bulawayo. For 10 per cent of the sample the whereabouts of the households was unknown. Given that these were probably more likely to have left Bulawayo, the SPT calculated that this meant that a maximum of 17 per cent, and a minimum of 6 per cent, of households displaced went to rural areas. Of the rest, a few individuals went to other towns or to South Africa or Botswana, but the vast majority of the IDPs remained in Bulawayo, with 38 per cent remaining on the stand where their backyard structure had been demolished, and a similar number going to another stand. A few households were split up within town. To be accommodated within Bulawayo, once the backyard shacks which had provided crucial housing space had gone, meant the most desperate overcrowding within the formal, legal housing stock, which had already been very overcrowded. The SPT report provides exacting and moving details of this, including examples where living space per person had reduced to around 2 square metres, or even less. The initial displacements also had a cascade effect, as the first strategy for those rendered homeless was, if feasible, to move in with relatives who lived in a formal house somewhere in Bulawayo. This could be on the same stand on which their former backyard room had been destroyed, or elsewhere. However, as most rooms in most houses were already 'fully' occupied, accommodating relatives meant thousands of unrelated lodgers, who had been unaffected *directly* by Operation Murambatsvina demolitions, were asked to leave.

The SPT also followed up on certain groups displaced to rural areas from

Killarney and Ngezi Mines in Bulawayo, and from Victoria Falls. These surveys occurred in October 2005; others with small groups followed at various intervals up to August 2006. Of 106 people surveyed in October, the researchers predicted that only 21 per cent seemed likely to remain in the rural areas. This assessment was borne out by the other surveys, albeit that these covered different IDPs, which found that 19 per cent of those displaced from urban to rural areas were still there, and that 75 per cent were known to have returned to town. The remainder were untraceable. The case study material provided shows clearly that very few had been able to devise an alternative livelihood in a rural area and this was the primary reason for their urban return. In most of the followed-up case studies, the displaced apparently had no previous links with the area to which they moved, let alone assets there. As discussed above, it is therefore unsurprising that they had to return to town as the elements needed for a rural livelihood to be a feasible option were absent.

Apart from the work discussed above, systematic research on the fate of those displaced by Operation Murambatsvina was rare. In Bulawayo the City Council was sympathetic to the plight of the displaced, which helped, but in Harare the city is run by a government-appointed commission that makes such research more difficult. Nonetheless, many civic groups and NGOs there played advocacy roles and are able to provide general information about Operation Murambatsvina. The Combined Harare Residents Association (CHRA) has also conducted, in collaboration with other groups, two major surveys on the impact of Operation Murambatsvina on housing in Harare (and elsewhere) and those remaining on the affected stands. I interviewed a range of such organisations in July and August 2006, as well as some individuals and groups directly affected by Operation Murambatsvina.[4] All noted the impossibility of being precise about the numbers displaced *out of* Harare by Operation Murambatsvina or how many had subsequently returned, but all were also of the opinion, from anecdotal evidence and observation, that the majority of those who lost their housing remained in town. As in Bulawayo the main strategy has been further densification of occupation within the formal, planned housing stock in the HDAs (Chenjerai 2006) and a significant rearrangement of living spaces, with many lodgers unrelated to landlords being displaced in their turn.

On the other hand, all informants were also aware that a proportion of the displaced *had* gone to rural areas. For example, one housing scheme that had members in Mbare, Harare's most densely settled HDA which was terribly affected by the demolition of backyard shacks, had had 68 members before Operation Murambatsvina and only about 20 a year later, and some were known to have left for rural areas. A small focus group of people who had been displaced from backyard shacks and were now mainly living in hostels, such as the Joburg Lines in Mbare, explained that 'indeed many went to rural areas. Many of our friends are now not here' (pers. comm.).[5] This group emphasised the terrible suf-

---

4   Interviews with church-based informants, 30 July 2006, 2 August 2006.
5   See footnote 1.

fering that Operation Murambatsvina had caused, and that people they knew had died because of the disruption to their livelihoods and health. Another informant, who had herself been displaced from Dzivarasekwa, told of the difficulties faced by IDPs there who wished to go to rural areas but could not afford to transport their goods there. A survey in Mbare found that many IDPs had had to sell their furniture at knockdown prices because of this; 33 per cent of those interviewed had actually bought such furniture (Chenjerai 2006).

One issue that emerged from this research in Harare was that there was an element of 'sifting' during the processing of IDPs who ended up in the holding camp of Caledonia Farm. These tended to be a selective group – as one informant put it, they were the 'IDPs with no alternative'.[6] In other words, these IDPs could not find a legal dwelling space in town, perhaps due to lack of urban relatives or because other, closer relatives had been housed before them. Nor had they rural options, perhaps because they had no realistic links or, in some cases, because they could not afford the travel costs of leaving town. These were the most desperate people who were living on the streets, on waste ground, or in the ruins of their former dwelling units. In the holding camps, they were quizzed about their rural 'roots', and it is apparent that it was somehow deemed that some should not be 'returned' to rural areas. The criteria remain unclear but lack of rural links does seem, albeit arbitrarily and imperfectly, to have played a part for some. An informant from one church-based organisation involved in humanitarian interventions after Operation Murambatsvina, who generally held the view that most people do have a rural home, nonetheless argued that it was felt that urban-born residents and those of foreign descent should be 'set aside'. As this organisation was involved in providing transport for IDPs in the early stages, although this was later rethought, possibly such views had some influence. Certainly not all of these IDPs in Harare were 'ruralised' for some were taken to Hopley Farm, another holding camp in southern Harare, along the road to Chitungwiza. Hopley has a secretive reputation, is not openly accessible, and was described by one informant as pseudo-militarised;[7] its population in August 2006 was variously estimated at 1,000 and 4,000 households and it was becoming more formalised with housing stands being allocated[8] (see also Zimbabwe Lawyers for Human Rights 2006). Nonetheless, as already mentioned, others *were* dumped near communal areas, but far from their actual villages. One informant stated that some IDPs from holding camps were transported to government farms to become a source of cheap labour.[9]

One form of urban–rural movement noted in Harare was people moving not to distant rural 'homes', but to the communal areas nearest Harare such as Domboshawa, Goromonzi and Seke.[10] The issue of rural kinship links and assets

6   Focus group respondent, member of NGO savings group, 30 July 2006.
7   Interview with church-based informant, 30 July 2006.
8   Interview with civil society group informant, 4 August 2006.
9   Interviews with NGO informants, 3 August 2006; informal interview with Hopley Farm residents, 7 August 2006.
10   Interview with civil society group informant, 30 July 2006.

for an alternative livelihood are of little relevance to this sort of out-migration as the aim is to maintain physical access to the city and *urban* livelihoods via commuting. Purchasing a plot to build a house, thereby avoiding the planning restrictions of a residence within city boundaries, is often possible in the communal areas, despite land purchase being at odds with indigenous tenure.

An extraordinary feature of forced evictions and migration in Harare relates to Hatcliffe Extension, where thousands of people's houses were demolished under Operation Murambatsvina (see Potts 2006c; 2007). Most of those at Hatcliffe had a history of prior removals and evictions from within and around Harare – a process that may have already sifted out most with viable alternative livelihood options beyond the city. The settlement was entirely destroyed by Operation Murambatsvina. Yet, by August 2006 most of Hatcliffe Extension's evicted residents were back, on their original stands, with government permission, living largely in plastic-sheeted, timber-framed housing with asbestos roofs provided by NGOs and then, on a large scale, by the United Nations (UN) International Organization for Migration. The process involved in this dreadfully pointless eviction and return was that many of the residents at this settlement had been given leasehold permission by one authority or another to build houses. Most of the houses were unserviced, rendering them strictly illegal, and did not conform to various other legalities (Potts 2006c) but, nonetheless, the government finally agreed that people who had *papers* proving their 'legal' status there before Operation Murambatsvina, could return. Returnees told me that many of them had been moved to Caledonia Farm, 'processed' and some 'dumped in the bush' (pers. com,).[11] Subsequently, leaseholding evictees, now scattered, heard about the government's about-turn and returned. However, some Hatcliffe residents had *not* had leases, and informants believed these groups were more likely to have ended up in rural areas, although in line with the argument above about 'sifting' at holding camps, some were also known to be at Hopley. These informants, like those in Mbare, stressed that people had died during these displacements.

Conclusions

The economic security offered by rural landholdings remains important for many urban dwellers in sub-Saharan Africa, even if many of them do not turn to this option with much enthusiasm. The evidence that rural–urban linkages have strengthened in the face of urban economic decline relates mainly (but not necessarily only) to first-generation migrant cohorts who nowadays form only a minority of urban residents. Thus such links can be reducing for the urban-born majority at the same time as they are strengthening for this component.

The continued and renewed importance of such links has, however, in the

11   Interviews with Hatcliffe Extension residents, 31 July 2006.

case of Zimbabwe been deliberately utilised to disadvantage the urban poor.[12] It has also been deliberately misread and exaggerated. Some people, especially those who have come into town in recent years, will have potential or active *livelihood* links. However, to characterise all the urban poor as having such links is quite wrong. As each successive new generation is born in towns, the proportion of the total population who can 'return' to rural 'homes' reduces. Gender, nationality and land availability are other important factors influencing rural linkages.

Linkages between African rural and urban areas can serve many positive socio-economic functions *if there is freedom of movement and settlement.* In those circumstances those who can derive advantage from these connections can choose whether or not to actualise them (albeit within the functional constraints operating within their society and economy). However, to displace urban people forcibly, in the manner and scale of Operation Murambatsvina, breached human rights, was destructive of livelihoods and caused enormous suffering. As has been shown, not surprisingly, the majority of those displaced remained in, or had returned to, the towns within a year.

[12] While Mbiba (2001) makes an interesting argument that communal land rights are *inherently* disadvantageous for Zimbabwe's urban communities, I would contend that the evidence of the migrant surveys in Harare over the years, plus the very negative trends in African urban livelihoods throughout sub-Saharan Africa, show that, on balance, they are advantageous and remain an essential economic security net for millions.

Bibliography

ActionAid International/CSU/CHRA/ZPP. 2005. An in-depth study of Operation Murambatsvina/Restore Order in Zimbabwe. November 2005.
ActionAid International/Combined Harare Residents' Association, 2005. A study on the impact of 'Operation Murambatsvina/Restore Order' in 26 wards of Harare High Density Housing Areas, July. www.sarpn.org.za/documents/d0001388/index.php.
ActionAid International/CHR see ActionAid International/Combined Harare Residents
Becker, C., A. Hamer and A. Morrison. 1994. *Beyond urban bias: African urbanisation in an era of structural adjustment.* London: James Currey.
Bryceson, D. and D. Potts (eds) 2006. *African urban economies.* Houndmills: Palgrave.
Central Statistical Office. 2004. Census 2002: National report. Central Census Office, Harare.
Chenjerai, L. 2006. Post-Operation Murambatsvina: A study of the housing problems in Harare. BA dissertation, Geography Department, University of Zimbabwe.
Ferguson, J. 1999. *Expectations of modernity: Myths and meanings of urban life on the Zambian Copperbelt.* Berkeley: University of California Press.
Habitat International. 2005. Habitat International Coalition Housing and Land Rights Network Urgent Action Appeal: 200,000 people evicted in two weeks and another million threatened in Zimbabwe: Case ZIM100605.
Human Rights Watch. 2005. 'Clear the filth': Mass evictions and demolitions in Zimbabwe, September. http://hrw.org/backgrounder/africa/zimbabwe0905/.
Mbare Report. 2005. 'Discarded people', *Mbare Report* 12, June 27.

Mbiba, B. 2001. 'Communal land rights in Zimbabwe as state sanction and social control: A narrative', *Africa* 71 (3): 113–31.

Potts, D. 2005. 'Counter-urbanization on the Zambian Copperbelt? Interpretations and Implications', *Urban Studies* 42 (4): 583–609.

Potts, D. 1995. 'Shall we go home? Increasing urban poverty in African cities and migration processes', *Geographical Journal*, 161 (3): 245–64.

— 2006a. 'Urban growth and urban economies in eastern and southern Africa: trends and prospects' in Bryceson, D. and D. Potts (eds) *African urban economies*. 67–104. Houndmills: Palgrave.

— 2006b. '"All my hopes and dreams are shattered": Urbanization and migrancy in an imploding economy; The case of Zimbabwe', *Geoforum*, 37 (4): 536–51.

— 2006c. '"Restoring Order?" The interrelationships between Operation Murambatsvina in Zimbabwe and urban poverty, informal housing and employment', *Journal of Southern African Studies*, 32 (2): 273–91.

— 2007. 'City life in Zimbabwe at a time of fear and loathing: Urban planning, urban poverty and Operation Murambatsvina' in Myers, G. and M. Murray (eds) *Cities in Contemporary Africa*. Houndmills: Palgrave.

Potts, D. and C. Mutambirwa. 1991. 'Rural-urban migration in contemporary Harare: why migrants need their land', *Journal of Southern African Studies* 16 (4): 177–98.

— 1998. '"Basics are now a luxury": Perceptions of ESAP's impact on rural and urban areas in Zimbabwe', *Environment and Urbanization* 10 (1): 55–76.

Rakodi, C. (ed.) 1997. *The urban challenge in Africa: Growth and management of its large cities*. Tokyo: United Nations University Press.

Sachikonye, L. 2003. The situation of commercial farm workers after land reform in Zimbabwe: a report prepared for the Farm Community Trust of Zimbabwe. www.indcatholicnews.com/zimlan.html.

Schlyter, A. 1990. 'Women in Harare: Gender aspects of urban–rural interaction' in Baker, J. (ed.) *Small town Africa: Studies in rural urban interaction*. Uppsala: SAIS.

Solidarity Peace Trust. 2005. 'Discarding the filth: Operation Murambatsvina; Interim report on the Zimbabwean government's urban cleansing and forced eviction campaign', May/June 2005.

— 2006. '"Meltdown": Murambatsvina one year on'. August. Unpublished.

Tacoli, C. 1988. 'Rural–urban interactions: A guide to the literature', *Environment and Urbanization* [special issue on 'Beyond the rural–urban divide], 10 (1): 147–166.

Tacoli, C. (ed.) 2006. *The Earthscan reader in rural-urban linkages*. London: Earthscan.

Zimbabwe Lawyers for Human Rights 2006. *Hopley Farm residents: A life without dignity*. Harare: ZLHR.

5

Eschatology, Magic, Nature and Politics
The Responses of the People of Epworth to the Tragedy of Operation Murambatsvina[1]

Mickias Musiyiwa

Operation Murambatsvina caught many people by surprise, particularly the residents of Harare's high-density suburbs. This chapter examines the responses of the people of Epworth to the clean-up campaign. The intention of Operation Murambatsvina, as argued by the government, was to rid the country of illegal structures, crime, filthy stalls and squalor. However, this aim was completely overshadowed by its catastrophic aftermaths, which included homelessness, loss of property, forced migration, destitution, starvation, disease and children dropping out of school. For the majority of the people of Epworth, Murambatsvina was not a unique and unprecedented event because they had experienced similar tragedies in the form of 'Operation Clean-up' launched in 1983[2] and the 1991 clean-up.[3] The former evicted thousands of people deemed squatters countrywide, particularly in urban centres. The latter rounded up squatters and vagrants in Epworth, Mbare Musika and other parts of greater Harare.

Except for those residents who had not encountered the previous operations, there was less hopelessness and fear than in other suburbs when the tragedy struck their area. As during the early 1980s and 1990s clean-up campaigns, many of the people of Epworth resorted to nature, religion, magic and politics in an attempt to cushion the course and effects of this man-made disaster. As regards religion, there are numerous apostolic sects who through prophecy, forewarn their adherents of any impending troubles. *N'angas* (traditional healers and diviners) keep traditional religious practices alive and many people

---

1   *Murambatsvina* is a Shona noun meaning 'one who doesn't like dirt'. It was used to refer to city council workers who cleaned the streets and who would punish everyone they saw throwing litter everywhere. The word was attached with different political meanings and came to describe illegal urbanites.

2   It was launched to restore order in the country since hundreds of thousands of people displaced by the 1970s war of independence had settled illegally in urban centres and commercial farms.

3   It was organised by the Harare City Council to clean the city in preparation for the arrival of Queen Elizabeth II attending the Commonwealth Heads of Government Meeting (CHOGM).

consult them. The high political consciousness in Epworth has seen people's political allegiance shifting from United African National Council (UANC) to ZANU(PF) in 1980 and to the Movement for Democratic Change (MDC) in 2000. Ordinary people have exploited this political contingence to survive evictions. The continued stay of the majority of Epworth residents hinges upon their ability to utilise these different strategies and acquired knowledge systems and the manipulation of political symbols.

Operation Murambatsvina in history

Coverage of Operation Murambatsvina in the local and international media barely historicised the event, in spite of the fact that there have been many such operations in the past. Besides, other Murambatsvinas, though of a smaller magnitude, are carried out almost every year.[4] In order to appreciate the various responses of the people of Epworth to the 2005 Murambatsvina it is important to examine briefly the history of clean-up campaigns involving forcible eviction and the destruction of homes, which date back to the colonial period. The alienation of African land by colonial settlers, particularly after the passing of the Land Apportionment Act of 1930, triggered many evictions throughout the country. Africans were forced to settle in areas designated as 'reserves' which later were called Tribal Trust Lands after the 1969 Land Tenure Act. There were also colonial laws to deal with vagrancy, loitering and squatting in urban areas.

Africans found violating these laws were rounded up, arrested or sent back to the rural areas. Homelessness, which resulted in the mushrooming of squatter areas, was exacerbated in the 1970s with the intensification of the liberation struggle. Tens of thousands of people fled rural areas seeking refuge in urban centres. At independence the new government inherited a complex problem involving hundreds of thousands of displaced people who were now staying at places considered illegal; in the outskirts of cities and towns, and also at Mbare Musika and on the banks of the Mukuvisi river in Harare. Tens of thousands of war refugees flocked into Epworth and were given temporary refuge by the Methodist Church, which owned the area. After independence most of the homeless people were unwilling to return to their rural homes. This worsened the problem of squatting in Harare.

In an attempt to restore order the government adopted a 'bulldozer policy' in 1983. This was conceived as 'part of a broader policy' to restore order and 'to reverse the flow of rural people to Zimbabwe's cities and towns'.[5] Thus the bulldoz-

---

4   In 2006 alone these included Operation Round-Up which rounded up squatters, vagrants and street youths in May; Operation Sunrise, which was launched in August to promote the new family of bearer cheques introduced by the Reserve Bank and also as a way to try and destroy the parallel market; Operation Squatters Clean-Up which was done in July to deal with illegal foreign currency dealers and squatters in Bulawayo; and Operation Chikorokoza Chapera to deal with illegal mining activities.

5   'Bulldozer Policy to Halt Trek to Cities', *The Herald*, 11 February 1984.

ing of all settlements considered illegal was carried out throughout the country in 'Operation Clean-up'.[6] Those people who had occupied white-owned farms as part of reclamation of the land, in accordance with nationalist wartime rhetoric, were also evicted. Despite these measures, the squatter problem persisted into the next decade as witnessed by the adoption of another large scale clean-up in various parts of Harare in 1991. Initiated by the Harare City Council, it removed people from Epworth, Mbare Musika and other parts of Harare and settled them at Porta Farm to avoid causing 'severe embarrassment'[7] to Queen Elizabeth II, who was coming to the country to attend the Commonwealth Heads of Government Meeting (CHOGM).

However, in the whole history of clean-up exercises, the people of Epworth have been spared, experiencing only selective evictions and demolitions of their settlements. This has happened in spite of the fact that at independence, more than 30,000 squatters were living in the area,[8] making it one of the largest squatter settlements in the country. Religion, culture, politics and nature have played an influential role in moderating the severity of clean-up operations in Epworth. In 1984, the government stated that Epworth was an exception to the bulldozer policy because it 'is a unique settlement that started as a mission station ... and expanded rapidly during the liberation war when missionaries permitted displaced persons to live on the station'.[9] During the 2000 parliamentary elections, President Mugabe declared at a rally in Epworth that no person was supposed to be evicted because Epworth 'is now state land and the government says we are all equal and those who settled here first should not bar others from coming in'.[10] This leniency on the part of the government has resulted in the perennial flocking of home-seekers into the area. Now it has a population of 113,884,[11] the majority living as tenants and squatters. Almost 75 per cent of the structures in the area are deemed illegal.[12]

The cultural composition of Epworth: A brief history

Epworth is located about 15 km south-east of Harare, beyond the low-density suburb of Hatfield. It was sparsely populated during the pre-colonial period. In 1891 the Methodist Church took control of the area, and it is now one of the most densely populated residential areas in Harare. In the colonial period the main areas of Epworth were Chizungu, Chinamano and Chiremba. At present,

6   'Ex-squatters go home'. *The Herald*, 19 December 1983.
7   Lovemore Ngoma. 'Squatters Could Embarrass Queen, Council Tells Judge'. *The Herald*, 13 September 1991.
8   Tendayi Kumbula. 'Hope for Epworth as Government Steps in'. *The Sunday Mail*, 9 January 1983.
9   'Bulldozer Policy to Halt Trek to Cities'. *The Herald*, 11 February 1984.
10 Nelson Chenga. 'No One will be Removed from Epworth: President'. *The Herald*, 1 February 2000.
11 2002 Census, Preliminary Report. Central Statistical Office. Harare.
12 Caesar Zvayi. 'Reports on Clean-up Vindictive'. *The Herald*, 7 July 2005.

it is sub-divided into a multiplicity of areas due to the perennial influx of people. Now, there are also some informal settlements popularly known as *magada*[13] that actually outnumber officially designated stands.

During the pre-colonial period, the area first belonged to the Harava people of the Shava dynasty under their chief, Neharava. However, as Beach (1994, 96) shows, in the early eighteenth century the Harava were conquered by another group of the Shona people led by Seke Mutema of the Shava totem, who considered themselves the rightful owners of the Epworth lands. After the colonisation of Zimbabwe in 1890, the area was converted into a Christian village in 1892 by the Wesleyan Methodist Church when Cecil John Rhodes gave the church 3,000 acres in the area (Zvobgo 1996, 5). In the late 1970s, the church allowed thousands of refugees to live in the area as non-rent paying residents. Although the local people and the Methodist Church expected these *vauyi/vapoteri* (refugees) to return to their rural homes after the war, the *vapoteri* decided to stay permanently; as supporters of the new ruling party, ZANU(PF), they were given a mandate to live in the area as the government took the ownership of the Epworth lands from the church in 1982. It is clear that the government's strategy in acquiring the area was purely political. If these refugees were to be evicted, the ruling party was not going to win elections in the area because the legal residents of the area were mainly supporters of Bishop Abel Muzorewa's UANC.[14]

This conflict between the local people and the *vauyi* still remains, and is exacerbated each time there are general elections. The tension was also manifested during Operation Murambatsvina, when the houses of alleged MDC supporters were destroyed, particularly in Dhonoro, Komboniyatsva and other areas (pers. com.).[15] In spite of the government's repossession of Epworth, landownership here is still quite complex because the local people, as represented by their traditional chiefs, continue to claim that the land is theirs and that the Methodist Church had no right to take it in the first place, and worse still sell it to outsiders. While the church was allocating stands, some local people were also clandestinely selling stands to the *vauyi*. With rural-urban migration increasing after independence, many job-seekers preferred to stay in Epworth, where accommodation was affordable. Although in the 1980s and early 1990s there were efforts to develop the area and build decent houses, with financial assistance from United States Agency International Development (USAID),[16] Epworth still remains a largely informal settlement.

Both traditional and modern belief systems coexist and sometimes contradict each other, particularly when it comes to the control of nature, land and rocks.

---

13 The word is derived from the Shona ideophone, gada, which means 'to fall backwards and lie or sit restfully' or 'to lie on one's back resting'. In the context of the problem of accommodation in Epworth, it implies the freedom people have in building their shelters where ever they please and then 'rest' comfortably, without having to pay much rent and encounter other problems associated with being a tenant.

14 Interview with Simon Mabukwa, Harare, 9 June 2006.

15 Anonymous Interviewee, Epworth, 3 June 2006.

16 'Bulldozer Policy to Halt Trek to Cities', *The Herald*, 11 February 1984.

The remnants of the Neharava people criticise both the Methodist Church and the government for appropriating their land, which they regard emotionally and culturally as their ancestral heritage. An area of conflict is the control of nature, especially the rocks in the area, a struggle with a pre-colonial precedent.[17] Traditionalists wish to build their homes even in the midst of rocks and to perform their religious rituals there. The government intends to use the rocks for commercial tourism. Different Christian faiths also want control of the rock areas in order to build their churches or to establish their *masowe* (secluded places of prayer). The most spectacular rocks have been fenced off to protect them as a natural heritage site, but many areas of Epworth such as Komboniyatsva, Kedhishi and also in the *magada* beyond Chizungu have similar rocks. The 318-metre flat-topped rock, Domboramwari, is the largest physical feature in the area and could be the reason why it was a sacred place for the Shona people of pre-colonial times.

Even today, Christian faiths compete to control the mysterious rock and have built churches around it. Traditionalists claim historical and cultural ownership of the rock, as reflected in the many legends they tell about it. One has it that on its top there is a footprint of Mwari (Shona High God). For this reason the rock was named *Domboramwari* (rock of God). Another legend says that on the bottom of the northern side of the rock was a *musasa* tree where people could be served with *sadza* and delicious meat. Traditionalists argue that because of the coming of Western values and the desecration of *chivanhu* (Shona traditional values), these miracles no longer happen. As if Mwari's intervention is the last hope for the people of Epworth to end their troubles, it is here at Domboramwari that people whose houses had been demolished gathered as they pondered on where to go; to the rural areas or to the transit camp of Caledonia Farm.[18]

Domboremaziso (The Multi-Eyed Rock) is another revered rock, found in Overspill. It was given this name because, looked at from the east it is shaped like a huge human head with multiple eyes. When rain falls, water fills the potholes and flows down the sides of the rock, leaving indelible lines resembling the tears of a weeping person. The cave at the bottom of the rock and its surroundings are an important place of prayer; people from Jacha, Secondary and Overspill in particular come to ask Mwari to intervene in their suffering. It is here that in January 2004 a prophecy was made concerning the advent of Murambatsvina[19]. However, in spite of the relentless Western cultural onslaught, Epworth is still strongly symbolic of Shona traditional cultural life. Some people still own livestock, and traditional ceremonies such as *kurova guva* (settling the spirit of the deceased), cleansing ceremonies and *mapira* (all-night ancestral spirit ceremo-

---

17   According to Beach, (1994, 97), Chief Savanhu of the Harava was killed by Chinhamhora's people over the ownership of the Domboramwari Rock.

18   The farm is in the northern outskirts of Harare and was used as a transit point for those people whose homes had been demolished. However, not all the homeless were willing to stay at the farm, afraid that their freedom would be restricted and that they would be forced to go to rural areas.

19   Interview with Jonah Nhema, Epworth, 16 April 2006.

nies) are still practised. *Mbira* music, one of the religious musics of the Shona people, is dominant in the area. *N'anga* are also common, and in the past have been at the forefront in helping people deal with Murambatsvina.

Christianity – in the area for over a century now – is dominated by the Methodist Church, which has a theological college, a children's home and a church at Chiremba as well as primary and secondary schools. Other denominational churches include Roman Catholic, Salvation Army, the Seventh Day Adventist, Apostolic Faith Mission and Family of God. As in most areas of socio-economic exhaustion, there are also numerous *vapositori* (apostolic) sects, particularly those of the Johane Masowe weChishanu[20] movement.

The course and aftermaths of Operation Murambatsvina

Although the residents of Epworth are quite familiar with clean-up campaigns, the 2005 Murambatsvina alarmed many of them. It was unique in the suddenness and rapidity of its demolition. Harare residents dubbed it *tsunami*.[21] In the past, people whose houses were considered illegal structures were first issued with eviction notices, as was the case in 1984. This time no such notices were issued. Operation Murambatsvina took place in the context of heightened political tension, the ruling party having lost the Hatfield constituency (to which Epworth belongs) to the MDC in the parliamentary elections of both 2000 and 2005. The people of Epworth, and indeed in the other parts of Harare, were afraid that Operation Murambatsvina was to punish them for voting for the opposition. Although many squatters resisted the evictions and destruction of shelters in the early 1980s,[22] this time the military nature of the exercise and the political polarity in the country precipitated deep-rooted fear amongst all who were affected. Only the residents of Porta Farm offered legal resistance, by taking the authorities to court, but they lost the case.[23] In order to survive the onslaught, people in Epworth resorted to the strategies they had used in the past: magic, religion, nature and politics. While some of these strategies did not work, others did, and the residents either saved their houses from destruction or moved to live in safer areas.

Prophecies are not new in Epworth. They find a ready reception in the ears of an ever-anxious audience, which has encountered evictions for many years and lives in constant fear of more. Among the *vapositori* and other Christian faiths in the area, Murambatsvina was interpreted in eschatological terms; its rapidity, the use of excavators, riot police and armed soldiers, and the rendering

---

[20] One of the largest African Independent Churches in Zimbabwe. It was founded by Johane Masowe in the early 1930s and has since spread to many Southern African countries.

[21] For the tidal waves which struck South-east Asia on 26 December 2004.

[22] Tendayi Kumbula. 'Hope for Epworth as Government Steps in'. *The Sunday Mail*, 9 January 1983.

[23] *Daily Mirror*, 18 July 2005.

of multitudes of people homeless in a matter of minutes, was analogous to no other event but *kuguma kwenyika* (the end of the world). The 1991 clean-up had been foretold in the late 1980s by a prophetess in the Johane Masowe sect of the Maseko area when she told her followers,

> *Vanhu vane dzimba dziri muno endai munovaka misha kumaruwa. Ndaona dzimba zhinji dzaparadzwa*
>
> (I advise all those with houses in this area to go and build homes in the rural areas. It has been revealed to me that many of these houses shall be destroyed.)[24]

The prophecies date back many years. They were said at *misangano yegore* (annual gatherings), especially of the Johane Masowe weChishanu sect. People were advised to go and build their homes in the rural areas. Phineas Nyamhuka (pers. com.) recalls that this 'end-time' prophecy was repeated at the 2000 *musangano wegore* held at Domboshawa, a few kilometres north of Harare, when *Mweya Mutsvene* (Holy Spirit) warned urban dwellers that:

> *Ndaona madhorobha akurambai*
>
> (It has been revealed to me that the cities and towns of this country will reject you.)[25]

Isaac Maupa (pers. comm.) says that Madzibaba Misheck, a prophet of a *sowe* in Hatfield, foretold the coming of Murambatsvina five years ago. People were informed that there would be much suffering, as many would be rendered homeless, that it would be too expensive for many to find shelter and that they would sleep in the open.[26] Jonah Nhema, an active member of this sect and a resident of Chiremba, confirmed (pers. com.) the prophecy when he said that their prophet had warned them in January 2004 at the *sowe* of Domborema-ziso about the impending cataclysm.[27] Thus when the operation was launched in May 2005, the people were at least psychologically prepared for it. Although some argue that parts of Epworth were saved from destruction by the arrival of the UN special envoy, Anna Kajimulo Tibaijuka, on 26 June, eschatology believers see this as a cosmic event. Both followers and non-followers of the *vapositori* churches were given prayers of sanctification so that Murambatsvina could have a 'Passover effect' on their houses. Others were prayed for and advised about where they could find alternative accommodation in the rural areas or at Caledonia Farm.

Although members of the different sects in the area see these tragedies as God's will, traditionalists in the area are quite adamant. They tried throughout the colonial period and to the present day to resist all efforts to urbanise their area. According to Bvumai Mashayamombe (pers. comm.), some *n'angas* used powerful magic to prevent their houses from being destroyed. In 1991, in the

---

24   Interview with Simon Mabukwa, Harare, 9 June 2006.
25   Interview with Phineas Nyamhuka, Hatfield, Harare, 11 June 2006.
26   Interview with Isaac Maupa, Epworth, Harare, 23 April 2006.

Secondary area, a *n'anga* used charms to confuse a bulldozer driver, who would see a pool of water or thick darkness when approaching 'magically protected' homes. In some cases, the walls of houses would fall in the direction of the bulldozer as if to crush the driver. One bulldozer driver is said to have died after demolishing a particular house (pers. comm.). These stories are certainly difficult to authenticate, but many people have testified to them. Komboniyatsva, the charismatic traditional healer, was the hope for those who believed in a magical escape from Murambatsvina. He advised people in his area to remain. He said no house was going to be demolished. Many believed that such charms had protective powers. Since he himself had many structures – including a bottle store, a 'hospital' and a house – there was little doubt among charm believers that their own were securely protected. Unfortunately, this strategy did not succeed. On June 18 Komboniyatsva succumbed to the might of excavators, save for a few structures built amongst rocks. The *n'anga* himself, a supporter of the ruling party, is said to have said that he could not resist the demolition of his structures because he did not want to use his charms against the government.

Ndezve hurumende izvi. Handingashandisiri hurumende mushonga

(This is a government exercise. I can't use my charms against the government).[28, 29]

It is in Dhonoro that occult resistance partially succeeded. One excavator driver died after he refused to heed a resident's warning that he would to die if he destroyed his home. Furthermore, in some houses there were baboons, makona (charms) and other magical paraphernalia . This scared the police and bulldozer drivers to the extent that they ordered people to destroy their structures on their own. This became the authorities' approach in the Secondary, Overspill, Kedhishi and Jacha areas and people were at least able to save their valuables from destruction.

Nature itself shielded some Epworth structures from the marauding excavators. From time immemorial, rocks, mountains, caves, forests and hills have always been hiding places in the face of danger for the people of Zimbabwe. In the nineteenth century the Shona people used them as refuge from Nguni raiding armies. The Ndebele sought protection in the Matopos Hills during the First Chimurenga, and both Zimbabwe African National Liberation Army (ZANLA) and Zimbabwe People's Revolutionary Army (ZIPRA) guerrillas used the same hills as bases during the Second Chimurenga. In Epworth, the same strategy is still being used today. Even if all the magada in Epworth were to be destroyed, some houses would to be saved since they are built between rocks, beyond the reach of excavators and bulldozers. This was the case with some houses at Komboniyatsva, whose occupants have since returned to stay. Even for those whose houses were demolished, the rocks provided a natural hiding-place while contemplating whether to go to the rural areas or wait for

---

27   Interview with Jonah Nhema, Epworth, Harare, 23 April 2006.
28   Interview, Tafadzwa Patrick, Hatfield, 15 April 2006.
29   Interview, Revolt Marembo, Epworth, 30 June 2006.

the passing of Murambatsvina before reconstructing their shattered homes. But for nature, every structure in Komboniyatsva could have been razed, as was the case in Dunsten and Dhonoro.

As in the past, people in Epworth exploited politics to prevent the annihilation of their homes. Suspicious that Murambatsvina was punishment for voting for the opposition, many posed as supporters of the ruling party. They were removed from the areas of Dunsten, Komboniyatsva and Dhonoro and given alternative accommodation in Secondary and Overspill. Even if some did not benefit from this scheme, in Dhonoro they were recalled to rebuild their structures after Murambatsvina was over. To speed up the process they were provided with tents. Unfortunately, those in the Komboniyatsva area who were supporters of MDC, had their shelters demolished on grounds that the government intended to build a museum at the place . The credibility of this story is high given that Komboniyatsva – the traditional healer himself - passively watched his home and business premises being destroyed when people were expecting a magical resistance from him. It appears residents who did not resort to any of the strategies above, were completely not spared by Murambatsvina. A case in point was the people at Belapezi Farm whose nearly 2000 houses under their Green Valley Housing Co-operation were crushed to pieces.

Conclusion

Religion, nature, magic and politics played a crucial role in mitigating the effects of Operation Murambatsvina among the residents of Epworth. In a residential area plagued by deep-seated poverty, Murambatsvina only served to exacerbate the adverse socio-economic life of the people of Epworth. Nevertheless, as people who had experienced evictions and demolitions of their houses on a large scale in the past, they now had strategies of dealing with such events. Prophecies among the vapositori sects not only predicted Murambatsvina, they also prepared people psychologically to deal with its effects. Prophets and prophetesses among the numerous masowe advised people where to go to avoid the tragedy, or after the annihilation of their shelters, and provided them with prayers to ameliorate the effects of Murambatsvina. Although the n'angas did not succeed this time, there was some magical resistance in Dhonoro, which forced the authorities to halt the use of bulldozers and instead have people destroy their structures on their own. Natural protection in the form of rocks also saved some people from having their homes demolished and provided them with places to hide. Political consciousness among many Epworth residents saved them from being evicted and their homes annihilated.

The reaction of the residents of Epworth to Murambatsvina demonstrates their capacity to deal with the disaster from the strategies at their disposal: cultural and religious beliefs, politics and nature. Their ability to withstand the brutality of such an operation, challenging as it did their very existence, is a remarkable feat of historical significance. It is apparent that without this religio-cultural and political preparedness, the effects of Murambatsvina could have been even more psychologically and socio-economically devastating to the residents of Epworth.

References

Beach, D.N. 1994. *A Zimbabwean past: Shona dynastic histories and oral traditions.* Gweru: Mambo Press.

Central Statistical Office. 2002 Census, preliminary report. Harare, Zimbabwe: Central Statistical Office.

Ranger, T.O. 1999. *Voices from the rocks: Nature, culture and history in the Matopos Hills of Zimbabwe.* Harare: Baobab Books.

Zvobgo, C.J.M. 1996. *A history of Christian missions in Zimbabwe, 1890–1939.* Gweru: Mambo Press.

6

Murambatsvina's Assault on Women's Legal and Economic Rights
An Interview with a Cross-border Small Trader

Beauty Vambe

Women's perceptions of social and historical processes that impinge on their daily lives and businesses matter a great deal. In situations where a culture of fear and intimidation has been bred, people become permanently suspicious of their government. This breakdown of dialogue between a government and its people was manifested through Operation Murambatsvina in Zimbabwe in 2005. In the mayhem, women's legal rights were fundamentally dislocated and compromised as their economic activities based on cross-border trade to and from Zambia were permanently damaged.

This chapter traces the story of one woman, Mai Saddy (not her real name) resident in Kuwadzana Extension; it tells how she endured the disruption of her trade and how she survived the nightmare. Her story is representative of those of many women who saw their trade destroyed, their houses demolished and are now unable to pay fees for their children or care for the sick, including themselves. The interview form is used because women's own voices need to be heard (Staunton 1990), particularly in contested political contexts such as Operation Murambatsvina in order to bring their impact to the surface for critical scrutiny.

The historical context of African women's legal rights in Zimbabwe

Women in pre-colonial Zimbabwe did not have rights equal to those of men. Once married, African women were often viewed as an extension of the men's property. Women could be made captives, pawns and held as hostages (Schmidt 1992, 30). African women were perceived as 'lazy', 'slothful' and 'uncivilised'. Colonialism worsened the legal situation by limiting the movement of African women. It was considered lawful that 'European men could have sex with African women of any marital status without being liable to charge' (ibid., p. 105).

Even African women who trained as nurses were still under the supervision of European nurses and doctors.

At independence in 1980 African women were thus living under a system of legal dualism comprising customary law and the common law of Zimbabwe (Stewart et al. 1990, 166-67). The Legal Age of Majority Act, 1982 (Act 15 of 1982) partially unhinged the legal constraints on black women, giving majority status to those who had reached the age of 18. This enabled women to enter into financial transactions with third parties without necessarily having to receive the permission of their fathers or husbands. They could now start and run businesses on their own. A revised 1996 Constitution of Zimbabwe further entrenched the democratic legal rights of black women to own property either in community of property or as individuals. The government further promoted the legal status of women to engage in informal trade by the introduction of Statutory Instrument 216 of 1994 (Regional Town and Country Planning (Use Groups) Regulations) that allowed anybody to set up businesses so as to promote the economic development of the country at a time when the economy was shrinking rapidly.

In a context of national economic decline since the 1990s, and of the high mortality rate from HIV/AIDS, black women from the urban townships and rural areas participated increasingly in the economy as informal traders. Informal trade had, by Zimbabwean standards, became 'formal' trade. In 2004, the government conceded that informal trade with neighbouring countries constituted 40 per cent of the country's employment. Many black women became breadwinners overnight.

In 2005 Operation Murambatsvina targeted this informal sector and undermined the economic rights and legal status of women. Young black women not yet married or those in marriages out of community of property who ran the thriving flea markets were hit hard by Murambatsvina when the authorities confiscated their goods. Without anybody to turn to, and unable to raise capital to restart their businesses, most of the women lost their economic independence and some were forced to choose the hard option of prostitution. Those women married under community of property lost income from rent as their houses were razed. The laws used to violate the women's rights to trade were derived from colonialism but manipulated by the Zimbabwean ruling patriarchy. By the time the Tibaijuka report was published in July 2005, it simply confirmed the pains that women had gone through when it concluded that 'most of the victims were already among the most economically disadvantaged groups in society ... particularly among widows, single mothers, children, orphans, the elderly and the disabled persons' (Tibaijuka 2005, 45).

Operation Murambatsvina's assault on the legal rights of black women

Although Feltoe (2004) has written on the erosion of women's democratic rights in the context of the breakdown of the rule of law in Zimbabwe, Operation Murambatsvina severely compromised specific legal rights enshrined in the Constitution of Zimbabwe. For example, Article 16 (1) of 1996 states that, 'No property of any description or interest or right therein shall be compulsorily acquired' (Constitution of Zimbabwe 1996, 15).

By confiscating traders' goods from the flea markets, the authorities violated this right. Vendors at designated flea markets actually complied with council regulations by paying monthly fees for the spaces assigned to them by the local authorities. According to Article 16 1 (ii) (b), the Constitution, 'requires the acquiring authority to give reasonable notice of the intention to acquire the property, interest or right to any person owning the property' (p. 10).

In the initial stages of Murambatsvina, the police demolition teams gave insufficient notice to homeowners until later when the authorities ordered the owners of property to destroy their own buildings. Women were not notified in time to be able to collect their goods before they were destroyed. Article 16 7 (i) (f) makes provision that national and local authorities may interfere with private property provided that, 'by reason of the property in question being in a dangerous state or prejudicial to the health or safety of human, animal or vegetable life or having been constructed or grown on any land in contravention of any law relating to the occupation or use of that land' (p. 16).

By inference, this provision was used by the authorities during Murambatsvina to negate Statutory Instrument 216 of 1994 that had made it legal for small traders to organise themselves and create businesses. By most accounts, prior to Murambatsvina no health hazards had been reported as a direct result of the activities of these traders.

These violations of the Constitution of Zimbabwe by the authorities put in doubt the legality of Operation Murambatsvina. Also, and more importantly, they lead one to infer that it may have been conducted in order to undermine black women's economic initiatives. The aim was to make sure that women who form the majority of Zimbabwe's electorate remain poor and therefore dependent on state patronage. These inferences are lent further credibility by the conversation below, which illustrates the contradictions of Murambatsvina as seen by at least one woman who has had a long history of trade between Zimbabwe and Zambia.

The Interview

Question: When did you come to live in Harare?

Answer: I was born in Harare and I lived with my parents in the surburb of Mufakose. I did my grade 1 to 7 at Mugundu in Mufakose. After that I went to our rural home in Domboshava. It is there that I met the man who became my husband. I was married in 1981 and my husband took me to Highfield, in Harare. We lived in Highfield from 1981 to 1986, and we had our first-born child there. We then moved to Glenview 4 and my husband lost his job. We went home in the rural areas until 1987 when my husband was helped by his uncle to get a job. By then we were renting one room in Kuwadzana 1. Once again, my husband lost his job, and then we decided to stay in Kuwadzana 3. Luckily, he got another job. We then planned to grow maize in the rural areas. From the 8 bags of maize we got 1,800 Zimbabwean dollars which was then a lot of money with which one could buy many things. That was 1992. I approached my husband and told him that I wanted to get a passport to go to Zambia where other women were going. Seeing that life was difficult with his little salary, my husband agreed. This is how I started the business of going to sell shoes in Zambia.

Q: Now you are living in your own house here, in Kuwadzana Extension. How did you come to own this house and build that small one made of bricks?

A: When we bought this house from the Zimbabwe Building Society (ZBS) it was made of prefabricated material. We started by building a small three-roomed house of bricks behind the main house. This small brick house is the one that was to be destroyed by Operation Murambatsvina. We had built this house from the money that I got from selling shoes in Zambia and from the savings from my husband's salary. From Zambia, we also 'hoarded' shoes that we sold in Zimbabwe. Whatever small profit we got, we put aside. Whatever cent we got as profit, we saved. Then we would buy more shoes from Norton, here in Zimbabwe, to sell in Zambia. When we came back we sold our wares to those traders in the flea markets. Apart from shoes, we also brought T-shirts for men that we sold to traders at the flea market. If the traders gave you all the money then you were lucky because you would buy more shoes to take to Zambia. With this money we then bought cement, asbestos and bricks bit by bit.

Q: You have said you are the ones who destroyed the prefabricated houses that you rebuilt using bricks, long before Murambatsvina set in. Was your rejection of the substandard prefabricated houses not a form of Murambatsvina?

A: This was Murambatsvina but not in the negative sense. We realised that the prefabricated houses would not last for long because cracks developed, the iron rusted, and there was the danger that one day the houses could fall on top of us while we were sleeping. So we decided to destroy the prefabricated houses and build a new one with an approved plan.

Q: Who then destroyed your small brick house?

A: Although it is us who destroyed the house, I can say it is Operation Murambatsvina. What happened is that when Murambatsvina started, the police used to demolish the houses. Then they changed and ordered people to destroy their own property. If you did not destroy your structures you were beaten by the soldiers and the police, so out of fear we saw it as better to destroy our house. We also hoped to salvage some materials from the destroyed house because the police used to break doors and crack windows, asbestos, willy-nilly. So it was better to 'destroy' the house before you were beaten.

Q: And how did you feel about being forced to demolish a house for which you had suffered and struggled so much to build, going as far as Zambia, to trade shoes to get the money?

A: Up to today the pain of having to destroy our house is still with me. That pain is a very big wound that refuses to go away, because if you think that you worked so hard, sleeping on the hard ground in Zambia, harassed by fleas – you know in Zambia there is cholera – and you see where we sleep, you feel pity, all striving to build your house, and then after finishing, you are told to destroy it. You remain with many internal wounds that will never heal. So we felt the pain of destroying the house, we still feel that pain in the form of stress and even high blood pressure, all of which can kill. We are sick people. You end up wondering what country you are living in. You get confused and the pain continues because you were forced to destroy what you suffered for when building the house. But the authorities are not sympathetic to your efforts because we expected that since we had already build the structures, the authorities would give us conditions to say since you have built beautiful houses that had ceilings, with well-painted walls and with all facilities then you should regularise by getting a plan approved for them. This was not to be. Somebody's voice from the municipal and government authorities just said we should destroy those houses. It pained us because they should have given us time. Nobody was given sufficient time. We just heard that Mbare structures have been destroyed. And then they came for us. There was no opportunity given us to develop plans that would be approved by the authorities so that we can stay in the houses, because they were beautiful. They were not like the prefabricated houses. Our houses were of bricks, well plastered and had ceilings.

Q: When you were building these houses did you go to the council to seek their permission so that you would build according to the urban housing by-laws?

A: No, we did not because we believed that since we had bought these houses from the bank on cash, now they belonged to us and that we could do what we want with our property.

Q: What about the allegation that in Zambia you buy foreign currency that you sell here on the parallel or black market?

A: As I said before, we bought shoes from a factory in Norton, here in Zimbabwe. We then sold these shoes in Zambia. We sold school shoes, tennis shoes for women and children's shoes. We sold other goods, but mainly shoes. From Zambia we brought women's sandals, and tennis shoes which we then sold to flea market traders in Harare.

Q: So it was when you came back from Zambia that you saw that your customers in Harare had been chased away and their goods taken? Explain how Murambatsvina changed your business and that of your customers in the flea markets.

A: We heard of the devastating destruction caused by Murambastvina in the flea-markets when we were on the bus coming from Zambia. While in the bus we heard that flea markets had been closed and since we had goods to sell we did not know what to do with them. Also, we had sold goods to our customers on credit hoping that when we returned from Zambia we would collect the remainder of our money. Most of our customers, therefore, had not yet finished paying us our money. So these people, our customers who were chased from the flea markets, went away with our money. We could not locate them. We began to worry also about the goods we had because we did not know who to sell to. So when we arrived in Harare, we stayed with our goods. We did not have money to spend because the flea markets where we used to sell our goods had been closed. We started to sell our goods indoors, one by one until all were finished. But we were also spending the capital and it got finished. We had to start mobilising new funds to restart the business. Extended members of the family helped us to raise the money. Some of the money went to paying school fees. So life became very difficult, especially when there was nobody to sell stuff to. Police were arresting anybody found selling stuff.

Q: *To what extent were your customers at the flea markets affected by Murambatsvina?*

A: I think we who went to Zambia were left a little better off by Murambatsvina than those who had, and sometimes shared, tables at the flea markets. These people were found right on the ground, at the flea markets. All their goods were taken by the police and dumped at the central police station. These people lost everything. They did not recover anything. The people did not know what to do. Even today if you see them they are poor and struggling with life. To think that these are the people who used to do well, whom we used to describe as our 'white men' or *varungu vedu*, now they are the ones whose life was 'killed' and destroyed forever. They are now at point zero, the lowest standard of living that one can ever imagine. However, some of them are starting to gather themselves, initiating a business and starting to sell goods bit by bit at the Mpedzanhamo. But their businesses were ruined much more than ours because these people had their goods confiscated and those goods were never recovered. The flea market traders ended with nothing, and today most of these traders have nothing.

Q: *Do you mean, therefore, that you the traders are part of what the authorities describe as the dirt that they are removing through Operation Murambatsvina. How do you feel about being described as dirty?*

A: This word Murambatsvina is actually wrong. The reality is that the authorities' operation actually introduced dirt and disorder in our lives, something I can call Muisatsvina (One Who Puts Dirt in People's Lives). The operation introduced dirt because of our houses that the authorities destroyed and the rubble has not been removed. All the rubble is heaped everywhere and even the rubbish from the bins is now being emptied on these heaps of rubble. Then the people whose houses were demolished were rendered homeless. They started living in the open, where there were no toilets, so this operation was not rejecting dirt but, in fact, increased and put more in people's homes and lives. So, I can say the authorities put dirt on top of other dirt.

Q: With regard to the laws that are supposed to encourage women to enhance their lives to what extent would you say Murambatsvina undermined them?

A: Operation Murambatsvina actually came to destroy people's living. Authorities saw that women were carrying out initiatives on their own, boosting the standards of lives for their families. So, Operation Murambatsvina actually targeted women in order to undermine their efforts, in the process depriving people of their money, livelihood and property. But the people whose businesses were destroyed are peace-loving. They did not do anything bad to the authorities. Yet, today, the people who were once thriving traders are now financially broke and dejected. The laws meant to protect the well-being of women were used to punish us women. In fact, these laws are suppressed and not well known by the public so that women should not know the full extent of their rights.

Q: Before Murambatsvina how did you and the traders at the flea markets help to develop Zimbabwe?

A: We used to help develop the country since we bought shoes from Norton. We created employment for Zimbabweans working at shoe companies. We also sold the shoes in Zambia and when we paid customs duty the country received revenue. We used to declare our goods at the port of entry in Zimbabwe and then pay our duty to the revenue authorities. When we arrived in Zimbabwe we created employment for traders who owned the flea markets. These traders who owned business stands called 'tables' from which to sell at the flea markets started to employ men and women to do the selling of the wares to the people. Ordinary people benefited from buying clothes that were not costly from us. Sometimes they took goods on credit, something that made payment easy. In Harare one trader could own four or five 'tables' depending on the trader's money. That also meant that the trader would employ four to five people to sell the goods on the tables. So, the country was being developed that way since these employed people could now have something to eat. The government was also helped because it did not have to worry about creating employment for people who had created their own employment. But, unfortunately, these four or five people who had been employed were pulled down to nothing and back to the status of unemployment by Operation Murambatsvina. Right now these people are unemployed. Before the Murambatsvina of 2005, it was better for these people because at least they were employed by somebody. These four or five people also helped their immediate and extended family with their income. What this means was that the government's load or burden to look after orphans had been reduced because people helped themselves, working for themselves in those small jobs. But all these were destroyed by Murambatsvina.

Q: Women are a large percentage in the Zimbabwean population. What then is going to be your future relationship with political parties especially in the aftermath of Murambatsvina?

A: Those people who come soliciting for our votes are the people who used a law to push for Murambatsvina which destroyed our businesses. Therefore, it is better not to vote for these people when they come next time asking for our votes. Because after we give them our votes, they will use the laws to destroy our lives. We use our vote in the hope that those up there will represent us. But you come to realise that these are the same people whose policies undermine your business.

Q: Some people say that because of Operation Murambatsvina the country is now clean and towns are now smart. What do you think?

A: The country can be clean and smart while people are dying of hunger. How can the country be 'clean' when people do not have somewhere to build their houses? The country can be clean but people do not have places where they can sell their wares and do business. In fact, there are now more girls doing prostitution after Murambatsvina because they do not have jobs to look after themselves. Deaths have increased. Men cannot get jobs, nor can women. Those who used to provide services like selling sadza and polishing shoes can no longer do that. These people used to provide for their families. So I do not understand when people say the country and towns are clean, when people are no longer living and going about their business freely. What, therefore, is the boast that the country is clean when people are suffering?

Q: Others say that small traders like yourself used to bring foreign currency and exchange it at the parallel market, thereby fuelling inflation. What do you say to that?

A: Yes, the issue of exchanging money at the parallel market is there. But the problem is that people buy their clothes from here in Zimbabwe and they are expensive. When they sell in Zambia they get little profit. As a result, people started bringing foreign currency in Zimbabwe. But the main problem is that the exchange rate in the bank is so low it erodes whatever little profit any trader can hope to have. Also, the major problem is that the central bank has stipulated a fixed rate of exchange that is far below the rate at which things are getting expensive in the shops. It is responsible for the parallel market because it gives very little money when exchanging your hard-earned foreign currency. If banks had put in place higher rates of money exchange so that a trader would be satisfied like what was happening in the 1990s people would be encouraged to sell their foreign exchange to the banks and bureaus. The fixed price of foreign exchange supported by the government gave to traders very little money. If we go back in the 1990s we see that the exchange rate was better. So what is it that is causing people to shun the banks and go to the parallel market?

Q: In your view, what kind of laws should be put in place in order to encourage and promote businesses by small traders like yourself?

A: There must be a law that when a trader crosses the border from one country to another, the trader must be charged a small tax so that the trader will continue to prosper in business. The more the trader goes out with goods, the more the trader comes in with goods and forex. This will make it possible for money to flow to the government and the banks. But the opposite happens because the government will say since you have come from outside we will charge you a lot of tax money at the border. This will kill my business. There must also be a law that scrutinises exactly what the informal sector is contributing to the economic development of the country. If they put that law, they will realise that the women who go to trade in neighbouring countries are actually benefiting the country by way of raising their own children, sending them to school without asking government to do so. This will allow the government to put money in other areas.

Q: Murambatsvina came and passed, so how are you surviving today?

A: Yes, Murambatsvina came and passed. We are now piecing our lives together. We go to Zambia to sell shoes, come back with goods and sell in Zimbabwe at Mpedzanhamo open market where some small traders were given tables. We also sell to the Indian shop owners in town. But the problem is that as you sell you are running away from the police because if they see you selling the goods they will take them and tell you that you do not have papers to sell these goods in town. So, things are still difficult. We are continuing to sell regardless. But at the borders it is now better, you can declare your goods and they will let you go. But it is here in town where police will harass you and say you should not sell your wares here. So the police end up taking the goods.

Q: In your view do the police understand what Murambatsvina is and the consequences of arresting small traders, preventing then from doing their businesses?

A: I do not think that the police thoroughly understand what Murambatsvina is, and the meaning of their actions. Actually, if the police arrest you selling the goods and you offer them a bribe, they will accept it and let you go. The police do not have a solid understanding of Murambatsvina because, for example, here in Kuwadzana Extension where we stay there is no supermarket, no shop and no public toilet, but they talk of Murambatsvina. So we do not know where Murambatsvina starts and ends. If there is no clinic, no public toilet, no place for a market, no shop from which to buy things, people end up setting up tuck shops at their homes to sell goods. From here in Kuwadzana Extension to Mutomba supermarket in

Kuwadzana 7 it is five kilometres. So, I think that the police do not understand what Murambatsvina means. In fact, the authorities should lead by example, by building a public toilet, a clinic, a supermarket that is clean, but there is nothing like this in Kuwadzana Extension and yet they talk of Murambatsvina.

Q: Women are at the forefront of voting for different political parties. With the experience from Murambatsvina, how do you view yourself, and feel, when you are described as dirty because it is you who were running away from the police, holding your goods?

A: We are not considered as human beings with rights to be respected. In fact, we are viewed as unthinking objects that authorities can uproot, displace and discard at will. If the authorities had ever considered us as Zimbabwean citizens with rights legally enshrined in the constitution, they would not have come early in the morning and ordered us to destroy our houses. They just said destroy your houses because they never see us as citizens with rights that protect them from being rendered homeless. When they destroyed houses mainly in the high-density surburbs that is when we saw and realised Murambatsvina was targeted at the poor people, because when it was said that Murambatsvina was now going to the low-density surburbs, they started from Waterfalls, and suddenly the authorities said Operation Murambatsvina was complete and should stop. So it means that they saw it fit to destroy the poor people's property so that we remain poor, as Oliver Mtukudzi sang, because we the poor are the ones whose properties were destroyed. Today, if you go to the low-density suburbs, the boysky, small illegal structures, are there. None of the rich people have their property destroyed. Those properties still stand. Murambatsvina should have started with the people from above, with government ministers because it is up there where corruption is concentrated. Then they should have come down to us. But they started with the poor people while not affecting the business of the rich people. Today, it is the poor who are suffering from the effects of Murambatsvina. Those in high places and who are rich are enjoying Zimbabwe.

Q: As a woman trader, in your view, how do traditional African belief systems and attitudes towards women promote or undermine efforts such as yours to become a successful trader?

A: If you have the misfortune to have a husband who does not understand, or fears, your contribution, you will never go out of the country for business. I was lucky because my husband understood and affirmed the necessity of me going out for business in Zambia. He also saw that my business was helping us raise our family, so he said go. Most women who go out of Zimbabwe to other countries for business are looked down upon as prostitutes. It is true that some women engage in prostitution but most are only willing to do their businesses in order to raise their families. Even in the suburb where we live and in the rural areas, people who hear and know that you are a cross-border trader do not take you seriously. They do not respect you like those women who remain at home waiting for the husband's pay. They whisper that this cross-border woman is no longer 'straight'. She is indulging. Most people, but mainly other women, believe that us who go to other countries for trade are going there to prostitute ourselves. But the fact is that you cannot start prostitution just because you are now out of the view of your husband and those you live with. This thinking is wrong because even some of those women who remain at home actually have love affairs with other men. In the rural areas some women are not allowed to go and do business outside the country because their husbands have heard that those who go out have love affairs in those countries. So this man ends up not allowing the wife to do business outside Zimbabwe. We go to Zambia ourselves. Zambia is a good country with people who are well behaved. The people of Zambia follow their culture and they have no time for outrageous behaviour like prostitution. To think that just because women are going out of the country, so they engage in love affairs is therefore very wrong. People have little knowledge about the business of cross-border women. That is why they end up assuming that everybody who goes out of the country is flirting. But also, sometimes some women who go to Zambia may not trust their husbands who remain in Zimbabwe thinking that he is going to take a girlfriend in her absence. But if the wife and the husband trust each other and think of one thing – business – then your lives will change for the better.

Q: How is your business now, after Murambatsvina?

A: We are now continually looking for new places to sell our goods. We are now at Murambatsvina number two where the government is saying people should not change money on the parallel market. The authorities are saying that people are not allowed to walk with bulk money, but how can I not do that when I have to buy goods? How can I go outside the country without bulk money? They say I should declare five million Zimbabwean dollars per month. But when I get there what do I eat? Without carrying more money how do I pay for my bus fare? How do I pay my customs duty at the border if I do not carry bulk money? When they discover my large amount of money they take it. It is painful because this is being done to the poor people only. At the border we see rich people driving government vehicles with white number plates carrying lots of money and they are saluted when we the poor are arrested. Poor women are the ones helping the country to develop. There must be laws that say that the rule of law should be respected physically and not just say we have laws that people flout at will. Somehow and somewhere the laws in place are meant to suppress the rights of women. The men know that they are not working and yet they order the woman to stay at home. This disregards the woman's rights and what she thinks about her life. When the female vice-president was installed, we women thought things are going to be good for us. My wish is that the new vice-president should work closely with

Comrade Oppah Muchinguri because she helps women on the ground and that Oppah Muchinguri is helping female footballers in the country.

Conclusion

This chapter has used the story of a single woman who has been in the business of informal trade and had her business disrupted by Murambatsvina. The interview is considered as a window through which it is possible to uncover other buried narratives of women who suffered because of Murambatsvina. Obviously, some women – especially rich ones – benefited from Murambatsvina, but that was not the focus of this chapter. From this conversation with a Zimbabwean female trader a case can be argued that Operation Murambatsvina did indeed disrupt the business of small traders. It can only be suggested that women who were thriving in business were pushed back into poverty so as to remain poor and dependent on the state for patronage in exchange for future votes. Given that it was women who welcomed Statutory Instrument 216, embracing the Mpedzanhamo option through vending and small cross-border activities, it can be averred that the state was terrified to see its last 'colony' – the women – threatening to desert it in favour of self-improvement that is not dependent on state handouts. Operation Murambatsvina did indeed come and 'go' but it left indelible wounds in the hearts of Zimbabwean women.

Perceptions of the event gleaned from the conversation with the interviewee suggest that in their bid to do good, sometimes the state and the local authorities overstep their mandated authority. When that happens, as it did in 2005, the state runs the risk of being perceived as the 'Muisatsvina' (bringers of dirt) as opposed to being the rejecter of dirt which is what the word Murambatsvina is supposed to mean in its legal, literal and metaphorical senses.

Bibliography

Constitution of Zimbabwe. 1996. rev. edn, Harare: Government Printers.
Feltoe, G. 2004. 'The onslaught against democracy and the rule of law in Zimbabwe 2000' in Harold-Barry, D. (ed.) *Zimbabwe: The Past is the Future*, pp. 193-225. Harare, Weaver Press.
Schmidt E. 1992. *Peasants, traders and wives: Shona women in the history of Zimbabwe, 1870–1939*. Harare: Baobab Books.
Staunton, I. 1990. *Mothers of the Revolution*. Harare: Baobab Books.
Stewart, J. 1990. 'The legal situation of women in Zimbabwe' in Stewart, J. and A. Armstrong (eds) *Women and law in southern Africa: The legal situation of women in southern Africa*, pp. 165–222. Harare: University of Zimbabwe Publications.
Tibaijuka A.K. 2005. *Report of the Fact-Finding Mission to Zimbabwe to assess the scope and impact of Operation Murambatsvina by the UN Special Envoy on Human Settlements Issues in Zimbabwe*. New York: United Nations.

7

Bulldozers Always Come
'Maggots', Citizens and Governance in Contemporary Zimbabwe

Tinashe L. Chimedza

This chapter explores *citizenship*, *citizenship rights* and *governance* in post-colonial Zimbabwe in the context of Operation Murambatsvina. The focus is on how public law reform and coercive public policy has been deployed by nationalist elites to revive a waning hegemony resulting in excessive interference with the rights of citizens. Operation Murambatsvina must be interrogated and understood historically and empirically as an elite and uncivil nationalist project of establishing and conjuring 'identities' which make inclusion and exclusion possible and mess democratic governance. The consequence has been to enable the brutal policing and ordering of access to and enjoyment of citizenship. Resolving that 'citizenship deficit' lies not only in democratic public law reform and struggle but crucially in the contestation for history – to challenge the official scripts that are used to legitimate who is in and who is out. That way an exclusionary mode of citizenship is challenged and inclusive and democratic citizenship is drawn within reach.

Introduction:
'maggots' must be cleaned up[1]

I Robert Mugabe with *ancestral generations far back, I be dragged to court by a settler who only came 90 years ago*, who will claim the land we are taking is his. Morally, we can't accept that.[2] (my emphasis)

---

1   Police Commissioner Augustine Chihuri explaining the objectives of Operation Murambatsvina. See article by Dzikamayi Chidyausiku, 2005, 'Clearance Victims left in Limbo', Institute for War & Peace Reporting, *Africa Reports No 38*.

2   'No Unfairness in Land Policy, Says President', *The Herald*, 7 February 1991, cited in Moyo, J. 1992. 'State Politics and Social Domination in Zimbabwe', *Journal of Modern African Studies*, Vol. 30, No. 2, pp. 305-30.

For several days in June and July 2005 I sat in the Special Broadcasting Services (SBS) studios in Sydney going through unending hours of footage covering the devastating effect of Operation Murambatsvina[3] or Drive out the trash in Zimbabwe.[4] Since then I have endured reading and watching grotesque and sadistic pictures, reports, journal articles, documentaries and press coverage of the devastation caused by 'government by operations' in Zimbabwe.[5] As I sat in that studio, far removed from the experiences of being *cleaned up*, I thought of the young women and men who often sold 'buddie cards' or 'juice cards'[6] to me and my friends at the corner of Julius Nyerere and Samora Machel Streets in the Harare city centre. I thought of the young man who sat outside the entrance to a big internet café on the same street where I bought bananas and apples, sometimes on credit. I thought of the women along Sam Nujoma Street where we bought cheap *sadza* (thick porridge, Zimbabwe's staple meal) at lunch from an 'illegal' cooking business. I thought of them because I asked myself what it means to be Zimbabwean and what rights they and we are entitled to as citizens of Zimbabwe.

While growing up in rural Zimbabwe we used to ridicule anyone who was 'ignorant' as coming from the 'farms' where most of the people have family roots in Malawi, Mozambique and Zambia – a lasting effect of the labour migration patterns of late colonialism in southern and eastern Africa. While at high school as a 'Zimbabwean' I had often seen Municipal Police raid 'foreigners' on the streets in the eastern border town of Mutare and they applied a crude language 'test' to distinguish the 'natives' from the 'foreigners', marking the border between the 'insiders' (with the right to stay since they *belonged* to Zimbabwe) and the 'outsiders' (who had no right to stay since they did not *belong* to Zimbabwe). Those who failed the crude test, speaking 'Shona'[7] or often the meaning and pronunciation of particular words like 'eggs' in the local language were immediately bundled into police trucks and deported to Mozambique. Others were simply identified by how they looked and asked arbitrary questions about where they 'came from'. The failure to either identify the 'rural area' where one came from or to produce a 'national identification card' (*chitupa/ situpa* in colonial Zimbabwe) qualified one as a foreigner and thus an outsider.

3   For a comprehensive report on Operation Murambatsvina or Drive Out Trash see *Report of the Fact-Finding Mission to Zimbabwe to assess the Scope and Impact of Operation Murambatsvina by the UN Special Envoy on Human Settlements Issues in Zimbabwe, Mrs Anna K. Tibaijuka*. http://www.unhabitat.org/documents/ZimbabweReport.pdf and also http://www.kubatana. net/html/archive/urbdev/050601evictdex.asp?sector=URBDEV – contains several reports on the operation including parliamentary debates (accessed 25 August 2005).

4   On the 25 August 2005 SBS –Australia broadcast a Dateline programme, '*Zimbabwe: Operation Tsunami*', filmed secretly by Jinn Stein, on Operation Murambatsvina.

5   Moyo, J. 2005. 'Mugabe must go now', *The Independent*, 15 July. http://www.theindependent. co.zw/news/2005/July/Friday15/2757.html (accessed August 2005).

6   'Buddie cards' are mobile phone recharge cards that are sold on the streets.

7   The category 'Shona' itself rides recklessly over the complex differences and similarities that exist across the social groups referred to as 'Shona'. In this instance the test was a question in the 'Manyika' dialect. See Ranger, T. 1985. *The Invention of Tribalism in Zimbabwe*, Gwelo.

The simple equation was that 'there is no Zimbabwean without a rural home'.[8] Years later, as a university student in Harare, I often witnessed Municipal Police raiding street vendors, violently taking their stock and beating them for being 'illegal' traders. As soon as the Municipal Police passed, a few whistles and sign language would be enough to ignite this army of the 'subalterns' surviving in the 'informal economy' to emerge and fill the pavements and continue their trade as if nothing had happened.

This 'informalised' or 'peripheral' economy supplies everything efficiently almost without fail: scarce textbooks for students, newspapers (those that have survived[9]), marijuana, foreign currency, sugar, bread, fruits and goods that are in short supply in the supermarkets.[10] In the 'townships' at nearly every corner, house and open space there was a small street stall or a tuckshop selling clothes, bread, tomatoes, vegetables, cigarettes, fresh meat and so on. The signs were everywhere: 'mazai pano' (eggs sold here), 'huku pano' (chickens sold here), 'drinks sold here' and so on. It is a huge economy on which many survived and will continue to stubbornly survive on. This pavement economy, which includes illegal foreign currency trading, is highly efficient, escapes the 'taxman' and is tightly connected with the elites in power, with many of its networks extending to 'people in high places'.[11] It is this economy and these livelihoods that *Opera-Murambatsvina* targeted and attempted to annihilate. The solution was, in the words of the Police Commissioner, '[to] clean the country of the crawling mass of maggots bent on destroying the economy'.[12] This 'crawling mass of maggots' is overwhelmingly composed of the economically weakest groups of all: women, children, the unemployed and underemployed, recent migrants from the rural areas escaping droughts and hunger and hordes of former farm workers made jobless and landless and those that have resided in the towns after migrating from countries like Zambia, Malawi and Mozambique who are referred to as '*mabhurandaya*', '*machawa*', '*mabwidi*', and so on.[13]

8   On 28 May 2005 the police commanding Harare told journalists the same message, 'No one in Zimbabwe comes from nowhere. Everybody belongs somewhere.' See *Daily Mirror*, 21 June 2005.

9   The introduction of the Access to Information and Protection of Privacy Act (AIPPA, as amended, 2003) 'licensed' state harassment of journalists and the closure of several independent newspapers. A dramatic case is that of the *Daily News*. See, generally, Nyarota, G. 2006. *Against the Grain: Memoirs of a Zimbabwean Newsman*, Zebra Press.

10   In downtown Bulawayo, Zimbabwe's second biggest city, the parallel foreign currency market is dubbed the 'World Bank' because foreign currency is easily available at the 'black-market rate'.

11   There have been several reports of how Solomon Mujuru and his wife, Joyce Mujuru, are intricately linked to illegal foreign currency trading. See for example, Institute of Peace and War Reporting, *Africa Reports*, 91, January 2007) and allegations that Solomon Mujuru was 'reaping' Z$40 billion a day from foreign currency trading.

12   Police Commissioner Augustine Chihuri, June 2005, http://www.iwpr.net/?p=acr&s=f&o=25 352&apc_state=heniacr2005 (accessed 20 August 2005).

13   See, for example, an unsubstantiated claim, by the Member of Parliament for St, Mary's, the Hon. Job Sikhala that, '... [in] my constituency of St Mary's, 95 per cent of people I represent in this august House are aliens from Malawi, Zambia and other countries, they do not have any home wherever their origin is. The majority of the people do not know what a rural home looks like', Extracted from *Hansard*, Vol. 32, No. 4. Parliament of Zimbabwe, 22 June 2005 (www. kubatana.org – accessed 20 August 2005).

Why citizenship and rights?

Resolution 2151 (XXI) of the United Nations General Assembly reaffirmed the 'inalienable right of *the people of Zimbabwe* to freedom and independence (my own emphasis)'.[14] But who were these 'people of Zimbabwe' who had an'inalienable right' to 'freedom and independence'? That question was not settled then and has remained contentious. There is no better time to revisit this question than within the context of Operation Murambatsvina. Government actions and rhetoric before, during and after Murambatsvina provide an insight into the contestations, expressions and tensions around citizenship and citizen's rights in post-colonial Zimbabwe. Coercive public policy in the form of Operation Murambatsvina must be interrogated and understood historically and empirically as a complex reproduction, recasting and conflation of pre-colonial, colonial and post-colonial social and political identities. These identities are coercively authored and imposed to legitimate an arbitrary boundary between *who is in* and *who is out*. Democratic citizenship is undermined to serve the political needs of the elites and enclose accumulation processes to those related and interwoven with the ruling party structures. The consequence is the creation of a political-military-business cabal that has the state at its disposal to discipline any opposition.

The denial of democratic citizenship must be interrogated within the context of the revival of an often violent, ethnicised and authoritarian nationalism. To effectively carry out this project the elites need history on their side. To this effect Raftopoulos (2003) has pointed that the government is now engaged in a 'selective narrative of liberation' which appropriates symbols, myths and anti-colonial projects to the service of the ruling elite.[15] To this concept of selective narratives I would add Ranger's (2004) notion of 'patriotic history'.[16] The selective narrative of liberation is (re)packed by 'patriotic history' and is delivered by an equally controlled and disciplining 'patriotic journalism'. Furthermore the boundaries of these conflated social and political identities are entrenched through repeated public law reform the effect of which has been to diminish the rights of citizens.[17] Within the economy, the undermining of democratic citizenship serves the obvious role of building and cementing lines of clientilism and paternalism, in the name of indigenisation, that feed into an almost closed accumulation struc-

---

14   Official Documents, Southern Rhodesia: United Nations General Assembly *The American Journal of International Law*, Vol. 61, No. 2. (Apr., 1967), pp. 652-53.

15   See Raftopoulos, B. 2003. 'The State in Crisis: Authoritarian Nationalism, Selective Citizenship and Distortions of Democracy in Zimbabwe' in Hammar, A., Raftopoulos, B. and S. Jensen (eds) *Zimbabwe's Unfinished Business: Rethinking Land, State and Nation in the Context of Crisis.* Weaver Press, Harare. See also Raftopoulos, B. and I. Phimister. 2004. 'Zimbabwe Now: The Political Economy of Crisis and Coercion', *Historical Materialism*, Vol. 12, No. 4, 2004, pp. 355-82.

16   Ranger, T. 2004. 'Nationalist historiography, patriotic history and the history of the nation in Zimbabwe: Struggle over past', *Journal of Southern African Studies,* Vol. 30, (2), pp. 216-34.

17   See De Bourbon, A. 2003. 'Human Rights Litigation in Zimbabwe: The Past, Present and Future', *African Human Rights Law Journal* (AHRLJ), pp. 195-221.

ture which is interwoven with the political fortunes of the ruling elites.[18]

Citizens without rights: the 'totem-less people'

This inquiry is focused on this underclass of 'foreigners', 'pavement/street people', 'people without totems', 'shack dwellers', *mabhurandaya*', '*mabwidi*', '*machawa*'[19] who do not belong or are regarded as not belonging. Such attention is motivated by the fact that the exclusionary and often violent nature of post-colonial public policy and public law reform makes grappling with the 'crisis of post-colonial citizenship' necessary in attempting to address the 'democracy deficits' of the post-colonial Zimbabwean polity. In order to understand the nature of the contestations around citizenship and citizens rights it is necessary to look at some of the social groups from whom citizenship and rights have been brutally taken. Before Operation Murambatsvina the government was already skilled in the business of excessively interfering with citizens' rights.[20] The precarious balance between a state which supposedly protects rights and citizens who must enjoy that protection had already been tipped in the favour of the state. Citizenship and how it has been experienced differently can be analysed in relation to (i) women, (ii) farm workers, and (iii) the 'Ndebele'.[21] The experiences of these social groups will help unravel the nature and practice of citizenship in post-colonial Zimbabwe. There has been an increase in the study of citizenship in the 'South' and in Zimbabwe in particular and it needs be so because the question of democratic citizenship is central to understanding the brittleness of post-colonial states.[22] The need to interrogate the question of citizenship is made more urgent in the face of

18 On what can be called 'crony capitalism' see Raftopoulos, B. and D. Compagnon. 2004. 'Indigenization, the State Bourgeoisie and Neo-authoritarian Politics' in Darnoff, S. (ed.) *Twenty Years of Independence in Zimbabwe*, Gordonsville, VA: Palgrave Macmillan.

19 Zimbabwe is plagued with a vast array of prejudiced names given to different social groups; these names immediately qualify one as the 'other', as someone who is not from here, who does not belong and is thus not entitled to citizenship.

20 Some human rights organisations recorded horrifying stories of brutalities that were committed by government forces in the early 1980s. See, for example, 'Zimbabwe: Wages of War' by *Lawyers Committee for Human Rights Human Rights Quarterly*, Vol. 9, No. 1 (Feb. 1987), pp. 115-16.

21 This list is by no way exhaustive. To this list one can certainly add sexual minorities who have been brutalised with state complicity. This exclusion is 'popular' in the sense that religious bigotry and 'traditionalism/custom' have been used to legitimate these social groups as the 'others'. This is not withstanding that democratic citizenship entails that the 'ties that bind' are only civic and universal, that is, they are to be found in universal rights than elsewhere (religion, ethnicity, sexuality, gender, race, class etc.). See Epprecht, M. 1998. 'The 'Unsaying' of Indigenous Homosexualities in Zimbabwe: Mapping a Blind spot in African Masculinity', *Journal of Southern African Studies*, Vol. 24, No.4, pp. 631-51.

22 See for example: Mamdani, M. 1996. *Citizen and Subject: Contemporary Africa and the Legacy of Late Colonialism*; Chan, S. 2005. 'The Memory of Violence: Trauma in the Writings of Alexander Kanengoni and Yvonne Vera and the idea of unreconciled citizenship in Zimbabwe', *Third World Quarterly*, Vol. 26, (2) pp. 356-389; Nkiwane, T. 2000. 'Citizenship, Gender and Constitutionalism in Zimbabwe: The Fight against Amendment 14', *Citizenship Studies*,

intense global pressures. Related and bound to the nation state the emergence of global governance structures has opened new challenges on the citizen – yet there might also be opportunities because the '…arrival of world citizenship is no longer a mere phantom, though we are far from achieving it'.[23]

Citizens and the nation state: a cursory consideration

The concept of citizenship is tied to the historical development of the modern nation state and thus its enjoyment or frustration has always been related to the state of that polity. The concept of citizenship can be traced to ancient Greece and more recently to the American and French Revolutions.[24] One is a citizen when one is neither a 'slave nor a subject'. Citizen has come to be regarded highly as a protection from excessive interference by the state. As such it can be aptly summed up as '… the legal and political shield of the free person'.[25] But citizenship also entails certain obligations – loyalty to the state, paying taxes, observing the law and so on. Aristotle defined citizens as 'all who share in the civic life of ruling and being ruled'.[26] T.H. Marshall's classic work has been influential in defining who is a citizen and what rights they are entitled to, defining citizenship as 'a status bestowed on all those who are full members of a community. All who possess the status are equal with respect to the rights and duties with which the status is endowed'.[27]

By virtue of this status, as citizen, one is entitled to a range of rights – civil, political and social. Indispensable in this conception of citizenship is that citizens live under the rule of law and consent to that rule through universal suffrage. Discrimination and exclusion on the basis of ethnicity, gender, race, and sexuality are regarded as antithetical to democratic citizenship. The 'ties that bind' are no longer defined absolutely by blood and territory but by universal law and rights[28] – hence constitutions and statutes are paramount in defining who is a citizen, who is not and who may become a citizen.

In post-colonial states fragmented by wars of liberation, ethnic nationalisms and material deprivation, citizenship becomes attractive because it offers a universal category that can dilute or eradicate exclusions and hierarchies. The

22 ctnd Vol. 4; McFadden, P. 2005. 'Becoming Post-colonial: Women changing the meaning of Citizenship', *Meridians: Feminism, Race, Transnationalism*, Vol. 6, No. 1, pp. 1-18.
23 Harbemas, J. 1992. 'Citizenship and National Identity: Some Reflections on the Future of Europe', *Praxis International*, Vol. 12, pp. 1-19.
24 For a comprehensive study of the development of citizenship see Heater, D. 1999. *What is Citizenship?*. Malden, MA: Polity Press.
25 Feliks, C. 1999. *Citizenship and Ethnicity: The Growth and Development of a Democratic Multiethnic Institution*, Contributions in Sociology, No. 128. London: Green Wood Press.
26 Aristotle 1946, *Politics* (ed. E. Barker), Clarendon Press.
27 Marshall, T.H. 1963, *Sociology at the Crossroads*, London: Heinemann.
28 Not to say that this concept of 'citizenship as rights' and therefore 'equalising' has not been without its critiques. See for example; Young, I. 1989. 'Polity and Group Difference: A critique of Universal Citizenship', *Ethics*, No. 99, pp. 250-74.

question of citizenship and citizenship rights is at the core of the theory and practice of democracy and hence it has an analytical value in inquiring into the transformations of the post-colonial state. More than that, citizenship offers a substantive possibility of equality. Hammar and Raftopoulos have argued that the 'Zimbabwe crisis' must be interrogated within the context of the politics of 'land and resource distribution; reconstructions of nation and citizenship; and the remaking of state and modes of rule'.[29] Chan has pointed in this direction also arguing that rather than focusing on the 'chronology of the Zimbabwe decline' it is time 'to reflect on its impact upon the idea of citizenship and the idea of individuals as citizens'.[30] The nature and question of citizenship is also fundamental because the idea of a state or nation state cannot be meaningful without citizenship[31].

Late colonialism and citizenship: the 'savage' and the 'civil'

Citizenship has always been exclusionary, gendered, racialised, ethnicised and has thus been sharply contested.[32] On one hand are ruling elites, often racially defined, ethnic nationalists and anti-immigration groups seeking to restrict or manipulate accessing citizenship. On the other hand are social classes (refugees, ethnic minorities, sexual minorities, religious minorities) who contest their exclusion, arguing and contentiously acting for their inclusion as citizens – to be 'equalised'. In Zimbabwe, as in most of southern Africa, the emergence of nationalist, anti-colonial and anti-apartheid liberation movements in the late 20th century marked an important period in the contestations over citizenship. From 'subject to citizen' was the thrust of these contestations in order to access rights and entitlements and to be protected by the law. In colonial Rhodesia, as in apartheid South Africa, citizenship was differentiated primarily on the basis of race. Laws, regulations and institutions were fashioned to the exclusive service of the settler state and white minority. Civil law was meant for 'settlers' while customary or native law was meant for 'savage' 'natives'. This demarcated the 'subject' from the 'citizen': one was a subject if under native law and a citizen

---

29 Cited in Hammar, A. 2005. 'Disrupting Democracy: Altering Landscapes of Local Government in post-2000 Zimbabwe', Discussion Paper No. 9, Crisis States, Development Research Centre, London School of Economics http://www.crisisstates.com/download/dp/dp09.pdf (accessed 20 August 2006).

30 Chan, S. 2005. 'The Memory of Violence: Trauma in the Writings of Alexander Kanengoni and Yvonne Vera and the Idea of Unreconciled Citizenship in Zimbabwe', *Third World Quarterly*, Vol. 26, No. 2, pp. 362-89.

31 Adejumobi, Said 2001, 'Citizenship, Rights and the Problem of conflict and Civil wars in Africa', *Human Rights Quarterly*, Vol. 23, No. 1, pp. 148-70.

32 In the United States of America, for example, while the Fifteenth Amendment 'guaranteed' the right of citizens to vote regardless of '*race, colour, or previous condition of servitude*' it took almost another century and the agitation of the Civil Rights Movement to get Congress to enact the National Voting Rights Act of 1965 to remove barriers to voting such as the poll tax, the requirement of 'good character' references, literacy tests and so on.

if under civil law.[33] Nkiwane has argued that citizenship is about entitlement stating that, 'Gender with respect to citizenship equally is about entitlement. Clearly only those who are citizens are entitled, and therein lay a complex web of relationships between the state and its citizens'.[34] Citizenship is thus essential because not only is it about rights, it is about power – universal suffrage and the right to hold public office are integral to the (re)distribution of political power.

Undemocratic citizenship: post-colonial arbitrations and the doomed post-colonial state

Zimbabwe's nationalist movement hovered between liberal nationalism and some fluid forms of 'African socialism' and Marxist-Leninism.[35] One of the mobilising slogans for the liberation movement was 'one man one vote'. Phimister and Raftopolous (2004: 362) point out that 'in the broader mobilisation that characterised the mass nationalist movement from the 1950s, while popular demands were incorporated into the nationalist agenda, the central organising force behind it all remained the emerging elite with their demands for sovereignty, equal citizenship and economic advancement'.[36] Citizenship was attractive – it offered the prospects of rights, civil, political, social, and economic. Just as the French revolution had sought to demolish the old order, for the ordinary black Zimbabwean it meant being regarded as a human. As such at independence, in 1980, there was a widespread legitimate expectation that the colonial state would be dismantled and with it the attendant institutions and laws that had served white minority rule. This was not to be so.

Zimbabwe's citizenship is constitutionally provided for in Chapter 2 of the Constitution.[37] Dual citizenship is unlawful.[38] Zimbabwean citizenship has often been braided by other limitations beyond these legal definitions. Thus, while analysing the legal limitations on citizenship is necessary, it need not be the exclusive route through which the citizenship crisis in Zimbabwe can be

---

[33] Mamdani, M. 1996. *Citizen and Subject: Contemporary Africa and the Legacy of Late Colonialism*, Princeton University Press.

[34] Nkiwane, T. 2000. 'Citizenship, Gender and Constitutionalism in Zimbabwe: the Fight Aginst Amendment 14', *Citizenship Studies*, Vol. 4, No. 3, pp. 324-35.

[35] For extensive inquiries on the 'ideology conflations' and 'struggles within the struggle' see Astrow, A. 1983. *Zimbabwe: A Revolution That Lost Its Way?* London: Zed Press; Sithole, M. 1979. *Zimbabwe Struggles within the Struggle*, Salisbury, Rujeko; Moore, D.

[36] Phimister, I. and B. Raftopolous. 2004. 'Zimbabwe Now: The Political Economy of Coercion', *Historical Materialism*, Vol. 12., No. 4, pp. 355-82.

[37] Constitution of Zimbabwe, October 2005 http://www.kubatana.net/html/archive/legisl/050914consti.asp (viewed August 2005).

[38] See the case of Judith Garfield Todd vs Registrar-General of Citizenship & Minister of Home Affairs: Case No. HC 55/2002. In that case the government appealed against a finding by the High Court that the Registrar General had acted unconstitutionally by refusing the applicant, who had claim to New Zealand citizenship, to renew her passport. Todd was left with no option but to renounce her Zimbabwean citizenship and acquire New Zealand citizenship.

unravelled. Rather there is need to interrogate the experiences of certain social groups in order to adequately follow how accessing and enjoying citizenship has become a mode of rule for the governing elites in post-colonial Zimbabwe. Hindess has painted the grim picture observing that, '... [the]condition of citizenship in post-colonial states in particular is also seriously constrained by the governmental institutions and practices inherited from the colonial period, most of which were predicated on a view of the subject population as considerably less civilised than their rulers'[39]. To critically interrogate post-colonial citizenship one has to peer into Zimbabwe's post-colonial state-society-law relations. The best vantage point is to focus on social groups like women, farm workers and 'ethnic politics'. One is likely to meet the glaring evidence of a masculine-discriminatory and ethnicised state unready to function under the rule of law and always ready to diminish citizens' rights.

Farm workers

Farm workers are perhaps a social group whose claim to citizenship has been doubted. Farm workers' identity is linked to what Amin called the *Africa of labour reserves* that was characterised by the migrant labour system to serve the capitalist development needs in the mines and agriculture.[40] Rutherford has characterised the farm workers as existing within what he calls *domestic government*.[41] Farm workers have existed on the margins in colonial and post-colonial Zimbabwe. West and Rutherford have captured this marginalisation in the following words:

> They [farm workers] are citizens whose claims to belong to Zimbabwe have been treated with suspicion by the government and many other Zimbabweans because of the history of labour migration and, more importantly, the form of administration under which they fell. The former meant that many farm workers in the colonial period were foreign-born, while the latter has meant that they have been closely linked to white farmers and not necessarily the post-colonial nation.[42]

Rutherford has also clearly argued that the status of farm workers, both as 'foreigners' and 'the wretched', was appropriated by nationalist anti-colonialism and by the constitutionalism and liberal discourse of human rights. In the language

---

39   Hindess, B. 2002, 'Neo-liberal citizenship', *Citizenship Studies*, Vol. 6, No. 2., p. 337.

40   The *Africa of the labour reserves* consists of the eastern and southern parts of the African continent: Kenya, Uganda, Tanzania, Rwanda, Burundi, Zambia, Malawi, Angola, Mozambique, Zimbabwe, Botswana, Lesotho, Swaziland and South Africa (Amin, 1972: 502-23).

41   Rutherford, B. 2001. 'Commercial Farm workers and the politics of (Dis)placement in Zimbabwe: Colonialism, Liberation and Democracy in Zimbabwe', *Journal of Agrarian Change*, Vol. 1, No. 4, pp. 626-51.

42   West, A. and B. Rutherford. 2005. 'Zimbabwe's 'New Clothes': Unraveling the Fabric of Identity and Power Among Displaced Farm Workers', *Sarai Reader 05*, pp. 398-411.

of the former, both colonial and post-colonial Zimbabwe saw the farm worker as part of the reason for the liberation struggle and in the language of the *Third Chimurenga* the farm workers must be liberated from the *murungu*. In the latter, within the discourses of constitutionalism and liberal rights, the farm worker is put at the centre of debates, still exploited and still wretched, his/her status appropriated in the language of displaced persons. While the government of Zimbabwe took some initiative to make provision for farm workers to renounce their claim to dual citizenship and be Zimbabwean citizens, due to lack of education the affected farm workers remained out of the process.[43] The initiative was half-hearted and has not largely altered the marginality of most of the farm workers and 'foreigners' whose genealogy is mingled with migration labour patterns of late colonialism.

Second-class citizens: women, customary law and citizenship

Citizenship has often been exclusionary, highly gendered, based on property ownership and racialised. It was not until the early 20th century that citizenship was formally extended to women. In the US it would take the civil rights movement to secure a vote for the blacks. The racialised and patriarchal nature of citizenship in colonial Zimbabwe was executed by many laws, including pass laws that ensured that racially exclusive definitions of identity, nationality and citizenship were enforced.[44] This exclusion of women was not a monopoly of the settler state. Zimbabwe's liberation movements often confined women to 'womanly duties' like nursing and teaching, and women cadres were often raped by men in the training camps.[45] Writing on 'war narratives' by Zimbabwe People's Revolutionary Army (ZIPRA) ex-combatants, Alexander and McGregor observed that 'ZIPRA's women battalions never left the camps'.[46] In the case of the Zimbabwe Africa National Liberation Army (ZANLA), initially women were confined to the camps as support staff growing food, cooking and carrying supplies to the front. This situation was to change in the late 1970s as women became commanders of guerrilla units and there was an attempt, however minimal, to liquidate the sexual division of labour.[47]

Zimbabwe's independence in 1980 saw major legal reforms to improve the

---

43 Citizenship of Zimbabwe Amendment Act, 2003. See Kandororo-Dingani, E. 2006. 'Voter Apathy Dilutes Value of Democracy', *The Zimbabwe Independent*.

44 Barnes, T. 1997. '"Am I a Man?" Gender and the Pass Laws in Urban Colonial Zimbabwe', *African Studies Review 1930-1980*, Vol. 40, No. 1, pp. 59-81 (at p. 59).

45 See, for example, the award-winning film *Flame* (1996) produced by Zimmedia and directed by Ingrid Sinclair.

46 Alexander, J. and J. Macgregor. 2004. 'War Stories: Guerrilla Stories of Zimbabwe's Liberation War', *History Workshop Journal*, Vol. 5, pp. 79-100.

47 Seidman, G.W. 1984. 'Women in Zimbabwe: Post-independent struggles', *Feminist*, Vol. 10, No. 3, pp. 419-40.

status of women.[48] The passage of these laws has not provided sufficient stimulus to remove all forms of discrimination against women in Zimbabwe and they remain mostly trapped at the lowest socio-economic level.[49] The evidence of this exclusion and blaming women as the 'sources of moral and cultural degeneration' was the 'clean up' of 1983 and the struggle over Constitutional Amendment 14.[50] Women have contested the nature of this post-colonial citizenship. The state, dominated by black males, was and is determined that women stay in the rural areas and perform 'motherly duties' – keep them in the domestic arena.[51] *Operation Clean Up/Chinyavada* was meant to clean the streets of '*pfambi/ mahure*' (prostitutes) and force them to the rural areas where they 'belonged'.[52] Win, a feminist activist, charged that 'For some of course things have never changed. 1983, [was] the first signal that women's rights were to be bestowed and taken away as and when the state wished'[53]. Further, women who participate in politics are labelled as *mahure* (prostitutes) or that they want to be *like* men. That the post-colonial state was not interested in democratic citizenship was subsequently evident in the case of *Magaya vs Magaya*.[54] The Zimbabwe Supreme Court upheld a decision by the magistrates court that 'Venia [Magaya, the plaintiff] is a lady and therefore cannot be appointed (heir) to (her) father's estate when there is a male'.[55]

The effect of this judgement was to place customary law above constitutionality tests. Sithole (1999: 59)[56] argued that the implications were not only in inheritance issues but allowed discriminatory customary law to apply. Sithole argued that, 'the Supreme Court's approval of the constitutional provisions that support discrimination based on sex in the area of customary law poses a serious threat to women's rights in Zimbabwe because women can no longer expect to use the constitution to challenge discriminatory customary law'. Further to that the state made it clear that women were not equal citizens, as children born of a marriage between a Zimbabwe woman and non-citizen foreigner could not be entitled to citizenship.[57] In the context of land reform, in which the majority of women live in the rural areas and therefore are under 'customary law', the

---

48 See Moyo, O. and S. Kawewe. 2002. 'The Dynamics or Racialised, Gendered, Ethnicised and Economically Stratified Society: The Socio-Economic Status of Women in Zimbabwe', *Feminist Economics*, Vol. 8, No. 2, pp. 163-81.
49 Ibid.
50 Nkiwane, T. 2000. 'Citizenship, Gender and Constitutionalism in Zimbabwe: the fight against Amendment 14', *Citizenship Studies*, Vol. 4, No. 3, pp. 324-35.
51 See, for example, Gaisela, 1995. 'Troubled Sisterhood: Women and Politics in Southern Africa: Case Studies from Zambia, Zimbabwe and Botswana', *African Affairs*, Vol. 94, No. 377.
52 Watson, P. 1988. *Determined to Act*, Women's Action Group, Harare.
53 See Win, E. 2004. 'Celebrating Independence – is 24 years not enough?', www.justassociates. org/the%20national%20anthem.pdf (accessed August 20, 2005).
54 1999 (1) Zimbabwe Law Reports 100 (S).
55 http://www.worldlii.org/int/cases/ICHRL/1999/14.html (accessed 20 August 2005).
56 See Sithole, E. 'The Ongoing Struggle for Women's Rights in Zimbabwe', http://findarticles. com/p/articles/mi_m2872/is_1_26/ai_62793786 (accessed 26 August 2006).
57 See Gaidzanwa, R. and A. Cheater. 1996. 'Citizenship in Neo-Patrilineal States: Gender and Mobility in Southern Africa, *Journal of Southern African Studies*, Vol. 35, No. 3, pp. 189-200.

discriminatory effect is devastating and disempowering for women. Nkiwane has argued that the resolution of women's subordination and exploitation lies beyond the state simply because 'the state is not a neutral arbitar ... The state represents class and gender interests that are central to its maintenance'.[58] Women have contested the nature of this exclusionary citizenship, making some modest gains against extreme opposition.[59] Indeed for many feminists the state has been designated a site of sustained struggle.[60]

Who belongs?: citizenship and ethnicity

The post-colonial state is 'doomed' because 'it is the uncritical successor of the colonial state and therefore lacks legitimacy'.[61] Mukau (1994) argues that much of the crisis of the post-colonial state is that it is ahistorical, amoral and an imposition of the nationalist elite. In that regard the post-colonial state is a fragile state plagued with ethnic tensions that continuously threaten its stability. Ethnic tensions threaten to overwhelm the Zimbabwean state. These tensions are pointers to the fact that where democratic citizenship is withered by resort to narrowly mobilising ethnic identities and using them as the basis of 'access' to the state and national resources then the post-colonial state is effectively doomed. In the four months between August and December 2005 a regular visitor to web forums hosted by New Zimbabwe and Zimdaily[62] would have been confronted with the evidence of this 'doomed' postcolonial state.[63] On various occasions the forum editors, administrators and managers of the chat rooms and the websites had to intervene. One person shared his disdain of Shonas saying that 'all Shonas must be killed' and the response was swift and equally escalatory, urging the Shona to 'send all the Ndebeles' to South Africa.

This cyber-antagonism cannot be immediately ascribed to particular individuals, yet it reflects one of the most bitter contestations over belonging and citizenship in Zimbabwe. The 'Ndebele' are regarded as pre-colonial 'invaders' who routinely raided 'peace-loving Shonas'. The Shonas in turn are charged for dominating, often violently, the post-colonial polity. Cyber-space provides a comfort zone for people to be faceless and thus take advantage of that anonymity to vent their frustrations. This zone of comfort is relatively new because during the liberation war the contestations for power based on ethnicity were often

---

58 Nkiwane, T. 2000, 337.
59 The latest of this is the Domestic Violence Bill 2006. See the fiery debates and opposition it has generated at http://www.kubatana.net/html/archive/gen/061012domvdex.asp?sector=LEGISL&year=0&range_start=1 (viewed November 2006).
60 In late 2006 the Women in Politics Support Unit (WIPSU) launched the '50-50' campaign with the slogan 'The Time for 50% Representation is Now'.
61 Mukau, M. 1994–1995, 'Why redraw the map of Africa: A moral and Legal Inquiry', *Michigan Journal of International Law*, Vol. 16, pp. 1113-76.
62 See www.newzimbabwe.com and www.zimdaily.com.
63 In the late 1990s debates around constitutional reform also included heated debates within the National Constitutional Assembly (NCA), around calls for a 'federal state' in Zimbabwe.

violent. The sharpest break came in early post-colonial Zimbabwe with the 'problem of dissidents' in Matabeleland and Midlands. The human rights abuses committed there, with impunity, by Zimbabwe's security forces with sanction from government are horrifying. The causes of the conflict itself might be complex and need not detain us here but there is general agreement that there was a systematic disregard of the Rule of Law in dealing with the conflict and as such many were brutalised. Those affected were overwhelmingly from the minority Ndebele.[64] Ethnic divisions, tensions and mistrust might have worked well for colonial administrations because they supported a policy of 'divide and rule' – but its effect was to entrench an almost unresolvable contestation on claims over 'Zimbabwe'. The brutal war to stamp out the 'dissidents' exacerbated ethnic mistrust and Robert Mugabe was later to admit that it was 'a moment of madness'.

Based on one's ethnic or racial identity, one's belonging to Zimbabwe is doubted. 'Others' are immediately seen as 'less Zimbabwean' while others with 'ancestral generations going back' regard themselves as more Zimbabwean.[65] Maroleng (2005) has argued that Zimbabwe's political fortunes are tied to how ethnic tensions are mediated and or reproduced in the attempts to secure power.[66]

'Patriotic History': chequered nationalism and truncated citizenship

We need to understand the nexus between citizenship, citizenship rights and entitlements on one hand and post-colonial public policy and public law on the other and how an often racialist nationalism has been used to effect exclusion. This exclusion cannot be complete unless it can be legitimated by editing and presenting a history that validates the claims made by the ruling elites. Ranger has robustly interrogated the development of 'patriotic history'.[67] One has to be 'patriotic', meaning the rejection of dual citizenship and renouncing any possible claim to other citizenship. A claim to foreign citizenship is considered disloyalty to the national patriotic project. For Ranger, patriotic history '... then

---

64 Berkeley, B. 1986, 'Zimbabwe: Wages of War: A Report on Human Rights', Lawyers Committee for Human Rights, New York; Catholic Commission for Peace and Justice and Legal Resources Foundation 1997, 'Breaking the Silence, Building True Peace: A Report on the Disturbances in Matabeleland and Midlands 1980–1989', Harare. www.hrforumzim.com/members_reports/matrep/matrepsumm.htm (accessed 20 August 2006).

65 The power of ethnic mobilisation has been aptly captured in an analysis of the succession tensions by Chris Maroleng, who summed it up as a 'Zezuru-sum' game.

66 See the following: Maroleng, C. 2005. 'Zimbabwe's Zezuru Sum Game: The Basis for The Security Dilemma in which the political elite finds itself', *African Security Review*, Vol. 14, No. 3; Gatsheni-Ndlovu, Sabelo. J. 2005. 'The post-colonial state and Matabeleland: Regional Perceptions of Civil-Military Relations 1980-2002', Institute of Security Studies, South Africa, Briefing Paper http://www.issafrica.org/pubs/Books/OurselvesToKnow/Ndlovu.pdf (accessed 20 August 2005).

67 See Ranger, T. 2004. 'Nationalist Historiography, Patriotic History and the History of the Nation: The Struggle over the Past in Zimbabwe', *Journal of Southern African Studies*, Vol. 30,

is a complex phenomenon. It ranges from the brutal over-simplifications of the militia camps, through presidential campaign speeches, through the work of ministerial historians, to the sophistications of Mahoso, and to addresses to world conservationists. It is equally variously propagated – in courses taught by war veterans in the camps, in collections of Mugabe's speeches, in Chigwedere's syllabi and textbooks in the schools, on state television and radio, and in the writings of Mahoso and others in the state-controlled press. As we have seen, it is proclaimed as a remedy to the failures of parents and teachers and especially of universities to instil the revolutionary spirit'.[68]

Patriotic history is supposed to discipline consciousness before it emerges, de-legitimise and vilify where it has emerged and to write a remembering syllabus of what can be remembered and what cannot be remembered.[69] 'Patriotic history' is delivered by an equally interested and tightly controlled 'patriotic journalism'.[70] One can be included as long as one agrees with this narrative and bows to its rituals like buying a ruling party card, participating in meetings voluntarily or otherwise and accepting that only the party of liberation, the ruling party, carries with it the 'historic mission' of nation-building and defending 'our' sovereignty. At its most crude and brutal level and mainly during election time patriotic history is taught at the *pungwe* (night-time political (re)education meeting). For those who (re-)join the ruling party, whether compelled by fear or otherwise, they are said to have 'repented' and are welcomed 'home'.[71] From patriotic history emerged the concept of the '*Third Chimurenga*', in which Zimbabweans are pigeon-holed as 'revolutionaries' or 'sell-outs'.[72] Allegiance to and voting for the 'party of liberation' becomes the yardstick of patriotism. Those that do not agree automatically become *vatengesi,* (sell-outs/informants) are lumped with the 'foreigners', 'imperialists' and they become the 'other' – their rights can always be abused, diminished and taken away because as long as they are not members of the ruling party then their loyalty to the nation is doubted and can be easily stripped away.

Imminent contestations: citizenship as a struggle

Hammar succinctly observed that '… ZANU(PF)'s current vision of redistribution and authentic African government is radically partisan and partial, and rests on

No. 2, pp. 215–34.

68 Ibid.

69 See Dansereau, S. 2004. 'Liberation and Opposition in Zimbabwe', in Melber, H. (ed.) *Limits to Liberation in Southern Africa: The Unfinished Business of Democratic Consolidation.* South Africa: HSRC Press.

70 Ranger, T. 2005. 'The rise of patriotic journalism in Zimbabwe and its possible implications', *Westminster Papers in Communication and Culture.* London: University of Westminster, Special Issue, pp. 8-17.

71 BBC. 'Mugabe Urges Critics to Repent', 11 August 2003. http://www.news.bbc.co.uk/1/hi/world/africa/3140801.htm (accessed 20 August 2006).

72 See also Fanon, F. 1963. *The Wretched of the Earth* (especially 'The Pitfalls of National

dramatically altered and narrowing boundaries of *national citizenship and belonging*.[73] Citizenship is about power and the exercise of that power. It determines 'who governs'. The entitlement to and exercise of democratic citizenship constitutes an anchor of a modern democratic polity. Democratic citizenship potentially dissolves hierarchies because 'citizen' is an equalizing word.[74] Yet, becoming a citizen involves a process of, as it were, getting into society as an outcome of social struggle.[75] An idea shared by McFadden when she argues as follows:

> Through active citizenship, expressed in the continued contestation over all facets of what it means to be a citizen – a life free of sexual and physical violence; the ability to travel and be identified as an autonomous being; to be registered and acknowledged as a rightful heir to familial and public resources; to engage in political practice and have access to the key institutions of the society in order to restructure them in more inclusive ways – these are among the many tenets of a modern citizenship that Africans want and which they have been denied by successive regimes almost without exception.[76]

Beyond public law reform and building robust government institutions poverty is a central issue. This is essentially because '... poverty is perhaps the most severe obstacle to the full realisation of citizenship rights'.[77] Turner also points to the importance of social participation arguing that 'Citizenship involves essentially the question of access to scarce resources in society and participation in the distribution and enjoyment of such resources'.[78] In Zimbabwe some of the people who have been routinely cleaned-up and 'resettled' do not even know whether they are 'aliens' or citizens. Mostly engaged in the everyday attempts to survive they almost constitute an 'underclass' which is severely deprived of social mobility.

Conclusion: peacing the pieces

Coercive public policy and pubic law in Zimbabwe must be interrogated and understood historically and empirically within the context of a rising racialist and authoritarian nationalism. Further, that this nationalist authoritarianism selectively and often violently appropriates symbols, discourses and ideologies of the liberation struggle and conflates them with pre-colonial and colonial modes of citizenship. This is often effected through violence and (re)packaging history, what Ranger has called 'patriotic history', and is delivered through a

Consciousness', pp. 148-205). New York: Grove Press.

73   Hammar, A. 2005, 28.

74   Kerber, L.K. 1997. 'The Meaning of Citizenship', *Journal of American History*, Vol. 84, No. 4.

75   Turner 1986, 11.

76   McFadden, P. 2002. 'Becoming post-colonial: African women changing the meaning of citizenship', Presented at Queens University, Canada. http://www.queensu.ca/snid/mcfadden. doc (accessed 20 August 2005).

77   Nkiwane, 2000, 329.

monopolised media where an equally interested 'patriotic journalism' executes it. The boundaries of who is in and who is out are continuously made fluid and shifted expediently to fit the immediate needs of anxious nationalist elites. Almost bordering on class, certainly bordering on gender and sexuality, almost bordering on ethnicity the boundaries are arbitrary, brutal, disciplining and ordering. Public law reform is equally employed to the same effect: exacting identification and loyalty by making dual citizenship illegal. In such a terrain citizenship entails struggle. However, the exclusion of 'the others' must also be analysed fully in awareness of the fact that the ruling elites, having cornered national symbols and history, have sought to create and exploit a national psyche where others see themselves as more Zimbabwean and therefore with the right to belong, and others are seen as less Zimbabwe and thus with no right, or a diminished right, to belong.

Operation Murambatsvina spectacularly demonstrated the continued erosion of certain rights that are and must be protected by national and international laws, including the fundamental right to human dignity; to shelter; to employment; to education; to health care; and the right to freely engage in business activities. Zimbabwe is a party to several regional and international legal conventions that were clearly violated in the wake of Operation Murambatsvina.[79] These include but are not limited to the African Charter on Human and People's Rights, the Universal Declaration of Human Rights, the International Covenant on Economic, Social and Cultural Rights and the International Covenant on Civil and Political Rights[80]. In the aftermath of Operation Murambatsvina, Recommendation 8 of the UN Special Envoy stated that, 'the Government of Zimbabwe should grant full citizenship to those former migrant workers and their descendants who have no such legal status'. Zimbabwe is an artefact, its borders are the creations of colonial incursions into Africa and thus the negotiation over identity, belonging and citizenship must be informed by that sad reality of the fragmentations that existed in pre-colonial Africa.

It is very clear that access to citizenship has become a 'technology' of monopolising state power in Zimbabwe. It is used to police social groups, to control and to keep surveillance on those who dare to challenge its parochial definition. Women, minorities of different kinds (ethnic, racial and sexual) and those whose genealogy is 'mingled' in the colonial migrant labour system, or those pejoratively called 'coloureds' have never been considered full citizens of either the colonial or the post-colonial state. History has been effectively cornered to legitimise these exclusions; as such the liberation of that history is necessary so that prejudices and 'wrong' narratives can be challenged and countered. Whatever the case, it is through struggle that democratic citizenship can be brought within reach and the state in these matters will never be a 'neutral arbiter'.

---

78 Turner 1986, 85.
79 Action Aid Internationa. 2005. *An Analysis of the Demolitions in Zimbabwe*, pp. 29-39.
80 See Zimbabwe Human Rights NGO Forum, 'Order out of Chaos, or Chaos out of Order:

PART THREE

REPRESENTATIONS OF MURAMBATSVINA IN POPULAR MEDIA

8

Worlds apart
Representations of Operation Murambatsvina in Two Zimbabwean Weeklies

Tendai Chari

After winning a crucial election in March 2005 the Government of Zimbabwe embarked on a controversial cleaning-up exercise to spruce up its towns and cities. Code-named 'Operation Murambatsvina'[1,] or 'Tsunami', the exercise excited the emotions of both the local and international media. This chapter compares and analyses the coverage of the clean-up operation by two Zimbabwean newspapers, one state-owned and the other privately owned. This chapter argues that representation of Operation Murambatsvina mirrored the polarised political environment prevailing at the time. *The Sunday Mail*'s and *The Standard*'s coverage of Operation Murambatsvina during a six-week period beginning 22 May up to the 13 November 2005 is covered using qualitative methods, mainly content analysis and discourse analysis. The aim of this chapter is to ascertain the ideological motivations that inform representations of Murambatsvina in these two newspapers, and explore the implications of these representations to issues of media democracy in the country.

Introduction and background

The Government of Zimbabwe's clean-up campaign code named *Operation Murambatsvina/Operation Restore Order* launched in May 2005 immediately became a major talking point among the Zimbabwean body politic, local and international media. The campaign was supposed be a joint initiative between the Zimbabwe Republic Police and the City of Harare municipal police. The first media report about it appeared in the state-owned daily *The Herald* of 19 May 2005. The report suggests that the clean-up campaign was meant to rid all cities and towns of 'criminals, illegal dealers, touts, street people and unlicensed flea market operators'. A police spokesperson was reported to have said, 'Naturally, if

[1] *Murambatsvina* is a Shona word which means 'drive out filth'.

people are left to do things as they wish, chaos will be the order of the day. The city of Harare, once on record as the 'Sunshine City', is now virtually an eyesore'. This statement issued by the police is probably the closest one can get to the official policy encapsulating the stated objectives of Operation Murambatsvina.

The Sunday Mail

The Sunday Mail is a broadsheet published by Zimbabwe Newspapers Pvt Ltd (1980), a government-owned publishing company with a wide range of publications. It has been in circulation since 1935 and has maintained its position as the most widely read newspaper since independence. At the time of writing, the newspaper's circulation stood at 90,000 (Chagutah 2007, 25). Readership of the newspaper stood at about 100,000 in 2005, which is the year in which the clean-up operation was carried out. In order to live up to its motto as 'the most widely read newspaper', the paper has different sections catering for different tastes. The main sections of the paper are general news, business news, Sunday Metro and entertainment. Most of the news articles on Operation Murambatsvina appeared in the general news and Sunday Metro section. By virtue of being the 'leading voice for the sunshine city' the Sunday Metro section focuses mainly on metropolitan Harare, which is where the manifestations of the clean-up operation were more apparent. *The Sunday Mail* is guided by the parent company's editorial policy which, among other things, states that newspapers:

- must be credible, giving readers information that is as accurate as possible
- must be as complete as possible, publishing reports of the major local national, regional, and international events, whether news, sport or cultural
- must be fit reading for all, requiring sensitivity in the handling of sensational and lurid stories
- will be supportive of Zimbabwe and its goals, generally supportive of the elected government of the day. (Chagutah 2007, 25)

As is stated in its editorial policy *The Sunday Mail* does not at all disguise its pro-government stance. Like all publications that fall under the ambit of the government, its duty is to vigorously defend government policies, regardless of how unpalatable those policies may appear to others. It is against this background that the newspaper's coverage of the clean-up operation should be seen. The pro-government stance was quite evident during the clean-up operation in 2005 when it functioned as the government's mouthpieces.

The Standard

The Standard is published by the Zimind Publishing Group which is owned by Zimbabwean business mogul Trevor Ncube. Formerly *The Sunday Standard*, the newspaper was launched on 13 April 1997. The paper is a tabloid with several sections that include general news, health, motoring, special features, business and leisure and entertainment. At the time of its launch, the circulation of the paper stood at 10,000, rose to 41,000 in 2004 and to 50,000 in 2006 (Chagutah 2006, 23). The Zimbabwe All Media Products Survey (ZAMPS) survey for the third quarter of 2005 put *The Standard*'s readership at 420,552 (ibid.). It is guided by the Group's mission statement, which states that: 'Our duty is to serve and inform the public, which we strive to do professionally, courageously and responsibly while enhancing stakeholder value and upholding press freedom, human rights and cultivating democratic values' (ibid.). In its maiden issue the paper claimed that it intended to take a 'middle of the road' thrust by shunning what it called the 'doggedly pro-government' or the 'rightist' stance of independent publications. 'The newspaper we aim to produce is one of accuracy and fairness, a paper to be known for giving audience to all quarters, regardless of their chosen allegiances – be they political, cultural, religious or social' (ibid.).

The Standard and its allies in the private press (save for the Mirror publications) are stridently critical of most government policies. The private press views itself as 'independent' and claim that they play a 'watchdog' or 'fourth estate' role. It is against this background that *The Standard* adopted an outright anti-Operation Murambatsvina approach in its reportage. *The Standard* sought to expose what it perceived as 'policy bankruptcy' on the part of the ZANU(PF) government.

Methodology

This is a content and discourse analysis of two weekly Zimbabwean newspapers, which are the state-owned *The Sunday Mail* and the privately owned *The Standard*. These two newspapers are the most influential in the country. Both are based in the capital Harare. The two newspapers were selected because they are representative of diametrically opposed editorial policies and ideological viewpoint, and both play an important role in shaping public opinion. Twenty-four issues spanning a six-week period (22 May to 13 November 2005) were analysed.

Research questions

The research questions presented below where informed by the theoretical framework presented here and by the normative roles ascribed to the media in Zimbabwe.

How much coverage did the two newspapers accord to Operation Murambatsvina during the period under consideration?

How did the two newspapers represent Operation Murambatsvina to their readers and what did they seek to achieve through such representation?

To what extent was the coverage of Operation Murambatsvina representative of the diverse social groupings in Zimbabwe?

To what extent did the newspapers adhere to ethical and professional norms in their coverage of the clean-up operation?

Quantitative presentation/Story count

A story count in the two newspapers yielded the following results:

Date	Quantity	
	The Sunday Mail	*The Standard*
22/05/05	0	2
29/05/05	4	4
05/06/05	5	4
12/06/05	4	0
19/06/05	0	1
26/06/05	8	5
03/07/05	0	7
10/07/05	0	11
17/07/05	0	0
24/07/05	0	0
31/07/05	5	4
07/08/05	0	2
14/08/05	0	2
21/08/05	0	4
28/08/05	0	0
04/09/05	0	0
11/09/05	0	5
18/09/05	0	0
25/09/05	0	2
02/10/05	2	0
09/10/05	0	0
16/10/05	1	2
23/10/05	0	0
30/10/05	0	2
Total	**31**	**60**

Source: Zimbabwe All Media Products Survey, 2005

A story count on the clean-up operation showed that *The Sunday Mail* published 31 stories between 22 May and 30 October 2005, while *The Standard* published 60 stories during the same period.

Placement

Significant to note is the fact that out of the 31 stories published by *The Sunday Mail*, only 2 were lead stories. In contrast, *The Standard* contained 10 lead stories. This means the clean-up operation was given more prominence than in *The Sunday Mail*.

Commentary

A newspaper's commentary page is its heart and soul. It encapsulates the editorial line and ideology of the newspaper succinctly and robustly. A commentary usually dwells on the most serious issues of the day or week. It presents an undiluted and uncontaminated opinion of the publication. It is worth noting here that *The Sunday Mail* devoted only two commentaries while *The Standard* carried four commentaries on the clean-up operation during the period under review.

Qualitative findings & analysis on Operation Murambatsvina as a news agenda

While *The Sunday Mail* coverage was concentrated within the period of the clean-up, *The Standard* continued focusing on the clean-up operation well after it had been declared officially over. The coverage highlighted the after-effects of the operation and shortcomings of Operation Murambatsvina's successor – Operation Garikai/Hlalani Kuhle.[2]

Operation Murambatsvina in the news

The second question at the centre of this study is: how did the two newspapers represent Operation Murambatsvina to their readers and how did they seek to influence public opinion? *The Standard* largely represented it as 'policy bankruptcy' on the part of government. The newspaper also likened the operation to 'state terror', 'state apartheid', 'a crime against humanity', 'barbaric', 'evil', 'insensitive' and a 'violation of human rights'. The newspaper unreservedly condemned the clean-up operation and sought to direct public opinion towards what it called its 'disastrous consequences' by devoting significant space to the impact. The government was often described as 'uncaring', 'evil', and 'bloodthirsty'. The clean-up was represented as having sparked public outrage and condemnation. News headlines such as 'Survey exposes evils of Operation Murambatsvina' (14 August 2005), 'Clean-up violated basic human rights' (24 July 2005) and 'Clean-up disables the disabled' (31 July 2005) are testament to the newspaper's uncharitable view of the clean-up operation. These representations sharply contrast those of *The Sunday Mail*, which legitimated the operation as 'a noble' exercise necessary for the restoration of law and order in cities and towns. In some instances, *The Sunday Mail* promoted it as a 'blessing in disguise', or as having paid dividends by removing all illegal activities by paving the way for the introduction of a government programme of reconstruction. News headlines in *The Sunday Mail* mainly projected the clean-up operation as something beneficial to the nation. The newspaper accentuated the necessity of

2   *Garikai* and *Hlalani Kuhle* are Shona and Ndebele respectively, meaning 'Good Living'.

'order', 'legality', 'cleanliness', 'proper housing' and 'proper business practices'. While *The Standard* highlighted only the negative aspects of the clean-up operation, *The Sunday Mail* glorified it without any reservations.

Operation Garikai/Hlalani Kuhle: Optimism and cynicism

When the Government officially announced the conclusion of Operation Murambatsvina on 25 June 2005, it was reported that it would immediately be replaced with Operation Garikai/Hlalani Kuhle, the objective of which was 'to provide residential and business accommodation to deserving people under a comprehensive reconstruction programme' (*The Sunday Mail*, 26 June 2005). The operation was to be implemented 'with immediate effect and would see the construction of houses, micro and small and medium enterprises, business facilities and attendant infrastructure in cities, towns, the growth points and resettlement areas by August 2005' (*The Sunday Mail*, 26 June 2005). The study revealed that *The Sunday Mail* celebrated Operation Garikai while *The Standard* trashed it at every turn. *The Sunday Mail* accentuated Operation Garikai's benefits to victims of Operation Murambatsvina. In some instances the newspaper fell short of declaring that Operation Murambatsvina was a 'blessing in disguise' to home seekers. Operation Garikai was projected in *The Sunday Mail* as a 'God sent' opportunity, heralding the dawn of a new era in the provision of houses. Thus, reportage on Operation Garikai conveniently situated Operation Murambatsvina as a programme that was mainly about sanitation and housing provision thus pushing to the margins earlier claims about removing illegal activities and restoring Harare's sunshine city status.

The Standard, in turn, represented Operation Garikai/Hlalani as a 'hoax', an exercise in duplicity, a smokescreen to disguise the evils of Operation Murambatsvina, a non-event, hot air, etc. The newspaper was not only critical of Operation Garikai but cynical too. Headlines such as 'Operation Garikai a pie in the sky' (7 August 2005), 'Garikai a scandal' (21 August 2005) and 'Furore over Operation Garikai beneficiaries' (10 October 2005) are indicative of the newspaper's cynicism. *The Standard* largely dwelt on 'corruption', 'lack of transparency', the 'slow pace of the programme', 'missed deadlines and targets'. It cast aspersions on the efficacy of the operation in resolving housing problems in the country and on the government's commitment towards the programme. The newspaper was studious in exposing government shortcomings in the implementation of the reconstruction programme. Operation Garikai was presented as having failed before it had taken off, in order to deligitimise it. The specific ways in which Operations Murambatsvina and Garikai are constructed and represented are discussed elsewhere in this book. Needless to say, *The Sunday Mail*'s representation of Anna Tibaijuka's report is poles apart from that of *The Standard*.

Victims of Operation Murambatsvina

The major features in the news were the victims of Operation Murambatsvina. *The Sunday Mail* played down the negative impact of the clean-up operation and avoided focusing on its victims. This created the impression that the operation had few adverse effects. Where the newspaper did highlight victims of the clean-up operation, it played down their 'suffering'. Some news headlines gave the wrong impression that citizens had obeyed orders to demolish their 'illegal structures'. A cartoon showed a man carting his belongings to some unknown but 'safe destination' telling his wife (who is also saddled with a heavy load) 'Mai Muchadura, I am moving and I don't want to be caught unawares' (*The Sunday Mail*). A picture in *The Sunday Mail* on 26 June 2005 shows victims of the clean-up operation loading belongings onto a lorry possibly headed for 'unknown destinations'. The caption reads, 'Tafara residents who were affected by the ongoing clean-up exercise load their property onto a lorry destined for their respective rural homes. Most of the residents have received assistance such as transport and access to essential facilities from the Roman Catholic Church.' This caption creates the false impression that people voluntarily complied with the law and were most probably happy to do so. Such stories mask the trauma and anxiety and resistance that characterised Operation Murambatsvina.

Even where *The Sunday Mail* sought to highlight the negative aspects of the clean-up operation, it did not hype the negative aspects, thus creating an artificial veneer of co-operation among the citizenry. In a news article published on 29 May 2005 a police spokesperson is quoted as having expressed gratification about the manner in which the clean-up was progressing. He is reported to have said, '[S]ome people who had resettled illegally within the outskirts of Harare had demolished their structures and were moving away in compliance with the city of Harare.' The effect of the news discourse was to create the wrong impression that people who were complying with demolition orders were in support of the clean-up. It can be argued that *The Sunday Mail* saw the plight of victims of Operation Murambatsvina through 'rose-tinted lenses' by not acknowledging their extensive pain and grief. The 'sanitisation' of Operation Murambatsvina by *The Sunday Mail* also entailed avoiding mentioning the number of victims and obliterating 'the technology of destruction' such as bulldozers and excavators, and what Leibes (1997, 71) refers to as the 'human consequences' of the clean-up operation.

Unlike *The Sunday Mail*, *The Standard* blew the victims' plight out of proportion by devoting amounts of space to the impact of the clean-up operation on diverse sections of society. News coverage was contradictory in the sense that it created the impression that Operation Murambatsvina was cross-cutting and transcended race, class, creed, gender, ethnicity and political affiliation while at the same time giving the impression that it was primarily directed at the opposition Movement for Democratic Change (MDC) supporters who constitute the majority in urban areas.[4] Much of the news focused on the physical pain and the 'callousness' of those who had inflicted it. News reports placed particular emphasis on the victims' shock and indignation, 'assertions of outrage' and 'demands for action' to be taken to halt what was described as 'a catastrophe'. Sympathetic attention was paid to those who had 'lost their homes, livelihoods or assets'. The plight of victims of the clean-up operation was accentuated through pictures, captions and news headlines. Headlines such as the following were used to whip up emotions among readers and to project the cruelty of the implementers of the clean-up operation:

'Crackdown on vendors ill-advised' (19 May 2005)
'Clean-up claims six' (19 June 2005)
'Clean-up disables the disabled' (25 September 2005)
'Clean-up worsens urban poverty' (24 July 2005)
'Demolitions leave thousands homeless' (5 July 2005)
'34 terminally ill at Hopley Farm' (13 November 2005)
'Clean-up forces 300,000 pupils out of school' (26 June 2005)

It is instructive to note that news reports about the victims were saturated with 'humanist rhetoric', epitomised by heavy sensationalism and dramatic coverage.

Reports about victims in *The Standard* conform to Herman and Chomsky's (1988, 39) notion of 'worthy victims', who are given generous coverage characterised by 'gory details and quoted expressions of outrage and demands for justice'. Reports on 'worthy victims' deploy the 'eyewitness account narrative technique to say what the newspaper reporters or editors want to 'dredge up' thus enabling the news reports to bring out a lot of detail about the so-called horrifying experience of the victim'. In the case of *The Standard*, the narrator is most probably a 'victim' of the clean-up operation who has first-hand experience, usually suffering from an ailment of some sort. He or she is either disabled, a woman, a child or a sick person. This dramatic and emotional representation helps draw the sympathy of the readers, thereby glossing over other pertinent dimensions of an event or issue.

Rhetorical questions such as 'what crime have we committed to deserve such penalty?' are used to whip up the emotions of readers. The villain – in this case the government – is named at every turn as a strategy of attributing agency. Great detail is given about the 'atrocities' through direct quotes. A case in point is a news article in *The Standard* of 3 July 2005 in which a news source (a victim of the clean-up operation) was given a long leash to expose the 'evils' of Operation Murambatsvina. He said, 'The government has been making money out of us, going around the world asking for donations in our name for the supposed housing scheme but we have never benefited.' We are told that although Porta Farm settlers were now used to evictions, this latest one was the most 'horrible and inhuman', having claimed 'three lives' and leaving 'half a dozen others at risk'. The callousness of the people who implemented the clean-up operation is further reinforced through humanist rhetoric. Detailed, blow-by-blow accounts of the circumstances in which victims of the clean-up operation met their fate are common. The following excerpt is a good example:

> On Wednesday, a five-year-old boy was crushed to death by a truck whilst assisting his grandmother to transmit their belongings to the bus stop. Another child was crushed to death on the rubble of a house in which she was. A pregnant woman is also reported to have fallen off a lorry that was ferrying their goods from the settlement. The same day, a woman gave birth in the open following the demolition of their house. *The Standard* has also established that the body of Loice Mandigora, who died on Thursday, was still in the open. The settlers could not bury her, as they were busy moving their belongings. A two-month-old baby was left unattended after the mother [had] 'disappeared' during the blitz. 'We found the baby and we looked for the mother in vain. We suspect that she abandoned the baby or the police took her,' said Jane Peter who is looking after the child. The envoy promised to send a consignment of milk and other groceries for child.

In *The Standard*, victims of Operation Murambatsvina are those considered vulnerable in society such as women, children, babies, the disabled, the unemployed and others considered impoverished or weak. This flies in the face of the reality – Operation Murambatsvina was cross-cutting and indiscriminate in its targeting. For example, some of the condemned structures were certainly not owned by poor people. The selective targeting of the weak and vulnerable of society as victims was meant to whip up the emotions of readers so that they would view Operation Murambatsvina as the worst humanitarian crisis that had been visited upon the Zimbabwean population. The news article, 'Clean-up claims six' (*The Standard* 19 June 2005) was a blatant example. Although the headline creates the impression that six people had been killed during the clean-up operation, the reader is told that the six had died 'due to circumstances related to the controversial operation'. Some of the dead (children) were 'crushed to death by structures that remained after police partially demolished homes', while others are said to have died 'after exposure to the cold'. All names of victims are given in full, and lurid detail is devoted to describing the circumstances in which they had died.

One of the purported victims is said to have committed suicide after a 'misunderstanding with his father following the demolition of his house'. We have mourners giving heart-rending graveside speeches at the burial of an 'eight-year-old child who died of pneumonia after excessive exposure to cold following the demolition of his parents' house'. The newspaper quotes graveside mourners extensively:

> This boy lying dead here was my only child and I don't know what to do. I am making efforts to see that justice prevails. I am a poor person but what happened to my son needs God's intervention because we are fighting a powerful force that does not care about human life. Had it not been for the destruction of our house, burning of blankets, food and other belongings this boy could not have died. We are poor but we are going to look after our child. (*The Standard* 19 June 2005)

The newspaper deploys the first person narrative technique to provoke the anger of the reader. The government is described as a monster capable of trampling on its victims, while the victims are projected as 'good natured', hapless and looking up to the Almighty God for salvation. The picture created in the mind of the reader is one of Good versus Evil. As has been noted by Joe Harvey (2005, 5) humanistic rhetoric uses highly emotive language to elicit the sympathy of the reader while masking the covert bias of the newspaper. The objective of this strategy is multi-pronged. Firstly, it is meant to secure consent by winning the hearts and minds of the audience. Secondly, it diverts the audience from other important aspects of the issues at hand by appealing to their sympathy. Thirdly, it masks overt bias by pretending that what the reader or viewer is getting is 'objective'.

Such representations mask the complexity of Operation Murambatsvina and create the impression that it was mounted solely to punish the most vulnerable segments of the populace. What were the real interests of the state in executing Operation Murambatsvina? What was the real motive from a political standpoint? These hidden dimensions were not unearthed in either *The Sunday Mail* or *The Standard*.

Humanitarian responses

Operation Murambatsvina attracted an overwhelming humanitarian response from civic organisations inside and outside the country. This was not surprising considering the coverage in both the local and international media. *The Sunday Mail* was predictably less enthusiastic in covering responses by civic organisations, because of their anti-government stance. It probably feared that giving the victims too much coverage would be seen as siding with detractors. Even when the paper did cover humanitarian responses it confined itself to rebutting allegations that the government was blocking assistance. However, the greater part of the coverage consisted of opinion pieces critiquing the intentions and reactions of civil society organisations, the major argument being that they were not sincere in their intentions but wanted to make political capital out of the exercise.

Civic responses were widely covered in *The Standard*. A number of pro-opposition NGOs such as Lawyers for Human Rights, Amnesty International, the Child Protection Working Group, and the National Association of Non-Governmental Organisations (NANGO), published press releases in *The Standard* and other privately owned newspapers, condemning the operation. Their view that it constituted a 'humanitarian crisis' was sensationalised in the newspaper. The MDC and officials of civic bodies were given a long leash to recount the horrors of Operation Murambatsvina and NGOs weighed in with lurid stories that magnified its impact.

The 'positive' work of these civic bodies is also generously covered in the newspaper. One news article claimed that a survey conducted by a civic organisation based in Harare revealed that '90% of the people living in Harare's high density suburbs' had been adversely affected (14 August 2005). The 'survey' is extensively quoted in the story implying that the paper had no grounds to query its findings. Press releases by civic organisations were reproduced *ad infinitum* without any sense of scepticism. A case in point is a statement by the Zimbabwe Catholic Bishops Conference (ZCBC), which was extensively reproduced on 26 June 2005. A large portion was taken from from the press release. Even MDC President Morgan Tsvangirai's claim that the clean-up was meant to 'punish urban dwellers after they [had] overwhelmingly rejected the ruling party in the March general elections'[3] was allowed to pass without any critical interrogation, in spite of the fact that Operation Murambatsvina affected even publicly known ZANU(PF) supporters,[4] war veterans, and members of the army and the police. Such media coverage creates and promotes a parochial understanding of the real motives of the clean-up operation. Thus, while the coverage in *The Standard* was biased against Operation Murambatsvina, *The Sunday Mail* decided to suppress information about it.

Global responses

International responses generated considerable news coverage. The *Sunday Mail* focused on 'repelling' what was perceived as hostile media coverage, particularly British and American. Its major thrust was that Western countries and their media were displaying their trademark hypocrisy and double standards and were trying to use Operation Murambatsvina as an alibi for 'regime change'. *The Standard* was more than willing to regurgitate the position of Western governments and their media. This was evident in its unqualified endorsement of statements made by Special Envoy Anna Kajumalo Tibaijuka and a visiting US ambassador, Tony Hall.

The Standard reported 'growing International outrage over Zim demolitions' by a 'horrified ... international community'. It stated that 'Zimbabwean stories have dominated British newspapers. relegating stories from Iraq to the inside pages'. The attention given by the newspaper to the international responses demonstrates that *The Standard* wished Operation Murambatsvina to be accorded 'international news status', while *The Sunday Mail* wanted it treated as a 'domestic story', a 'storm in a tea cup'.

The broader media reporting context

That *The Standard* published more than twice as many stories than *The Sunday Mail* is understandable. The less-than-enthusiastic coverage *The Sunday Mail*,

---

3 The MDC won both Harare and Bulawayo, the largest and second largest cities respectively.
4 War veterans and Zanu(PF) supporters who had been allocated stands in Harare had their properties demolished.

and *The Standard*'s zeal, should be understood in the broader socio-economic and political context, and the prevailing media polarity. Self-censorship is probably the most credible explanation for *The Sunday Mail*'s suppression of stories on Operation Murambatsvina. The hyping of the clean-up operation by perceived 'detractors' constrained the state media from giving readers unfettered coverage.

The ambivalent nature of Operation Murambatsvina exacerbated the predicament of the state media. As noted by Matshazi (2005, 9) the clean-up operation had, on the one hand,

> left hundreds of thousands homeless and suffering while on the other hand it destroyed structures of vice. The operation helped demonstrate elements that were both positive and negative within the nation including eliminating vice, the need to tackle the housing crisis and attracting international attention. Some of the negative elements include the ruthless manner [in which] the government pursued the agenda, in the process throwing people [out] in the winter cold; the exposure of the disarray in the administration of our local government and depriving children of education.

The state media found the 'negatives' of Operation Murambatsvina too unpalatable and chose to suppress them, while the private media decided to be blind to the 'positives'. The 'bigger picture' was missing in the two media camps and the public could not rely on them for a broad perspective that could have brought out the ambivalent nature of the clean-up operation.

The state media defends government policies at all costs, while the private media has signed a pact with the opposition under which it is supposed to be critical of what is wrong in both ZANU(PF) and MDC policies. The informational role of the media has been compromised. The style of reporting witnessed during Operation Murambatsvina is in many ways similar to the reporting on contentious events such as the referendum held in 2000, and the land reform programme and parliamentary and presidential elections held since 2000. The hostility of the Western media has engendered a siege mentality in the Zimbabwean state forcing it into a survival mode. This in turn has meant that redefining the relationship between the citizen and the state is problematic.

The state believes that it is at war with the West and has to deploy all its amoury, including the media, in order to survive the onslaught. Western countries, their media and the local private media reject the neo-colonial and imperial agenda, and cite democratic deficit, lack of governance and violation of human rights as the core problems in Zimbabwe. This explains international media and the private local media's projection of Operation Murambatsvina as a human rights and security issue, rather than, as the state media tended to treat it, a domestic issue meant to restore order.

Conclusion

This chapter has demonstrated that the two newspapers were selective in their coverage of Operation Murambatsvina. *The Standard* was interested in covering the oppression and the negative aspects of the clean-up operation, while the *Sunday Mail* tended to sanitise it. Coverage by the two newspapers mirrors the political and ideological polarisation characteristic of the media and the Zimbabwean society in general at that time. Neither represented Operation Murambatsvina in an objective, balanced and informative manner. They failed to project the clean-up operation in a manner reflecting its multi-faceted nature. Ownership constraints, a socio-political context characterised by hostile international relations, the waning power base of the ruling party, an economy under siege and other considerations appear to have played a crucial role in news reporting on Operation Murambatsvina. Operation Murambatsvina graphically illustrates how 'crises' and conflicts can impose technical limitations on the media. Although it has always been known that conflicts push journalists to extremes, the case of Operation Murambatsvina took them perhaps beyond the levels of 'permitted partisanship' in ethical journalism. The real danger with such reporting is the possibility of the media alienating one of their most key constituencies – the readers who look to them for information and wisdom.

References

Chagutah, T. 2006. Environmental reporting in the Zimbabwean press; A case of *The Standard* and *The Sunday Mail*. MA thesis, Department of English and Media Studies, University of Zimbabwe.

Dearing J.W.E and E.M. Rogers. 1996. *Agenda-setting*. London: Sage Publications.

Harbermas, J. 1989. *The structural transformation of the public sphere*. Cambridge, London, Polity Press.

Herman, E.S. and N. Chomsky. 1988. *Manufacturing consent; the political economy of the mass media*. New York: Pantheon Books.

Harvey, J. 2000. 'Media coverage of the Zimbabwe land crisis', *Deep South*, 3 (6).

Kean, J. 1991. *The media and democracy*. London, Polity Press.

Liebes, T. 1997. *Reporting the Arab–Israel conflict: How hegemony works*. London, Routledge.

Matshazi, K. 2005. 'The ambivalence of Operation Murambatsvina', *The Daily Mirror*, 1 July.

Mazhindu, E. 2005. 'Operation Murambatsvina calls for Civic Consciousness', *The Sunday Mail*, 1 July.

9

Cartooning Murambatsvina
Representation of Operation Murambatsvina
Through Press Cartoons

Richard Kudzai Nyamanhindi

Background

Cartoons are important tools that can be used to expose policy contradictions and defects in a democracy. A cartoon says 'more than a sermon of a thousand words'.[1] They can ridicule absurdities of political actions or other human frailties in a light-hearted manner. Pomposity, venality, hypocrisy and vanity are often the prime targets of press cartoons. This chapter examines the representation of Operation Murambatsvina in the form of cartoon in the Zimbabwean public and private press. Qualitative and quantitative content and discourse analysis on selected cartoons was used. This chapter concludes that the representation of Operation Murambatsvina in cartoons mirrors the ideological and political polarisation that characterises the Zimbabwean press. While public press cartoons, especially in the case of *The Herald*, emphasised the positive aspects of the operation, private press cartoons were cynical and emphasised a number of harmful themes of the operation such as human rights, democracy and the callous nature of government.

The background to Operation Murambatsvina

On 19 May 2005, with little or no warning, a military-style 'clean-up' started in the capital, Harare. It quickly developed into a nationwide campaign, wiping out what the government called illegal vending sites, structures, other informal business premises and homes. Many people were negatively affected as entire communities were at times destroyed, while others lost their source of income, property and at times their life. Residents, particularly those in the high-density suburbs of Mbare, Glen View, Mufakose and Budiriro, watched helplessly as

[1]   Lent, J.A. 1977. 'Rebirth of Cartooning in the South', in *Media Development*, 44 (4), pp. 3-7.

bulldozers and police officers in riot gear reduced their homes to rubble, while in some cases they were forced to destroy their own homes. The 'clean-up' campaign came to be called Operation Murambatsvina/Restore Order, while others cynically referred to it as 'Zimbabwe's Tsunami' in reference to its speed and ferocity, which was similar to the devastation that followed the tsunami caused by the 2004 Indian Ocean earthquake.

The first official announcement to start the operation was made in a speech by the Chairperson of the government-appointed Harare Commission, Ms Sekesai Makwawarara, on 19 May 2005 at the Harare Town House. She characterised the operation as 'a programme to enforce by-laws and to stop all forms of illegal activity in the city'.[2] She also made it clear that the police where going to be involved in the operation. Five days later, the City of Harare issued a notice indicating that all people in greater Harare who had erected illegal structures should demolish them by 20 June 2005.

The order was eventually extended to all urban and farming areas in the country. On 26 May, only a few days after the notice had appeared, and in complete disregard of the deadline of 20 June, a massive military style operation began in Harare, Bulawayo and other cites around the country – targeting first and foremost vendors' markets, flea markets, other informal market premises and 'illegal' housing structures. Reports of bulldozing, smashing and burning were made by the private media, while the public media tried unsuccessfully to justify the necessity for the operation. Throughout the months of June, July and August, the operation left a trail of destruction reminiscent of scenes where people flee war-torn regions. The subsequent report by the United Nations (UN) described how the team was 'shocked by the brutality' of what they had witnessed, particularly the indiscriminate and unjustified nature of the operation which was carried out during a severe winter.[3] Besides, the operation also took place at a time of persistent budget deficits, triple-digit inflation, critical food and fuel shortages and chronic shortages of foreign currency. Implementation was thus made in a highly polarised political climate characterised by mistrust, fear and a lack of dialogue between government and local authorities, and between the government and civil society.

The most devastating and immediate effect of this operation was the fact that hundreds of thousands (700,000 according to the UN report figure) were rendered homeless and left without any viable form of livelihood, creating a huge humanitarian disaster. Both domestic and international pressure mounted on the government to halt the demolitions. This pressure finally resulted in the UN Secretary-General Koffi Annan dispatching the UN Habitat Under-Secretary-General and Executive Director, Ms Anna Kajumulo Tibaijuka on 20 June 2005 to lead a fact-finding mission to assess the extent of the humanitarian disaster in the country.

---

2   *The Herald*, 19 May 2005, p.1.
3   Report of the fact-finding mission to Zimbabwe to assess the scope and impact of Operation Murambatsvina by the UN Special Envoy on Human Settlements Issues on Zimbabwe, 18 July 2005, p. 7.

Historical, political, economic and ideological justifications have been given for the operation, but most of these explanations, it must be admitted, are predicated on conjecture as the government has been surreptitious about the real reasons behind the clean-up campaign. Politically, it has been argued that the operation was retribution by a state which had 'unfinished business' with the urban dwellers who supported the Movement for Democratic Change (MDC). However, this reason seems to have been nullified because even the staunch supporters of the ZANU(PF) government, the war veterans, were negatively affected by the operation as their homes were also demolished. Economically, most analysts have argued that the operation was a result of a crisis that had been unfolding since the awarding of gratuities to war veterans in 1998; a situation which was perpetuated by the 'chaotic' fast-track land reform programme which resulted in a sprawling black market and galloping inflation. However, according to *New African* magazine, the operation was a Central Intelligence Organisation (CIO) initiative that was meant to foil a reincarnation of the Ukrainian Orange Revolution in November 2004.[4]

In contrast, official statements argued otherwise. The President, Robert Mugabe, justified the operation by stating that there was a need for 'a vigorous clean-up campaign to restore sanity and urban renewal'.[5] The Police Commissioner, Augustine Chihuri, also pointed out that the operation was meant to 'clean up the country of the crawling mass of maggots bent on destroying the economy'.[6] It seems as if it was this official line of argument that the public media followed in its reports on the operation. However, despite the justification given by any side, it seems as if Operation Murambatsvina was a 'smokescreen' for motives that had little to do with addressing the problems facing the majority and restoring order in both the urban and rural areas.

The media in Zimbabwe: a brief background

The media in Zimbabwe has over the past six years been caught up in a political vortex that is antagonistic to the doctrines of freedom of expression and media ethics, such as balance and objectivity. This environment, which has been further reinforced by such legislation as the Public Order and Security Act (POSA), Access to Information and Protection of Privacy Act (AIPPA) and the Broadcasting Services Act (BSA) has resulted in media polarisation, which has inevitably affected the way news is reported. The print media currently comprises nine national newspapers: *The Herald* (a state-controlled daily), *The Chronicle* (state-controlled daily), *The Sunday Mail* (state-controlled weekly), *The Sunday News* (state-controlled weekly), *The Daily Mirror* (privately owned daily, which has

---

4   Ankomah, B. 2005. 'Zimbabwe, a nation of many surprises', *New African*, October 2005 (444), pp. 53-4.
5   *The Herald*, 20 July 2005, p.1.
6   *The Herald*, 2 July 2005, p. 3.

been linked to state agents such as the CIO), *The Sunday Mirror* (privately owned weekly, which has also been linked to state agents), *The Zimbabwe Independent* (hereinafter *The Independent*; privately owned weekly), *The Standard* (privately-owned weekly) and *The Financial Gazette* ('privately-owned' weekly, which has also been linked to the CIO). One of the popular dailies, *The Daily News*, was closed down in September 2003 when it failed to register with the Media and Information Commission (MIC), which was created under AIPPA to regulate the media.

As regards broadcasting, the industry is entirely the preserve of the government. Despite promises that the government wanted to open the airwaves through the BSA in 2001, it seems as if the law was promulgated to stifle any competitors. The nature and control of the broadcasting media in the country have resulted in the emergence of alternative media such as Internet websites, which include Zimonline, Zimnews, newzimbabwe.com and zvakwana.com, among others. In addition, clandestine broadcasting radio stations such as Studio 7 have also emerged in a bid to offer an alternative voice.

The press and Operation Murambatsvina

When the government embarked on Operation Murambatsvina, the publicly funded media were in favour of the government, justifying in their reportage the need to carry out the operation. The private media, however, working in conjunction with the opposition parties, church groups and non-governmental organisations (NGOs) condemned the operation from its inception, arguing that it was an abrogation of basic human rights carried out by a government that had failed to respect the rule of law as enshrined in the constitution since 1999.

In reporting on Operation Murambatsvina, it is important to note that both the public and private press were reduced to instruments of partisan control and social engineering. In the case of the public press, for example, such partisan reporting was more striking in that journalists came to play second fiddle to patrimonial politics and in the end inevitably failed to play their 'public interest' role effectively in scrutinising adequately the shortcomings of the government during the operation. In other words, as argued by Tuchman (1979), the press during the operation proved to be a set of political organisations rather than neutral relayers of information as they sought the voices of the government or political elites rather than those of the victims.[7] The language in most stories covered by the public media during the operation did not adequately narrate the story of the victims, which included women, the elderly and children, and neither was there adequate analysis of the negative consequences of government's actions. The public media thus seems to have treated the operation as

---

7 Tuchman, G. 'The Production of News', in Jensen, K.B. (ed.) 2002. *A Handbook of Media and Communication Research.* London: Routledge, p.79.

though it were an everyday news event and yet it left many permanent scars on many people.

Thus, in the public media, it seems that as far as Operation Murambatsvina is concerned both journalists and cartoonists became 'professional politicians' as they were active accomplices in denying people the accurate and unprejudiced information on the causes, course and consequences of the operation. When the operation commenced, for example, there were no major stories in the public media that warned residents of the operation. Most of the stories that appeared in *The Herald* and *The Sunday Mail*, for instance, used such terms as 'illegal' and 'squatters' in reference to most settlements in urban areas as if there were no epistemological and historical underpinnings to the development of the illegal structures around the country. Hardly did the public media look at the adverse effects that the operation had on the vulnerable groups. Surprisingly, the public media argued that Zimbabwe was a victim of a conspiracy theory from the former colonial master (Britain), which sought to re-colonise the country through demonising a sovereign government, which was carrying out a justified clean-up campaign. That there was no shred of evidence for this conspiracy theory but the suffering of ordinary citizens was no insuperable obstacle to the government propaganda.

Cartooning in Zimbabwe

Political cartoons became popular in Zimbabwe in the 1990s with the new wave of democratisation and swept through the continent due to their ability to simplify and crystallise complex ideas across a variety of situations. Today it is rare in the Zimbabwean media landscape to find a newspaper without a cartoon or cartoon strip to augment its editorial. Most cartoons typically address issues ranging from the ever-widening gulf between the rich and poor to the high cost of food, ineffective utilities and dilapidated infrastructure. A political cartoon can be defined as a drawing, representational or symbolic, that makes a satirical, witty or humorous point. The cartoon, according to Low, may or may not have a caption and it may consist of more than one panel.[8] Cartooning styles also vary from the most accessible to the most abstract, as will be shown below in cartoons that appeared during Operation Murambatsvina. Most of the abstract cartoons appear in the private press, while those in the public media usually lack critique and complexity; a testimony of how government ownership in Africa affects media content.

Most people in Zimbabwe, literate and illiterate, trust cartoons to reveal the unstated underside of political actions, policies and events. Cartoonists such as Innocent Mpofu (*The Herald*), Knowleh (*The Daily Mirror*) and Tony Namate (*The Independent* and *The Standard*) have over the years come to hold the status

---

[8] Low quoted by R. Harrison. See *Cartoons: Communication to the Quick,* Beverly Hills: Sage Publications. 1981: p. 43.

of teachers; teaching the people the most important ingredients of civil obedience through caricature, irony and symbolism. Cartoons give a good insight into a country's political culture, because they often have wider, more robust views of political events facilitated by the wider audience they have. However, as portrayed in the cartoon by Namate in Figure 9.2, it is quite difficult in the light of the media polarisation in the country for cartoonists to be objective.

A sample of cartoons from the public and the private media was selected. The process resulted in a total of 43 cartoons over the period, of which 22 were from the two dailies and 21 from the weekly private papers. *The Herald* for example, had only 7 cartoons for the whole period under review, while *The Daily Mirror* had a total of 15. The cartoons selected were those directly dealing with Operation Murambatsvina.

Most cartoons in the press deviate little from the editorial content of the particular paper in which they appear. This analysis looks at several themes: cartoons on democracy and human rights abuses, cartoons on gender vulnerability and insecurity, cartoons on policy contradictions and a crisis of governance, and last but not least, cartoons on the naming of the president in relation to the operation.

Cartoons on policy contradictions and a crisis of governance

A number of cartoons in the private media dwelt on the crisis of governance in the country. The tone in most of them seemed to support the fact that the government was paralysed by lack of transparency, policy failure, contradictions and international isolation, which had forced it to maintain itself undemocratically in power through manipulating the electoral process. In the process, the values and ethos of democracy and good governance – a system of government that all Zimbabweans fought to install – became compromised. The cartoons appear to have been predicated on the fact that Zimbabwe faced a crisis characterised by a serious erosion of citizens' basic rights and policy failures of monumental proportions. The cartoons by Tony Namate are of great interest in this regard. For instance, the cartoon in *The Standard* (17 July 2005, 8), entitled 'A Government of the government, by the government, for the government' (see Figure 9.3) portrayed the ruling elite as people who were willing and determined to retain political and economic power at all costs without a single shred of respect for the wishes and rights of the people who had elected them into office.

The caption was a symbolic repudiation of democracy, which advocates 'a government of the people, for the people, by the people'. The brutality and lack of respect for basic human rights by the government and its machinery such as the army and the police was shown through the symbol of a large police/ army boot crushing a wooden shack – Home Sweet Home – for its occupants. Symbolically, the image is not difficult to measure, indeed at one level it can be argued that its effectiveness depends upon it. The use of a large black boot crushing the shack and its occupants concomitantly running for dear life portrayed the brutal methods the police used to evict families from their homes. Most people were beaten with batons and police boots if they refused or delayed destroying their homes. It is certain that if the government had respected the rights of its citizens it could have avoided using force through the police, army and CIO to remove people from the urban 'slums'. At the same time, it was also cruel for the government elected by the people – as portrayed by Knowleh of *The Daily Mirror* (29 June 2005, 6) in a cartoon entitled 'Welcome to the Sunshine City: Tsunami victims ahead' – to move the people in the middle of June and July when temperatures were at their lowest.

In other cartoons, such as the one in *The Standard* (10 July 2005, 8) entitled 'Rent a crowd', Namate boldly documents how the government violated the human rights of its citizens by arbitrarily forcing them to destroy their homes without notice, process or compensation and in the process displacing thousands into holding camps that lacked basic services such as health care, education, clean water or means of economic support. Holding camps such as Caledonia were in most cases reminiscent of the wartime keeps. Contrary to government reports that the camps were adequately equipped with resources, the UN Habitat team discovered that Caledonia was poorly equipped to cater for the thousands who were repatriated there.

As regards policy, cartoons from *The Financial Gazette* (16 May 2005, 8; 2 June 2005, 8) with the following captions: 'Is it true that only houses built by Ian Smith are being left intact' and 'These people have just heard that houses belonging to war veterans have been destroyed' respectively, and one from *The Daily Mirror* (9 June 2005, 8), which questioned: 'Whatever happened to the housing-for-all-policy?', showed the inconsistent and contradictory nature of government policy in respect of Operation Murambatsvina. When the government came into power in 1980, it called for a policy of education for all by the year 2000, health for all by the year 2000 and housing for all by the same year. The cartoon by Knowleh from *The Daily Mirror* on the housing policy alluded to above seemed to have been a sign of protest against the government's reneging on its earlier promises.

The cartoons from *The Financial Gazette* used cynicism in showing the inconsistency of government policy in that what the government was now leaving in the aftermath of Operation Murambatsvina were houses built during the Ian Smith regime, which the bitter liberation struggle had been fought to be rid of. By also destroying the houses built by the war veterans the government showed that it could not have permanent allies and thus could not be trusted to represent the interest of anyone but itself.

In this context, the cartoons on policy and poor governance were thus a microcosm of a crisis of governance, a panicking government whose record of policy failure, reversal of the promises of independence and social progress were now self-evident.

Positive cartoons on Operation Murambatsvina

As alluded to in the background, the public media seemed to have failed to produce an impartial assessment as far as the state of affairs in the country was during Operation Murambatsvina. *The Herald*, and to some extent *The Daily Mirror*, cartoons failed to warn the public of the possible occurrence of the operation and further failed to analyse the consequences of such a drastic policy on the ordinary citizens. The cartoons by Mpofu of *The Herald* revealed that his work lacked the key components and techniques that are essential for creating effective cartoons. These include irony or humour, encapsulation and metaphors. Political cartoons should in most cases provide a form of commentary, which combines the power of visual and verbal images. Unfortunately, from the seven cartoons that appeared in *The Herald* during the three months of the operation none of them critically assessed the negative consequences of Operation Murambatsvina.

Indeed, owing to the media polarisation in the country, all the cartoons on Operation Murambatsvina in *The Herald* emphasised the good side of the clean-up campaign. For example, *The Herald* cartoon of 22 June 2006 (p.8) had the caption 'Clean-up of dirty is good', contrary to the UN suggestion that the clean-up campaign lacked transparency and proper planning. Another example was the cartoon of 1 July 2005 (p. 8) in which Mpofu compared a shack in the then 'dirty' Mbare suburb to a formally built two bed-roomed house at White Cliff. The cartoonist insinuated that there was a conspiracy by Tony Blair, the then Prime Minister of Britain, to perpetuate the legacy of colonialism that treated Africans as second-class citizens. What is of interest is that most of these 'positive' cartoons on Operation Murambatsvina did not analytically assess why such illegal shacks and informal sectors had sprouted all over the country, and why the government had taken 25 years to provide decent accommodation.

Other positive cartoons in *The Herald*, such as those 20 May 2005 (p. 8) and 31 May 2005 (p. 8) showed the police and army involvement in Operation Murambatsvina in a non-violent fashion. The police and the army were represented as responsible, non-partisan and acting within the limits of their mandate in getting rid of the rot that was taking place in society, which included street and flea-markets, beggars, vendors, touts, and illegal foreign currency dealers. Besides, contrary to the evidence on the ground, the police were represented as innocent and not keen to use force. In this regard, cartoons seem to have existed in a system of networks and relationships internal to the language peddled by the government and the ruling elites who tried every means possible to justify the operation.

Figure 9.1

Figure 9.2

Figure 9.3

Figure 9.4

Figure 9.5

Figure 9.6

Figure 9.7

Cartoons on the compilation of
the United Nations Report

The compilation and publication of the UN report by Ms Anna Kajumulo Tiba-ijuka showed the most complex predicaments in Zimbabwe today of 'one event, three stories'. The cartoons that appeared in relation to the report showed very interesting aspects of the close relationship between the cultural and social organisation of meaning as far as political communication is concerned in most African countries. They revealed the importance of social semiotics in contrast to textual analysis as far as understanding the way it was interpreted, especially for those without social and cultural knowledge of what had been happening in the country since 1999. Without such a background, the cartoons would inevitably have led to speculative reading.

Both the public and private press demonstrated how their interpretations of the same event contained elements of ambiguity, inconsistency and a great deal of contradiction. *The Herald* cartoon of 5 July 2005 (p. 8) showed sarcastically a great deal of concern by the British Prime Minister Tony Blair when the UN envoy extended its stay in the country. 'Hope Tibaijuka is not finding it cosy over there!' was the caption Mpofu added. This was following what the public media and officials were saying, namely that the UN delegation's report would be biased because Tibaijuka was playing second fiddle to Blair as she was one of the nine members in the Blair Commission for Africa.

This cartoon was complemented by another one on 26 July 2005, which argued that the final UN Report was a product of Blair who was using Tibaijuka as a puppet. The same interpretation was also extended to *The Daily Mirror* cartoon of 2 August 2005 (p. 6) (see Figure 9. 4) which showed that the compilation of the report had been done in complete disregard of government's efforts to improve the living conditions of its people.

On the contrary, the private media's interpretation of the report revealed an ideological reading that was a negation of the public media. *The Financial Gazette* (28 July 2005, p. 6) carried a cartoon of a drunkard captioned: 'It won't be long before Tibaijuka's report is traced to Tony Blair's computer'; something that proved correct as the government in its response to the UN Report argued that it was grossly biased and showed a reflection of the colonial conspiracy already discussed.

The cartoonist's use of the drunkard seemed to have shown that it was obvious even to a drunk layman that the government would link the negative aspects pointed out by the report to its perennial enemies, the British and the Americans. As regards the relationship between Zimbabwe and Britain, the cartoons in the private media were used to document historical events such as the constitutional referendum of 2000 and the fast-track land reform programme.

The naming of Operation Murambatsvina
in cartoons

Fourteen cartoons that appeared in the private media showed how cartoonists (Tony Namate in particular) used representational or symbolic caricatures that made a satirical and witty humorous point about who was really responsible for the operation. For instance, in most cartoons in *The Independent* and *The Standard* members of the police and government officials – especially the president, Robert Mugabe – were signified as divorced from reality. The president, in *The Independent* cartoons of 10 June 2005 (p. 13), 24 June 2005 (p. 13), 1 July 2005, (p. 13) and 29 July 2006 (p. 13); and *The Standard* (12 June 2006, 8) was portrayed as powerful, dogmatic, and uncaring, while the ordinary people were signified as small, weak and open to exploitation. Namate also used pot-bellied fat politicians juxtaposed with thin desolate citizens to give visual expression to abstract ideas in relation to Zimbabwe's political and economic systems, which have been personalised to serve the interest of the elites.

The ruling elite and their allies were thus caricatured, lampooned and stigmatised, while their acronyms and slogans were creatively corrupted to negate what they claimed to stand for. A good example was the cartoon in *The Independent* of 27 June 2005 (p. 13), entitled 'We must destroy the whole village in order to save it'. Chinotimba, a supporter of the government and leader of the war veterans, was caricatured as saying, 'We defeated George Bush, we defeated Tony Blair, we defeated Morgan Tsvangirai. Now Comrades we are ready to defeat the economy!!'

The strength of most of the cartoons in this genre was predicated on the use of a combination of the visual and verbal aspects of language, which at times – as in the cartoon of *The Independent* of 24 June 2005 (p. 13) showing Mugabe pushing Zimbabwe over the cliff – had a greater impact on the audience. In this regard, the cartoonist chose visual images of an idea or issue, which might otherwise have been thought of in the realm of verbal abstraction. The use of abstraction as if it were a tangible reality enabled Namate to provide simple images in a clear and direct fashion.

In addition, Namate also represented the president as an uncaring, unavailable and unaccountable individual who delighted at the suffering of the masses in the cartoons in *The Independent* of 10 June 2005 and 29 July 2005; and *The Standard* of 12 June 2005. The one on 10 June 2005 entitled 'Operation Keep Warm' (see Figure 9.5) showed this by portraying an old, well-clothed Mugabe warming himself in front of a fire kindled from property destroyed during Operation Murambatsvina. The cartoon gave a visual demonstration of the president's 'sins' of destroying people's property and leaving them in the open during a severe winter. Consequently, this cartoon and another one from *The Independent* of 10 May 2005 (p. 13) with Mugabe saying, 'Well we told them to stop those illegal structures long, long ago. Why, we even showed them Tsvangirai's mushroom video during the March Election!!' were used to appeal to the intellect of most Zimbabweans by referring to what the leader of the opposition, Morgan Tsvangirai, had said earlier.

Thus, by revealing the President as an octogenarian while at the same time showing his arrogance, Namate made public the evil deeds of a leader whose actions were caricatured with force, and were presented in many instances with few words, or at times none at all, as in the cartoon on 'Operation Keep Warm'. It was the power of the images which appealed to most readers and other observers. The cartoons that appeared in *The Herald*, *The Daily Mirror* and to some extent *The Financial Gazette* during the operation tried to stick to 'safe subjects' when it came to naming in their cartoons. *The Herald* and *The Daily Mirror* never used the face of the president – or any other high official – as far as apportioning blame was concerned, despite the fact that approbation for the operation had come from the government.

Gendered cartoons on Operation Murambatsvina

More than 70 per cent of the population in Zimbabwe are estimated to be living below the poverty datum line. In this regard, most cartoonists from the private media showed how Operation Murambatsvina had further impoverished the majority.

As regards children, the cartoon in *The Financial Gazette* of 27 May 2005 (p. 6) showed how most children's rights to education, food and clothing had been affected by Operation Murambatsvina. The cartoonist seemed to have come to this conclusion in conjunction with some of the reports issued by the Progressive Teachers Union, which estimated that about 300,000 schoolchildren had been forced to drop out of school as a result of the forced removals, demolitions of homes, evictions and displacements. *The Standard* cartoon of 16 May 2005 (p. 8) entitled 'June 16: Day of the Evicted Orphan' also emphasised how orphaned children were exposed to crime, prostitution and mass poverty.

Entwined with the negative impact on children, other cartoons also looked at how family ties were disrupted. The operation negatively impacted on family life as either the mothers or children were forced to go to the rural areas leaving the father in town to fend for the family. Knowleh's cartoon in *The Daily Mirror* of 29 June 2005 (p. 6) entitled 'Tsunami victims ahead' showed how it had contributed to social dislocation of families; children were depicted sleeping in the open despite the fact that Zimbabwe is a signatory to conventions that protect the rights of children.

Other children also died during the operation, as represented by Namate in the cartoon in *The Standard* of 26 June 2005 (p. 8) entitled 'Collateral damage'. Collateral damage is usually associated with terrorism in terms of which those who die by accident are regarded as secondary. The cartoon followed the death of two children in Mbare and Chitungwiza after rubble had collapsed on them.[9] The fact that the government seemed to have viewed vulnerable groups such as children as secondary reinforced the iconoclastic and concrete reference to what most human rights groups were arguing as far as the treatment of children was concerned.

Besides children, another vulnerable group were women. Cartoons with a gender perspective totalled nine, and the majority of these showed how many women faced overnight destitution following the destruction of their homes. Cartoons such as the one in the *The Standard* of 5 June 2005 (p. 8) entitled 'The Shackville 'Massacre'' and the one in *The Daily Mirror* of 28 May 2005 (p. 4) with the caption 'For whose good?' (see Figures 9.6 and 9.7) showed how the loss of income and the lack of any other means of survival had made women in the country more vulnerable to exploitation. This was particularly the case given the fact that many of the evictees were pregnant women or women with small children. Thus, women were more vulnerable to shock, trauma and depression as a result of the dispossession and displacement caused by Operation Murambatsvina.

Namate and Knowleh also showed in their cartoons that the ability of women prior to Operation Murambatsvina to earn an independent income, however small, depended on the informal market. Thus, without any meaningful social welfare programmes and other sources of income, Operation Murambatsvina represented two steps backwards for womankind and one giant leap forward for ZANU(PF), as shown in the Shackville 'Massacre' cartoon. Thus as far as gender was concerned, Operation Murambatsvina – as portrayed by cartoonists in the private media – made it more difficult for women to break through the many socio-cultural barriers put up by a patriarchal society.

Conclusion

Cartoons in both the public and private media created contestable categorisations of public events and issues that reflected particular conceptual ways of experiencing Operation Murambatsvina. Political cartoons can thus be used to displace cherished influences in political communication. The images and models that manifested themselves through the cartoons – especially those on naming, scapegoating and foreshadowing – seem thus to have been catalysts in creating confidence that the political scene in Zimbabwe is understandable, as opposed to the disorder, murkiness and policy contradictions that usually characterise much of Zimbabweans' everyday experience. Many of the cartoons, especially those that appeared in the private media, portrayed the disorder and contractions in government policy towards the ordinary people and how this was dangerous for political survival.

Some of the cartoons depicting the operation, however, also clarified through

9   *The Standard*, 5 June 2005, p. 2.

simplistic portrayals the maligning character of politicians, especially how in their decisions they became effective, heroic, inept and at times acted against what they purported to stand for. A central figurehead such as Robert Mugabe, for example, was portrayed as a legendary figure who triumphed over the ordinary people, while the ordinary people were regarded as 'victims' who usually faded completely from the attention of the cartoonists. In a crucial sense therefore, the cartoons on Operation Murambatsvina became an example of how political cartoons in general can become a fountainhead from which political discourse, beliefs about politics and consequent actions ultimately spring.

Cartoons fulfil many functions in the creation of news and meaning, and have a great deal of reflection on ideology and the gatekeepers in the media. Operation Murambatsvina was just a single event, but on a daily basis cartoons showed that different complexities and meanings can be attributed to the institutionalisation of news and are necessary to study if their effects on the audience are to be determined.

References

Ankomah, B. 2005. 'Zimbabwe, a nation of many surprises', *New African*, 444 (October), pp. 53–4.
Berger, P. and T. Luckmann. 1966. *The social construction of reality*. Harmondsworth: Penguin.
Christian, H. (ed.) 1980. 'The sociology of journalism and the press'. University of Keele, *Sociological Review Monograph*, No. 29.
Firth, R. 1973. *Symbols: Public and Private*. London: George Allen and Unwin.
Gurevitch, M., Bennett, T, Curran, J. and J. Woollacott (eds) 1982. *Culture, Society and the Media*. London: Routledge.
Harrison, R. 1981. *Cartoons: Communication to the Quick*. Beverly Hills: Sage Publications.
Jason, N. and S. Steinberg. 1992. *Theoretical approaches to communication*. South Africa: Juta and Company.
Jensen, K.B. (ed.) 2002. *A handbook of media and communication research*. London: Routledge.
Lent, J.A. 1977. 'Rebirth of cartooning in the South', *Media Development* 44 (4), pp. 3–7.
Mbembe, A. 2001. *On the Postcolony*. Berkeley: University of California Press.
Nyamnjoh, F.B. 2005. *Africa's media, democracy and the politics of belonging*. London: Zed Books.
Tibaijuka, A.K. 2005. Report of the Fact-Finding Mission to Zimbabwe to assess the Scope and Impact of Operation Murambatsvina by the UN Special Envoy on Human Settlements Issues on Zimbabwe, 18 July.
Tuchman, G. 2002. 'The Production of News', in Jensen, K.B. (ed.) *A handbook of media and communication research*. London: Routledge.

10

The Chichidodo Syndrome
Rehearsals of Operation Murambatsvina in Zimbabwean Literature and Popular Songs

Maurice Taonezvi Vambe

Creative writers and popular singers in Zimbabwe have been sensitive to and critical of the colonial and post-colonial state's habit of assigning the identity of 'human dirt' to those that they consider dissident. The fictional works of Chidzero, Samupindi, Hove and Vera and some of the songs by Chipanga question the notion of describing humans as 'dirty.' Creative works place the reader and listener in a position of rethinking issues of citizenship, the subject and subjectivities in the period after Operation Murambatsvina. Zimbabwean writers and singers suggest that this operation had been rehearsed over the years by the authorities. The authors and singers in postcolonial Zimbabwe condemn the heavy-handed politics informing the ideology of the authorities that unleashed the operation on innocent Zimbabweans.

Bernard Chidzero's *Nzvengamutsvairo* (1957) is probably the first novel in Zimbabwe to capture creatively the colonial origin of the language of 'clean up' of the 'assumed dirty' in the cultural lives of African people. The novel's suggestive title can loosely be translated as 'Dodge the broom' and implies that the colonial socio-economic and political philosophy was based on an understanding that to usher Africans into the colonial modernity, their culture, political and economic systems had to be systematically undermined and swept aside. Father Biehler of Chishawasha mission wrote to Lord Grey in 1897 that the Shona people were the most hopeless of humankind. The revered father suggested that the only salvation was to kill all the Shona people from the age of 14 years in order to pave the way for a cultural renewal driven by colonial modernity.[1] In Chidzero's novel, colonialism is the physical as well as the metaphorical 'broom' that is supposed to sweep the 'dirt', described as African customs and ways of life.

However, many people in Zimbabwe tend to forget that the struggle for independence was a huge military operation akin to Murambatsvina, aimed as it

---

1   Vambe M.T. 2004. *African Oral Story-telling tradition and the Zimbabwean Novel in English.* Pretoria: UNISA Press, p. 1.

was at removing the exclusionary racial politics that characterised white rule in Rhodesia (Martin and Johnson 1981). Nonetheless, the actual conduct of the armed struggle by the liberation movements showed tendencies of 'sweeping' or persecuting those Africans whose ideas and views on the struggle were not aligned with the interests of the leaders of the political movements. This culture of suppressing alternative views within the liberation movement was, ironically, a form of Murambatsvina and it undermined attempts at broadening the ideological understanding of the cause, course and execution of the armed struggle.

Samupindi's novel, *Pawns* (1992) captures these contradictions within the struggle to an extent that when the novel is read after Operation Murambatsvina, the struggles within the liberation movements figure as preludes or official rehearsals of this operation. The novel is about Daniel, alias Fangs's spiritual/physical/mental journey to manhood until he joins the liberation forces on the side of Zimbabwe African National Liberation Army (ZANLA). Awaiting training and deployment at Seguranza, a guerrilla camp in Mozambique, Fangs and his comrades go through hunger and disease, and he witnesses the death of Peter, his friend. During these long months of waiting for training to become a freedom fighter, there were also 'defections' (p. 69) from guerrillas who feared being persecuted by their superiors for holding different views on the course and aims of the struggle. For example, once the masses were labelled as 'sell-outs' and reported to the guerrillas, they could be regarded as 'dirty', dispensable and murdered, in spite of the fact that they had provided fighting guerrillas with food. This violence against the masses is evidenced by comrade 'Logistics' who murders the old peasant, Mhangira, even as the guerrilla had no tangible evidence that the old man was a sell-out. By capturing this incident of heavy-handedness, Samupindi refuses to accord his guerilla creations the status of heroes. This is the author's strategy to debunk official nationalist myths that portrayed the guerrillas' relationship with the masses as always mutual.

In *Pawns*, the presence of the Vashandi guerillas complicates the nationalist narrative of war favoured by the old guard of ZANU(PF) who claim to speak in a unitary voice. The Vashandi were a group of young, educated cadres committed to dismantling privilege within the struggle. Part of the privileges of the leaders was the latitude they possessed to define how the war was to be conducted irrespective of the complications on the war front. Joseph, one of the converts to the Vashandi cause believes that theirs is 'a guerilla warfare within guerrilla warfare' (p. 100). The Vashandi also fought the tribalism fostered by their leaders within the movement. As the omniscient narrator notes, 'the language of the trainers, strange to most, was Korekore liberally smattered with Mozambican words and phrases. If you did not speak it, you were outside, you did not belong, you did not come from Mount Darwin' (p. 85).

Thus, language and ideology were used to police the Vashandi. In *Pawns*, the question of ideological self-criticism was central to the Vashandi because the old guard believed that 'as for ideology, this can be decided after independence' (p. 102). Fangs believes that the Vashandi have 'a good case' (p. 76). Unfortunately, while the leaders of the liberation movement speak of 'a people's war' (p. 72), the same leaders cannot 'countenance dissidence' (p. 20) from the rank and file of the military cadres such as the Vashandi. The process of 'cleaning up' the political elements such as the Vashandi because they support a plurality of war ideologies is a ruthless one. The person who executes the Vashandi is General Josiah Magama Tongogara, the guerilla who has entered into African song, dance, drama and folklore as the hero of the struggle for liberation in Zimbabwe (p. 102).

The loss of Nhari and Badza (p. 70), key members of the Vashandi movement, led David Moore to comment that the old guard of ZANU(PF) began to 'create its monopoly on violence from the conception of the guerrilla war' (Moore 1995, 376). Put differently, the language of cleaning-up dirt that became the informing official discourse of Operation Murambatsvina was already entrenched in a political movement struggling to create hegemonic control over the lives of other guerrillas as well as the ordinary people. Furthermore, in *Pawns*, after independence, Fangs's mother is ruthlessly harassed by the new government's police claiming to clean the city of its dirt and she is charged for selling vegetables by the roadside. The poor ordinary women eking out a living in Harare as depicted in *Pawns* are also described as human dirt and are harassed.

This persecution of ordinary people by the Zimbabwean authorities is further dramatised in *Shebeen Tales* (1997), a collection of short stories by Chenjerai Hove. The story, 'Cleaning the streets for the queen' (pp. 80–4) reveals that there have been several major historical 'Murambatsvinas' or clean-up operations before the ominous one of 2005. The first was conducted just before the Commonwealth Heads of Government Meeting in Harare to give the impression to the visiting Queen of England that Zimbabwe was a clean country. This operation was targeted at the residents of Mbare. As the authorial voices says in a mocking tone: 'A broom is a remarkable invention. Praise be to the inventors. The dirt in the house leaves as soon as a broom enters. Harare city council has a new broom, the law. The mayor was not talking of sweeping away real dirt. He was talking of the squatters in the Mbare area because of Harare's acute shortage of housing. The mayor's broom sweeps human beings, dumping them into some sort of rubbish pit so that the Queen does not see them' (p. 82).

Hove's fiction is being prophetic because this actually happened. The author enables the reader to put Operation Murambatsvina in a historical context so that readers can create connections between these actions and reveal a pattern in which the authorities can be said to have enjoyed inflicting systematic pain on their own people. In the same story, the second clean-up or Murambatsvina took place in 1986 when the country was preparing for the meeting of the Non-Aligned Movement. In this clean-up women walking alone at night were the targets as they were assumed to be prostitutes (p. 83). This particular clean-up exercise reveals the mysogynistic tendencies in the male rulers of Zimbabwe. They assume that women only can be prostitutes. No men were arrested. The third clean-up that the story mentions was undertaken to remove squatters from the Pope's sight (p. 83). These three clean-up exercises are used by the author to show the violent nature of the authorities who are depicted as disregarding the rights of the squatters and women as citizens of Zimbabwe. In this story, the squatters are punished by the 'broom' because they are poor, while the women are reviled because as females, according to the understanding of the authorities, they are degraded human beings. The impunity with which the authorities violate the lives of Zimbabwean citizens in this story recalls Achille Mbembe's (2001, 102) characterisation of the post-colonial leaders as using laws arbitrarily, and showing a tendency 'to excess and lack of proportion' in their 'sytematic application of pain' (p. 103) to those that they rule.

In the story, 'Vendors, policemen and death' (pp. 85–9), Hove deplores the violence meted out to ordinary citizens who are 'trying to earn an honest living' (p. 86). The police officer beats the boy vendor for selling vegetables on the town's pavements. When the crowd intervenes on the side of the vendor 'another policeman, more senior and with more medals, arrives' (p. 86). The question that the story raises is that the laws of the land are inhuman; the laws define vendors as dirty and as people without rights. The consequence for the boy in the story is that he has lost his vegetables to the police, and cannot go home with money to feed his family. Because the boy has spent a day in the police cells and lost his fruit and vegetables, 'he might even think of committing other more serious crimes, robbing a passenger at the bus terminus or something' (p. 86). The point of the story is that the actions of the authorities who send the police to chase after vendors actually create criminals out of innocent and law-abiding people struggling to fend for themselves when they are forced into penury. There are familiar echoes in the destruction of people's businesses that followed in the wake of Operation Murambatsvina.

The Stone Virgins and the creation of 'illicit versions of the war'

Yvonne Vera's novel *The Stone Virgins* (2002) recreates the historical antecedents of the Operation Murambatsvina, by focusing on the nationalist government's pacification of Matabeleland through another military operation called *Gukurahundi* (The September rains that remove chaff), which took place between 1981 and 1986. In *The Stone Virgins* what is swept by the military storm is what the authorities perceive as the 'illicit version of the war' (Vera 2002, 73) authored by Zipra women. In 1981, after the civilian population of Kezi had refused to submit and confess where the 'dissidents' were, 'soldiers sh[o]t them, without preamble – they walked in and raised AK rifles: every shot was fatal' (p. 121). In the process, Kezi is reduced to 'a naked cemetery' (p. 143). In this account of how the new government transgressed, violated and killed its own people, with women suffering the most, the triumphalism and celebrations that mark the new leaders' rule in the new nation is radically subverted and ridiculed.

Vera captures some sadistic aspects of Gukurahundi in the new nation's history through the portrayal of the desecration of the cultural life of Thandabantu by the soldiers of the new government. The violation of Thandabantu is, in fact, the violation of Matabeleland, the attempt at 'burying of memory' (p. 59) of the war narrative of Zipra women. The banality of the leaders' power is revealed through the soldiers who carry out systematic torture to 'intimidate, to kill, to extract confessions, to resurrect the dead' (p. 124). Two soldiers chillingly force a wife to axe her husband to save her two sons from death (p. 80). The brutal torture of Mahlathini is described in ways that suggest that it is the new government that is illegitimate and consequently is made up of a band of bandits: 'some of the men who are missing in the village *are said* to have certainly died there, the others, *it is said*, walked all the way from Kezi to Bulawayo ... having managed to escape, carrying with them the memory of a burning body and an impeccable flame .... *Others insist* that nobody fled to Bulawayo' (pp. 123-24).

Vera draws attention to the gratuitous nature with which the soldiers carry out the business of killing people whom the new government had branded 'dissident' or 'sympathisers of dissidents'. As regards the actual killing of the businessperson called Mahlathini, 'those who witnessed the goings-on at Thandabantu on this night said Mahlathini howled like a helpless animal' (p. 123). This graphic demonstration of power to suppress alternative views of life is depicted as a form of repression. A repressive regime uses cultural symbols such as Gukurahundi to label ordinary citizens as chaff that must be thrashed. However, this violent process of punishing people for holding different ideas about the potential directions of the running of Zimbabwe is further satirised in Hosiah Chipanga's lyrics.

Hosiah Chipanga, analogy and radical african independent musical theology

Popular songs in Zimbabwe handle the issue of Operation Murambastvina in a subtle way. For example, Hosiah Chipanga uses analogy to comment on Operation Murambatsvina. Analogy as metaphor brings into sharp comparison issues in the 'here and now' and theorises how the same issues were dealt with in past struggles. Analogy uses a different context to comment on the present condition. It extends the frontiers of meaning by sometimes refusing to name the source of social discord in open ways. In this way, analogy is best suited to comment in a hidden way on the politics of the day. On *Musikavanhu* (2005) Chipanga sings about the democratic deficit in Zimbabwean politics. On the same CD, he rewrites history through biblical analogy, comparing the unpreparedness of the Zimbabwean authorities to build enough houses for its people with the wisdom of Noah. Noah saw the storm coming and built the ark into which he put his family, his people and animals. During Operation Murambatsvina, the Zimbabwean authorities first destroyed the people's houses before building any houses for the victims. A government bereft of any redemptive strategy to confront the challenges of the country is satirised in the following lines from the song *Sodom neGommorroh*:

Noah akavaka ngarava, mvura isati yanaya, yakazosara yonaya Noah apinda mungarava
Mati nditange ndatsva, mozouya modzimura, sarai zvenyu mugarike, zvandatsva ndave Rota
Noah akavaka ngarava Mvura isati yanaya, yakazosara yonaya, Noah apinda mungarava
Mati nditange ndanyura mozouya mondibura, sarai zvenyu mugarike, zvandanyura ndave mudumbu rengwena

(Noah built an ark before the storm came and got into it with his family
Now you (the authorities) say I must burn first then you can help.
In that case you can live. I am burnt like Lot
Noah prepared and built his ark before the storm came?
You say I should drown first and then you will help me.
In that case you enjoy yourself because I am already
in the belly of the alligator.)

The vulnerability of those whose houses were destroyed by Operation Murambatsvina is identified with the misfortune of the biblical Lot, and the singer's protagonist who has been swallowed by an alligator. The wisdom of Noah finds its antithesis in the folly of the Zimbabwean authorities. The contrast is made that while the poor victims suffered harsh fates, the rich remain, alive; enjoying life And the moral of this critique of the authorities is to suggest that they are insensitive and a spent force that has outlived its usefulness. Instead of attending to collapsing medical infrastructure, the Government of Zimbabwe is depicted in *Utano Hwedu* as being obsessed with destroying the initiatives of the electorate. The danger or threat to the masses of a leadership bereft of any redemptive strategies to conquer poverty is that it ends up 'eating' its own people. The protagonist of *Utano Hwedu* laments that as Zimbabweans,

Tava parumana-nzombe isu
Vatadza kupedza urombo
zano ravo rasara, kutipedza varombo vacho

(We are now in trouble
The authorities have failed to destroy poverty
The only idea the authorities are left with is to destroy the poor themselves.)

State violence during Murambatsvina ensured that the authorities literally 'finished off' the masses by destroying the masses' thriving businesses. The government's claim that Murambatsvina was carried out to 'free' the masses from diseases, dirt and criminal activities is revealed as a hoax in the song, *Kutendeuka*, which tells the listeners that:

hapachisina munhu ari kusunungurwa
asi kuti, tave kusungirirwa

Ukambo sunungurwa, wozosunungurwa,
wakambo sunungurwa wave Kusungirirwa

Nobody is being liberated
But that we are being tied/oppressed
If you were liberated, then you are liberated again, when you were once
liberated, then you are being tied/oppressed.

Vacuous promises of freedom are made for, and on behalf of, the masses by
the leadership. What precedes *kusunungurwa*, or to be liberated, is a history of
oppression. Each of the acts of *kusunungurwa* is meant to constitute a negation of oppression, described in threesomes. In political terms, the rhetorical
device of litotes unmasks the dangerous mythology of state benevolence. The
'sterile' formalism of repeated acts of *kusunungurwa* – not *kuzvisunungura* –
implies tethering the masses to a cyclical history, and unbroken bondage to the
view that it is only leaders who have liberated masses from colonialism and *neo-
poverty* in post independence Zimbabwe. The government's claim to being the
sole institution that owns the words, tools and strategies of liberation is further
carnivalised and desacralised in *Kutendeuka*:

hapachisina munhu ari kutendeuka.
Asi kuti, tava kutenderera. Ukambo
tendeuka, wozotendeuka, wakambotendeuka
Wave kutenderera

(Nobody is repenting or changing
We are all going in circles
When you change, after having changed, when
you had changed in the past, then you were fixed on the same spot.)

Operation Murambatsvina is depicted as an act of individualising Zimbabwe's
history around a particular leader. Cheating, official patronage, and the delud-
ing of the masses about the sweetness of freedom that is not there constitute
a signicant aspect of the state's discursive arsenal to silence people by patting
them on the back: *bhabhadzirwa*. At this level, the masses *are* fed on political
promissory 'bearer notes'. When the masses see through official lies and want
to protest, Operation Murambatsvina is unleashed on them. However, governing the people by the gun through military operation is a symptom of governing
under stress. It reduces the state and the masses to the condition of powerlessness (Mbembe 2001).

For Chipanga, it is, therefore, not fortuitous or accidental that the nation
seems to be progressing despite it being in stasis; that a government can violate
the privacy of its electorate and that there is no foreign currency in the country.
The protagonist in *Musikavanhu*, the title song of Chipanga's CD, itemises the
breakdown of civil liberties and the disregard of popular aspirations for a better
life due to the lawlessness induced by the authorities' arbitrary amendments to
a defunct constitution that is used to promote the interests of a few individuals. The lawlessness that emanates from the leaders is transferred to the masses

who then take matters into their own hands and become a law unto themselves. Through his protagonists, Chipanga's grieving is so strident that even President Robert Mugabe (*The Herald* June 2006) is said to have addressed the churches of Zimbabwe urging: 'let there never be another 'Murambatsvina and Jambanja', and that in place of these, seeds of love and tolerance must be cultivated'.

In *Musikavanhu*, the protagonist advises the masses to consult the police in dealing with lawlessness: '*kana munhu atadzirwa ngaaende kumatare/* If a person is wronged, the person should go to the courts/*Musatonga mega vemutemo varipo/*Do not take the law into your own hands when the courts are there/*Kana musingavazive bvunzai mapurisa/*If you do not know the courts, ask the police'. The problem, however, is that the law is subject to tinkering and manipulation by careerist politicians. The jurisdictions of the police force and the courts of Zimbabwe have been undermined by politicians. These politicians can bend the law with impunity and in ways that render policing a mere formality. In such an unpredictable legal context, the most enduring and effective law is that immortalised in the founding ancestral figures of *masvikiro*, heroes and heroines such as Chaminuka, VaNkomo, vaZiyapapa, Nehanda, Tongogara and God, or *Musikavanhu*.

This call recognises that the present rulers have significantly deviated from the political goals and aspirations of those who died laying the foundation of a democratic society in Zimbabwe. A return to these visions – there is no one vision of what Zimbabwe can be – of fighters for freedom who yearned for peace and not war or violence in post-independence Zimbabwe suggests that there are potential *alternative versions of what it is to be Zimbabwean* that the leaders are suppressing. In the rhetoric of the song, these versions are informed by all-inclusive values of a post-nationalist discourse that must transcend ethnic loyalties, political patronage and favouritism. Some of the punchlines of the songs insist on a snycretic ideology for a new Zimbabwe that is difficult to ignore. The lines oppose the promotion of cultural identities based on political opportunism and ideological particularism:

Kana nyika yatadzirwa iyi/bvunzai baba Nkomo varipo
Musatonga mega baba Nkomo Varipo
Kana musingavazive bvunzai isu tinovaziva
Kana musingavaoni bvunzai isu tinovaona
Kana nyika yatadzirwa iyi bvunzai Tongogara
Musatonga mega Tongogara aripo
Kana musingamuzive bvunzai isu tinomuziva
Kana musingamuone
bvunzai isu tinomuona

If the country has been wronged ask Nkomo, he is there
Do not rule without also considering Nkomo's vision
If you do not know Nkomo's vision, ask us (singers, *povo*) who know it
If you cannot see Nkomo, ask us (*povo*, masses) who see him everyday in
   betrayed national interests.

As the country has been wronged, please, ask Tongogara
Do not rule this country without considering Tongogara's vision
If you do not know Tongogara's vision of what a good Zimbabwean
    should be, ask us (*povo*, masses) who know him
If you do not see him, ask us (*povo*, masses) who see him everyday in
    the people toiling.

To 'know' and 'see' Nkomo and Tongagara (though they are dead) is no longer a physical act. It is to uphold those values that they died fighting for. These values include the right of the blacks and whites to own land, to enjoy the democratic dividends of good governance, equality before the law, acknowledgement of civil liberties, freedom of expression, and of differing or having alternative opinions without being politically persecuted. The vision embodied in those values can only be achieved when leaders re-enter into dialogue with the people (*bvunzai isu tinovaziva*). The protagonist further insists on the need for dialogue between the self-proclaimed leaders and the gravid mass of the people. The masses actually claim moral superiority and urge the leaders to consult the masses in whose dreams are immortalised the aspirations for total freedom for which the founding ancestors had put their lives at stake.

Chipanga can be described as the 'voice of the voiceless'. His songs reflect a rare ability to debate issues of national importance in an analogical language with which most people are at home. For example, he can be brutally sarcastic when he pens lyrics that seem to be praising a character called Gushungo in *Gushungo Havana Mhosva*. The song must have enchanted the authorities because it is said that it was played at the 82nd birthday of President Robert Mugabe whose totem happens to be Gushungo of the Karigamombe clan. Some of the lines in the song:

Mapurazi mashanu mashanu wakapiwa nani?
Kutengesa diesel revarimi wakatumwa nani?
Kutengesa hupfu kuMozambique wakatumwa ani?
Kutengesa sugar ku Zambia wakatumwa nani?
Kana zvinhu zvashata woti Gushungo toita sei?

Who gave you those five farms?
Who sent you to sell diesel meant for farmers?
Who sent you to sell mealie meal in Mozambique?
Who sent you to sell sugar in Zambia?
When things are bad, you then say Gushungo, what can we do?

Diesel, sugar, and mealie meal are in constant shortage in Zimbabwe. The government has declared war on those who sell these commodities outside Zimbabwe. At the forefront of those leaders who are against speculation in vital basic goods and corruption in Zimbabwe is Gushungo, who in real life happens to be President Robert Mugabe. In other words, the barrage of the questions above rightfully challenge the assumptions in some people who suggest that Gushungo is always in the 'know' or that he also participates in the acts of graft and corruption described in the song. In this sense, the protoganist's voice tends to absolve Gushungo from the rot that Chipanga sings about.

But this surface meaning is cleft or qualified by the ironic and satirical voice of the protagonist who seems to be asking why Gushungo, who presides over the country, does not know what it is that is undermining his rule. In African oral literature in general, and Shona orature in particular, poets and singers have the verbal licence to rebuke authorities through telling a story using animal names or human totems. Put differently, in the song *Gushungo Havana Mhosva* (2006), the real politician has been been helped by the song to know that some of his senior ministers tasked with overseeing an equitable land redistribution have ransacked and are grabbing farms at the expense of the masses. However, the implied question in the song is about what Gushungo, the president of the country, is going to do in the immediate term.

The listener who *listens otherwise* or in a different way can see that the praise-denunciatory tone of the song is forcing the politician Gushungo to take a firm stand against rampant corruption. The listener who is searching for alternative meanings in the song might further ask when and what will happen to the 'big' fish implicated in amassing land as found out and recorded in the four land audits that President Robert Mugabe has instituted. In the rhetoric of the song, there can be no excuse for the politician Gushungo to say he did not know the underhand dealings of his ministers when the song has informed him. In other words, Operation Murambatsvina, according to Hosiah Chipanga, had less to do with actual dirt, but more to do with the survival of Gushungo in politics. Chipanga's songs bring out this fact in their lyrics, voice, tone, and pitch.

Conclusion

Operation Murambatsvina evokes the image of the Chichidodo bird that in the Ga mythology of Ghana is famed for its despising of human faeces while feeding on the worms that come out of human faeces (Armah 1967). The uncanny parallels here are the ways the authorities in Zimbabwe carried out Operation Murambatsvina to rid the country of what they described as 'human dirt'. The truth is that the state was using its coercive apparatus to police the electorate. The speed, vengeance and disproportionate use of force by the government on its people is an aspect of the the the aesthetics of vulgarity (Mbembe 2001), which not only carries with it the 'licence to violate' but also brings into question the extent to which and when, one can talk of being a citizen and a subject; of belonging and not belonging; of inclusion and exclusion in the new Zimbabwe.

The aim of this chapter was to show that the theme of clean-up operations that result in forced removals of innocent people is popular with creative writers and singers. The theme is popular in the sense that the constant return to it suggests the unfinished business of broadly defining the ethos of democracy in Zimbabwe. Chidzero's novel raised the problem of the colonial 'broom' and how it disrupted the social, economic and political lives of the indigenous people of Zimbabwe. Samupindi's *Pawns* draws attention to the political clean-ups that took place within the liberation movement between the old guard of politicians and the new and young politicians who felt that the struggle could be waged differently and be informed by different ideologies. *Pawns* suggests that any political persecution of alternative voices is a form of Operation Murambatsvina, and can ironically introduce more '*tsvina*', or dirt, in the lives of the people.

Chenjerai Hove's comic sketches in *Shebeen Tales* contain voices that can only be heard from the carnivalesque space of a shebeen. In the stories 'Cleaning the streets for the queen' and 'Vendors, policemen and death', Hove shows that the 'brutalisation of the Zimbabwean society' (p. 87) that people saw in Operation Murambastvina had already been rehearsed and refined in the earlier years of independence. Like Hove, Yvonne Vera's *The Stone Virgins* shows that Operation Gukurahundi in Matabeleland in the early 1980s was the veritable first evidence, after 1980, that a government possesses the power to kill its people in order to sustain its rule. Gukurahundi is, in Vera's novel, another name for Murambatsvina, for each of the terms is committed to rejecting dirt – defined as human beings whose values can no longer easily be policed by the authorities. Chipanga's lyrics suggest that when authorities govern under stress, they are likely to use force to finish the very people they claim Operation Murambatsvina was protecting from dirt. In these creative works the heavy-handedness of the authorities during various Murambatsvinas, and specifically the event of 2005, is deplored as reflecting the absence of an all-embracing democratic system in the country.

References

Armah, A.K. 1969. *The Beautyful Ones Are Not Yet Born*. London: Heinemann.
Chidzero, B.T.G. 1957. *Nzvengamutsvairo*. Cape Town: Longman, Green and Co., in association with the Southern Rhodesia African Literature Bureau.
Hove, C. 1997. *Shebeen Tales: Messages from Harare*. Harare: Baobab Books.
Martin, D. and P. Johnson. 1981. *The Struggle for Zimbabwe*. London and Boston: Faber and Faber.
Mbembe, A. 2001. *On the Postcolony*. Berkeley: University of California Press.
Moore, D. 1995. 'Democracy, violence, and identity in the Zimbabwean war of national liberation – Reflections from the realm of dissent', *Canadian Journal of African Studies* 29 (3) December, pp. 375–402.
Samupindi, C 1992. *Pawns*. Harare: Baobab Books.
Vambe, M.T. 2004. *African Oral Story-telling Tradition and the Zimbabwean Novel in English*. *Pretoria*: UNISA Press.
Vera, Y. 2002. *The Stone Virgins*. Harare: Weaver Press.

Discography

Chipanga, H. 2005. *Musikavanhu*. Harare: P&C Records and Tape Promotion.

PART FOUR

OFFICIAL RESPONSES TO OPERATION MURAMBATSVINA

11

The Zimbabwe Government's Responses to Criticism of Operation Murambatswina

Nhamo Mhiripiri

Operation Murambatswina was started by the Government of Zimbabwe on 19 May 2005 and quickly grew to include almost all urban centres in the country. Because of its timing and magnitude, it attracted much attention from both domestic and foreign media, and enjoyed various perspectives in terms of reportage. The prominent media visibility and condemnation from some sectors prompted the UN Secretary-General to dispatch a Special Envoy, Anna Tibaijuka, to assess the situation. The UN inspection culminated in a damning report that concluded that the Zimbabwean government and most urban authorities had breached both national and international human rights law provisions guiding evictions, thereby precipitating a humanitarian crisis. Many other local and global critics of the operation registered their own condemnations through different media and forums, accusing the government of human rights abuses, intolerance and insensitivity towards its own citizenry.

Internationally, it is now generally accepted that any government's responses to critical human rights condemnations should be taken seriously because they are a strong marker and indicator of the level of concern, tolerance and therefore democracy in that particular country. It also has strong implications for a country's reputation and image. Establishing the range of responses to local and global criticism to Operation Murambatsvina has implications for human rights, democracy and hegemonic rule in Zimbabwe. Such implications can best be deduced from the Zimbabwean government's responses, claims, denials and counterclaims to criticism as reported in the mass media and other sources.

Government responses range from public briefings, press releases and official statements to more restricted channels such as direct letters and meetings with delegations, and communications in regional or global agencies. The 'repertoire of government responses' includes any one or a combination of the following: the 'classic' discourse of official denial and rebuttals; converting a defensive position into an attack on the critic; disarmingly acknowledging the criticism;

and totally ignoring any public acknowledgement of the criticism and keeping isolated and quiet. Any one of these responses has implications for regime type, regime legitimacy and its claims to practising democracy.

The ZANU(PF) Regime and the urban populace

Some critics are convinced that the Zimbabwean government is commandist, despotic and undemocratic (see Sichone 1992; Raftopoulos 2004). Critics abound in different guises from local and international academics, civil groups and foreign governments, especially most Scandinavian countries, USA and the European Union (EU). Former liberation war movements tend to be quite often coercive, and this is because traditional political culture, colonial authoritarian inheritances and institutional structures and behaviour that best suited a commandist armed struggle (Melber 2004; Masunungure 2004; Kamete 2004; Dansereau 2004). Quite often in the post-colonial era the former liberation party has enjoyed a long tenure as a dominant single-party in a multiparty environment. Such a dominant single-party regime can only function if there is reasonable public consensus regarding its legitimacy. And the same political parties of liberation can progressively turn openly autocratic and resort to coercion in order to survive if their legitimacy is challenged fundamentally, especially when there is growing local and international criticism of the regime. This is the case with ZANU(PF) today.

Operation Murambatsvina was mainly conducted by the police, albeit with a heavy army presence. It is peculiar because it affected mostly Zimbabwe's urban constituencies who, ironically, are the strongholds of the opposition party, the Movement for Democratic Change (MDC). The hardest-hit were the working class, informal sector entrepreneurs and the lumpen proletariat. These urbanites are disgruntled by the status quo for a variety of reasons, most emanating from ZANU(PF)'s failure to provide the basis for a vibrant economy. The Zimbabwean economy's rapid deterioration, rising unemployment, skyrocketing cost of living, and spiraling inflation and urban poverty have resulted in considerable dissatisfaction, and at times open hostility towards and violent confrontation with, the government (Dansereau 2004; Kamete 2004). Since the government's first loss in any post-independence election in the constitutional referendum of February 2000, all elections have seen urbanites pass a vote of no confidence in the ruling party; the party has realised its loss of legitimacy and now views urbanites as sell-out agents of 'Western imperialism'. The evictions of 2005 can best be understood in the matrix and dynamics of Zimbabwe's national politics.

Authoritarianism tends to develop where there are unfulfilled (and unfulfillable) popular aspirations. The regime faces the erosion of national legitimacy as a result of the betrayal of a vision of renewal. In Zimbabwe since the start of the twenty-first century, ZANU(PF)'s legitimacy has undoubtedly been eroded, at least in key urban areas including the capital city. Legitimacy here means rule through the valid exercise of power and authority gained from consensual relations between government and its populace in both rural and urban areas. The crisis of legitimacy arises when there is an obvious breakdown in consensus (Shivji 1998, 23).

The battle to win hearts and minds

Speculations about and reasons for the demolitions and evictions include, among other things, political retribution against a recalcitrant urban population, weakening the MDC, controlling political protest, and regaining control of foreign currency dealings and the black market. The government's behaviour has invited incessant condemnation the world over. In turn, the government and ruling party have not taken criticism lying down. They have launched a coordinated battle to win hearts and minds of people, at least of those who are not their staunch detractors. Critics have once again charged that the latest propaganda strategy is an attempt by a rogue regime to confer legitimacy and moral decency on itself.

Zimbabwe is frequently scrutinised for violation of human rights not only because it is a bellicose chronic offender, but also because some 'violations' are more visible, especially where there are testimonies by observers and 'victims'. The country also has a high level of media accessibility, high literacy rates and remarkable Internet connectivity, especially for urban areas. Despite the restrictions on foreign journalists working in Zimbabwe, local human rights monitors and reporters act as whistleblowers. Local journalists publish in newspapers that are critical of the government, such as *The Standard* and *The Zimbabwe Independent*. Others write for e-newspapers such as *Newzimbabwe.com* or source stories for radio stations operating from outside the country such as *Studio 7*.

The government, in turn, uses state-owned or controlled media such as *The Herald* and *The Sunday Mail*, Zimbabwe Broadcasting Holdings' radio stations and television, and sympathetic publications such as the pan-African London-based *New African* magazine, to articulate its side of the story. Diplomacy that verges on social marketing[1] and briefings at international forums are part of the artillery.The government reiterates that the demonisation and vilification of its leadership is due to the land reform programme, which saw the white minority farmers, mostly of British ancestry, losing land to a minority black people from the ruling party, as a way of redressing imbalances created by colonialism. The coordinated condemnations of all types of Mugabe government-initiated policies and calls for 'regime change' by critics thus are inextricably linked to the land reform. Hence the very notions of democracy and human rights become contestable, and carry discursive and political implications, as they have always done (Sichone 1998, ii; Mamdani 1993).

The talk about democracy and human rights and the activities of social movements may be predicated on a political programme designed to undermine or neutralise genuine revolutionary initiatives that ensure equitable redistribution of wealth, resources and property. A conception of democracy that does not protect private property, such as that which had happened with the land redistribution programme in Zimbabwe, is contrary to the interests of the local and global bourgeoisie. In contrast, the struggle for reform could be the opening phase of a struggle against repression and dictatorship. Mamdani (1993, 175-6) aptly situates human rights in Africa not as a Trojan Horse to governments that regard themselves as revolutionary, but as a practical necessity, albeit with universal norms and values. He writes:

> No revolutionary struggle can gather steam if it proceeds by way of denouncing the agenda of human rights and the rule of law. The point is to struggle toward a definition of the agenda of human rights and the rule of law that will not displace the discourse of power and popular sovereignty, but will lead to it. To do so, of course, is impossible without arriving at an idea of rights that derives from a concrete conceptualisation of the wrongs on the continent.

For Mamdani (p. 178) the actual institutional guarantee for the defence of rights will depend on the balance of political forces and the nature of the process that leads to reform; this, in short, depends on how the question of power and politics is resolved.

Government responses: looking for acceptance from whom?

The classic discourse of official denial

According to Cohen (1996), three forms of denial appear in the discourse of official responses to allegations of human rights violations. These are (1) literal denial which is an insistence that 'nothing of the sort ever happened'; (2) interpretive denial which insists 'what happened is really something else'; and (3) implicatory denial which argues that 'what happened is justified'. The Zimbabwean government has used all forms of denial in varying degrees. President Robert Mugabe's response to journalists' questions at the Africa Union (AU) summit in Libya in June 2005 only just fell short of being crude literal denial. While any type of government can give such a response, it is usually used by repressive regimes that care little about their democratic credentials – regimes somewhat self-insulated from outside scrutiny and insensitive to their own international image or reputation.

After being questioned about reports that 'hundreds of thousands' of people had been made homeless by the campaign, Mugabe replied: 'Where are they? We don't know about those. It's just nonsense.' That response was unsustainable given the irrefutable video[1] evidence available, and testimonies by

---

[1]   Video evidence showing those displaced staying in spartan government holding camps such as that at Hopley Farm was quickly uploaded onto the internet.

local monitors, witnesses and the affected through a speedy reporting media. Euphemistic language is used by Mugabe as a form of reinterpreting the operation. This he presumably does to lessen the grave experiences of the affected. Orwellian analysis is relevant here to explain the anaesthetic function of political language, that is, 'how words insulate their users and listeners from experiencing fully the meaning of what they are doing' (cf. Cohen 1996, 527). 'There is no demolition campaign. It's a clean-up operation and that's what all countries do,' Mugabe quickly said after sensing the desperation of his initial response. The evictions and demolitions are sanitised in an interpretive denial; they are 'a vigorous clean-up campaign to restore sanity', suggesting 'what happened was really something else' (BBC News). In late August 2005, the government eventually released through pro-government newspapers a 45-page rebuttal of the UN report in which it accused the latter of political bias in favour of the opposition leadership and NGOs hostile to government.

In an implicatory denial style – 'what is happening is justified' – the government report, Mugabe and his stalwarts criminalised sections of the urban population, and argued that the operation was intended to bring back the rule of law and legality. The operation was meant to destroy illegal dwellings and structures, and to eliminate alleged illicit activities such as black market trading. The discourse of legality was proffered to make the affected appear like lawless people, and the government as law-abiding. Foreign Affairs Minister Simbarashe Mumbengegwi told journalists in Harare that the operation had been carried out in accordance with the country's laws and conformed to international standards. Local Government and Housing Minister Ignatius Chombo told the news agency IRIN that evicted people were in illegal settlements, and that he did not think the UN could sanction illegality. Government official spokesperson George Charamba (2005) wrote in an op-ed that displaced people had sought and lost a High Court ruling against the clean-up, suggesting that the rule of law prevailed in the country. In a disconcerting and dehumanising statement, Police Commissioner Augustine Chihuri said the operation was meant 'to clean [*sic*] the country of the crawling mass of maggots bent on destroying the economy' (*The Times*, 17 June 2005). In response to an administered questionnaire (28 September), the most extreme criminalisation of the urban populace came from Masvingo city's governor and resident minister, Willard Chiwewe, 'Slums which were proliferating in cities, especially Harare, and were becoming strongholds for urban-guerilla warfare. We were destroying the forest, which was going to hide the enemy.'

Threats of non-constitutional and hence treasonous attempts at removing the incumbent government have frequently been raised. *New African* applauded the Zimbabwean secret service for thwarting Western sponsored attempts at toppling the government through Ukrainian-style street demonstrations – the so-called yellow revolution. Citing anonymous 'reliable' government sources *New African* wrote, 'The metropolitan powers upped the ante by secretly channelling funds for an insurrection via opposition elements who were going to use vulnerable slum dwellers to confront the government in what they had hoped would be bloody street clashes'.

At the 61st session of the UN General Assembly, Mugabe charged that some countries and groups were concertedly destabilising Zimbabwe and imposing illegal economic sanctions to frustrate the country's development efforts. He resorted to the discourse of legality to dissuade those who may want to change his regime unconstitutionally.

The Zimbabwean government also reveals fears of military invasion and insurgence. Charamba hinted at the possibility of military invasion in his op-ed article. Acting Minister of Information and Publicity Paul Mangwana recently declared to visiting Russian journalists and diplomats, 'We will fight to the last person' in the event that the government's foes decide on military engagement (*The Herald*, 3 October 2006).

In proffering the discourse of counter-imperialism, the regime's stalwarts are claiming a form of righteousness. Forced displacements and the traumatic scuttling of urban populations were justified for the sake of the protection of national sovereignty. The regime feels justified that it is motivated by a transcendental ideology of patriotism. Their actions are exalted, extraordinary, and they possess a higher wisdom and morality that justify harmful behaviour for a higher good. The urban protest vote is regarded as ill-advised, hence politically conscious cadres have to intervene on the former's behalf. 'The question is ... whether to do good or bad with democracy. If people vote to commit suicide what should we do? Democracy should not be destructive but protect and preserve human life,' says Governor Chiwewe.

Loyalty to binding ideologies such as 'the revolutionary struggle, nationalism, ethnic purity', according to Cohen (1996, 530), 'provides a temporary or permanent release from the moral claims behind human rights prohibitions'. Ironically, and ostensibly on behalf of the Zimbabwe government, *New African* confessed that the operation was fraught with serious errors and bad planning, but was crucial for national survival.

ZANU(PF) counteroffensive strategies

Zimbabwe's government has turned its defensive position into strategic attacks on its critics. This is a method Cohen (1996, 534) has dubbed the 'shoot the messenger strategy', in which the government attacks the source of information by casting doubt on the truth of the allegations and questioning the right to criticise. The intention is to assert that the condemning report is 'biased, untrustworthy, tendentious, prejudiced, unreliable, and part of a campaign of vilification and evidence of an undeclared political agenda' (p. 535). The government's report does make exactly these allegations against the UN report. It points out that from the content of the report it is clear that submissions from government are dismissed as claims, allegations or rhetoric, whilst submissions from NGOs hostile to the government, donors and those opposition leaders who are critical of the government, are explicitly or impliedly treated as statements of fact. For ZANU(PF), the Tibaijuka report grossly exaggerates the numbers of people who were rendered homeless by the operation. A fact-finding mission must report on what it actually found on the ground and not infer homelessness from some fictitious formula or mathematical extrapolation.

Minister Simbarashe Mumbengegwi said Tibaijuka was 'two-faced' and she upheld 'a pro-opposition tone' in her report. Elsewhere, Mugabe was quoted as saying, 'Zimbabwe is left wondering whether the report by Mrs Tibaijuka was a UN report by a UN envoy or a Blair report by a member of Mr. Blair's Commission for Africa' (*New African*, August/September 2005). No sooner is Blair implicated for his unsavoury interference in Zimbabwe's internal politics, than the spectre of the land reform programme is conveniently raised. Every single issue about Zimbabwe is conflated with the sensitive land issue, unfortunately triggering racial undertones. Britain and her allies are purportedly aggressively against the government because their white kith and kin had lost out in the land struggle of the new millennium. Unfortunately, Britain and America have vindicated Mugabe in their dealings, and have been less than shrewd in making statements, especially at definitive moments. British Premier Tony Blair's tactless reminder to the UN Secretary-General that he hoped Tibaijuka 'will do a good job' – whatever that meant – is one such glaring example. Blair similarly called for the UN Security Council to debate the housing crackdown and what he said were ubiquitous human rights abuses, already implying the Zimbabwe government was guilty before the visiting UN envoy had even compiled her findings.

On another note, many European officials have put the MDC in a difficult position by indiscreetly announcing that they are working with the opposition to effect 'regime change' in Zimbabwe. This lends credence to Mugabe's allegation that the MDC agenda is not home-grown but spurred by international capitalist interest. This partly explains why most African and Southern African Development Community governments are reluctant to criticise the Mugabe regime openly, since they too believe that he is at times unfairly demonised for political purposes. Apparently, criticism of the Mugabe government specifically based on Operation Murambatsvina is fast losing steam.[2] Possibly the Zimbabwe government has won the battle for Operation Murambatsvina but it still has to fight the ultimate war to retain political power. In that case Operation Murambatsvina becomes a receding index of a larger political struggle.

The government has also used 'advantageous comparisons', which are essentially an oblique form of justification in which government compares itself to other groups or to its own critics (Cohen 1996, 533). The Zimbabwean government compared its 'mundane' and nearly not 'newsworthy' demolition actions to those of other governments and found nothing unusual. Charamba cited as comparative examples similar demolitions of illegal structures in Kenya, South

---

2   Several attempts by critics to put Operation Murambatsvina onto international agenda failed after African governments declared that the operation an 'internal matter'.

Africa, Nigeria and Britain itself for basically the same reasons that included eradicating crime. Operation Murambatsvina unfortunately had been politicised by detractors with ulterior motives. The real cause of the political and media frenzy surrounding Operation Murambatsvina was Zimbabwe's land reform programme in which whites lost out. 'And therein lies the key to the unusual reaction to the mundane clean up campaign which done elsewhere, would have passed unnoticed,' wrote Charamba (2005, 39).

In the typical strategy of 'condemning the condemners', Charamba challenges that Britain and the US have no moral legitimacy to criticise Operation Operation Murambatsvina, since they had always turned a blind eye to Israeli destructions of Palestinian homes. He accuses Britain and the US of hypocrisy, and blames them for having caused the problems in the Middle East in the first place. The same 'condemning the condemners' tactic was used against the UN when, after inspecting the scenes of demolition, they designed an asbestos walled model house for the displaced. Minister Chombo immediately criticised the house as 'sub-standard' and 'below human dignity'. He attacked the people who designed the structure as guided by a 'this-is-good-for-Africa' attitude (*The Herald*, June 2005).The government was in the process of building its own much more durable brick-and-cement core houses.

The conciliatory and disarming type of response that is supposedly characteristic of more democratic societies was used on friendly governments, allies and sympathisers, especially those who visited the country and were shown around. The initial reception of the UN special envoy was conciliatory. Of special importance is that the Zimbabwean government never opted for arrogant total silence typical of very autocratic beleaguered states.

Diversionary tactics

The government has also fully utilised the technique of parrying and ducking criticism. They have used diversionary tactics of giving focus to something favourable, which is the reconstruction, rebuilding and rehabilitating Operation Garikai/Hlalani Kuhle[3] that is expected to give hundreds of families new homes and to offer proper business and vending facilities to small- and medium-sector entrepreneurs. Government has tried to transform an alleged act of abuse into a philanthropic and socially responsible act where it has genuine concern for the welfare of its people. At a press conference, Local Government Minister Ignatius Chombo sidestepped criticism and focused on the government's corrective Operation Garikai, aimed at developing housing. 'Our people are much happier because the government is giving them land, they are getting stands, and are getting government assistance,' he said. The official government report dedicates a substantial amount of space to Operation Garikai, and accuses the UN report of not giving much attention to this corrective programme. Government

---

3   When literally translated, it means 'prosper' or 'stay comfortably'.

has taken every opportunity to show off Operation Garikai projects and resettled families to visiting sympathetic journalists, dignitaries and foreign allies such
as Russians and groups of African Americans, and asked them to tell the story as
it is when they return to their own countries.[4]

The discursive innuendos of the names of the two operations have been used
to full political effect by critics and government. The concept of *murambatsvina*
when used in government discourse means literally 'to clean up' – 'to restore
order'. Detractors, however, have often inferred that government perceives the
urban poor as dirt, maggots and trash. If a callous government views its own
people that way, it does not deserve to rule them since it is insensitive to their
plight. Such a government can only rule through coercion.

The regime is sensitive to suggestions that it has reduced its own poor people to
the level of trash. In his op-ed Charamba (2005, 38) was at pains to explain what
murambatsvina means, sanitising the concept. To him, the appendix to the whole
name – Restore Order – was supposed to 'convey a rehabilitative goal which was
to follow the clean-up exercise' – obviously hinting at Operation Garikai.

Conclusion

The question of power ought to be addressed and resolved first before serious
talk on human rights and democracy can be entertained. As long as the contestation for state control prevails in its different guises – including the battle
for legitimacy and moral authority – the Zimbabwe 'crisis' will persist. The
ZANU(PF) government is already aligning itself with those it thinks are
sympathetic to its agenda; those that it deems to understand the imperialist
machinations of the US, United Kingdom, and their local agents. The Zimbabwe question has been reduced to power politics, and the British openly declare
that they want regime change. The verbal war conducted in all types of forums at
the slightest opportunity is symbolic of the contestation for power and will only
end with some kind of consensual political settlement on who rules Zimbabwe.
The government may seem to act with impunity on several issues, but it is still
sensitive to criticism, as attested by the speedy implementation of Operation
Garikai. Its relentless image and reputation management shows government still
has a sense of integrity, and wishes to be acceptable amongst its peers in SADC
and the international community, albeit it that it seeks acceptance and moral
validation in a hostile environment where it is distrusted by powerful blocs. But
it remains to be said that the Government of Zimbabwe's denials of the brutalities that were attendant upon Operation Murambatsvina have not only damaged
the image of the party in the eyes of the electorate, but that such government

---

4   The Zimbabwe government possibly sponsors these trips to manage its international reputation.
    Indeed, Munyaradzi Huni asked the visiting chairman of the Canada-based Global African
    Congress, Cikiah Thomas, if his trip to Zimbabwe 'was some kind of free holiday' (*The Sunday
    Mail*, 15-21 October 2006).

denials actually undermine democracy in the country.

The contestation of power reached its climax when harmonised Municipal, Senatorial, House of Assembly, and Presidential elections were conducted on 29 March 2008. The MDC won a majority of seats in the House of Assembly, putting ZANU(PF) in opposition for the first time since independence, albeit with a pending presidential run-off between Robert Mugabe and MDC's Morgan Tsvangirai. It is arguable that the ghost of Murambatsvina still haunts ZANU(PF); people forcibly displaced to the rural areas most likely 'campaigned' for the opposition, and might still hold the key to the presidential election run-off. In the ensuing violence that has been reported in the rural areas research might need to establish how many of the victims were people with city links, especially those with direct or tenuous relations to Murambatsvina. Is it that ZANU(PF) has faced its nemesis in Murambatsvina, and that a 'reverse dispersal' of people might be a strategy to ensure 'loyal' votes in the rural areas? Murambatsvina victims who ended up in their rural 'homes' probably took their bitterness and disgruntlement with them, suggesting that ZANU(PF) had unwittingly spread elements of dissent in its traditional backyard.

References

Ankomah, B. 2005. 'Zimbabwe UN Report condemns demolition', *New African*, August/September, p. 23. Cohen, S. 1996. 'Government responses to human rights reports: Claims, denials, and counterclaims', *Human Rights Quarterly*, 18(3), pp. 517-43.

— 2005a. 'Zimbabwe, a nation of many surprises', *New African*, October, pp. 52-5.

Charamba, G. 2005. 'Zimbabwe – Operation Restore Order', *New African*, July, pp. 36-9.

Dansereau, S. 2004. 'Liberation and Opposition in Zimbabwe', in H. Melber (ed.) 2004. 2004. *Limits to Liberation In Southern Africa: The unfinished business of democratic consolidation*. Cape Town: HSRC Press.

Kamete, A. 2004. 'In Defence of National Sovereignty? Urban Governance and Democracy in Zimbabwe', in H. Melber (ed.) 2004. 2004. *Limits to Liberation In Southern Africa: The unfinished business of democratic consolidation*. Cape Town: HSRC Press.

Mamdani, M. 1993. 'Social Movements and Constitutionalism: The African context', in D. Greenberg, S.N. Katz, M.B. Oliviero and S.C Wheatley (eds), *Constitutionalism and Democracy: Transitions in the contemporary world*. Oxford: Oxford University Press.

Masunungure, E. 2004. 'Travails of opposition politics in Zimbabwe since independence', in D. Harold-Barry (ed.) *Zimbabwe The Past is the Future*. Harare: Weaver Press.

Raftopoulos, B. 2004. 'Current Politics In Zimbabwe: Confronting the crisis', in D. Harold-Barry (ed.) *Zimbabwe The Past is the Future*. Harare: Weaver Press.

Shivji, I. 1998. 'Problems of Constitution-making as Consensus-building: The Tanzanian Experience', in O. Sichone (ed.) 1998. *The State and Constitutionalism in Southern Africa*. Harare: SAPES Trust.

12

Reading the 2005 Tibaijuka Report on Zimbabwe in a Global Context

Tafataona Mahoso

The UN-sanctioned report by Anna Kajimulo Tibaijuka (Tibaijuka 2005), remains the most well-known document about Operation Murambatsvina. Both the critics and admirers of the Operation Murambatsvina make references to the report's 'authoritative' status when they make their judgements and arguments, especially in scholarly journals and in the public sphere where the report is also circulating. This means that in some important way, the report has become a discursive space through its constructions and representations of the facts of Operation Murambatsvina. However, the 'facts' in the report are discursively not beyond contest.

This chapter suggests that some hidden dimensions of Operation Murambatsvina, its antecedents, precedents and consequences for the future of democracy in Zimbabwe, can actually be revealed after critically analysing the facticity of the issues raised in the Tibaijuka report. A critical application of the linear perspective and its window; of framing theory and its frames; and of cognitive dissonance and its suppression of discrepant 'fact' can help scholars and ordinary readers to explain how so many 'reports' of 'fact-finding' missions have been predetermined by those who own the processes of report-making. In order to unravel the power discourses informing the Tibaijuka report and to underscore its constructedness and arbitrariness, it is important to foreground the 'international politics' that influenced the content of the report. This approach is useful because it helps the reader to situate the report in the discourses of globalisation of the human rights doctrine and see these as a pretext for intervention in international relations.

Tibaijuka's report is striking in at least three ways.

First, the report raises the question why something treated in most of the world as a routine event, namely slum clearance, should be turned into a 'global' incident, with the writer or writers wondering aloud how the event could qualify for UN Security Council attention and even for the International Criminal Court.

Second, the report contains a big gap, or contradiction, between its stated purpose and what it actually achieves. The stated purpose is to assess the magnitude of UN-organised assistance required by 700,000 to 2,400,000 people allegedly displaced or affected by the operation. This assistance is supposed to come from 'the international community' and 'the humanitarian community.' But no such assistance was sourced or received; the report in fact did not focus on the alleged assessment of the needs of the displaced people. Rather, it focused on, and achieved, the moral condemnation of the state to the extent of going beyond the terms of reference of the mission in order to achieve that condemnation. It went beyond the mission's terms of reference by bringing in the African land reclamation movement which is rural and has little to do with urban slum clearance; by introducing the question of how and when the Government of Zimbabwe talks or does not talk to its opposition; and by extensively exploring ways in which the state's actions could be criminalised on a global scale and brought before the UN Security Council.

Third, the report is striking as a form of communication: it is a piece of activist journalism rather than a technical, professional or diplomatic communication.

Theory

Linear perspective theory reveals that the cascading veto power of the UN Security Council has turned the UN mission into a closed imperial window for the occasional surveillance and scanning of a world that is now rarely expected to speak for itself. In Robert Romanyshyn's (1988, 37–43) words:

> [O]pen windows are, so to speak, halfway between doorways and windows that are closed. With a doorway one can follow one's eyes into the world. One can walk through a doorway. With a window that is closed one can only look at a world which is for that reason primarily a spectacle, an object of vision. The condition of the window implies a boundary between the perceiver and the perceived.

Framing is the process by which events may be converted into images and symbols; and likewise images and symbols may be converted into events. Put another way, framing is the process by which the communicator deploys events and signs selectively in order to evoke meaning(s) beyond denotative or objective meaning, making these assume precise connotative significance in a specific context.

When framing theory is applied to a reading of the Tibaijuka report, the following questions are provoked:

- What is the worldview that dominates and explains the report?
- Who are the nominal as well as substantive owners of the report and how does one locate them?
- Who is the figure being observed through the Tibaijuka window and on what sort of ground, on whose ground, does this figure stand, with what consequences?

- What aspects of the 'data' or 'facts' observed through the imperial window are highlighted and which ones are dimmed, with what effects?
- How does the language of the report contradict or confirm these other features of the frame?

The need to apply cognitive dissonance theory arises not only from the strained rhetoric of the report itself and the large volume of local and foreign opposition press coverage trying to make up for the perceived deficiencies of the official document. It also arises from the UN's response to the failure of Tibaijuka by sending yet another UN special envoy in the person of Mr Jan Egeland whose main job appeared to be to limit the damage already done to the credibility of Tibaijuka. Robert Jervis (1976) writes on cognitive dissonance:

> The basis of dissonance theory lies in the postulate that people seek strong justification for their behaviour. They are not content to believe merely that they behaved well and chose wisely – if this were the case they would only have to maintain the beliefs that produced their [previous] decisions. Instead, people want to minimize their internal conflict. This leads them to seek to believe that the reasons for acting or deciding as they did were overwhelming.

Cognitive dissonance theory is, therefore, ideal for post-decision situations, that is, what followed Tibaijuka's report or what previous actions the Tibaijuka visit and report sought to justify: 'First, dissonance theory asserts that, after making a decision, the person not only will downgrade or misinterpret discrepant information but will also avoid it and seek consonant information.' (p. 382).

This phenomenon is also known as *selective exposure*.

Shaping the frame and framing the South

Hans J. Morgenthau and Kenneth Thompson (1985, 274) suggest that the globalisation and universalisation of certain particular values is used by powerful forces as a basis for interference and intervention in the affairs of other countries: 'With fierce exclusiveness, all contestants equate their national conceptions of morality with what all mankind must and will ultimately accept and live by. In this, the ethics of international politics revert to the politics and morality of tribalism, of the crusades, and of the religious wars.' The authors continued thus:

> However much the content and objectives of today's ethics of nationalistic universalism may differ from those of primitive tribes or of the Thirty Years' War, they do not differ in the function they fulfil for international politics, and in the moral climate they create. The morality of the particular group, far from limiting the struggle for power on the international scene, gives the struggle a ferocity and intensity not known to other ages. For the claim to universality which inspires the moral code of one particular group is incompatible with the identical claim of another group ... (p. 274).

Tibaijuka's report represents the view of one particular group about governance in Zimbabwe. The British and US governments and their press commented
extensively on the report while the UN, whose envoy Tibaijuka was supposed to
be, said nothing or very little. The mission was premised on Anglo-American,
and not UN, values and objectives. It is not only 'human rights' that are framed
in the neoliberal and Anglo-Saxon manner; it is also the concept of law, rule of
law and legal culture that are similarly framed and defined, so that by the time
a Tibaijuka or Egeland comes to Zimbabwe these values have been set, at least
within the judiciary, the law society, and NGOs associated with 'regime change.'

Reading the Tibaijuka Report in a global context

If cognitive dissonance theory is applied to the Tibaijuka report, one would
notice that by the time of the mission too many influential governments,
organisations and individuals had been predicting too many dire things about
Zimbabwe for the predictions and interpretations on which they were based to
remain credible.

There was a need in the anti-Zimbabwe campaign to justify the campaign and
the unfulfilled predictions of the previous seven years. The New Labour regime
of Tony Blair in Britain announced through Clare Short in 1997–98 that it
was time Zimbabweans got rid of President Robert Mugabe and the liberation
movement in government that he represented. Since there were no elections in
1997 or 1998, New Labour was not only calling for unconstitutional ways of
getting rid of a government, but it was also inviting the white settler population
to engage in open opposition politics against a liberation movement they had
fought violently for at least 15 years. By 1998 New Labour was using British
media to predict a fall of the Zimbabwean government by June 1998 resulting
from 'implosion' caused by urban riots, economic sabotage by industry and the
cost of Zimbabwe's intervention in the Democratic Republic of the Congo.

In late 2000 *Megabuck* magazine adopted the New Labour line that the Government of Zimbabwe would be ousted unconstitutionally by Christmas. This
claim was credited to the newly formed and foreign-sponsored Movement for
Democratic Change (MDC). The *Megabuck* article was entitled 'Zimbabwe
doomed' and it occupied the cover of the paper. This constituted media terror
because it announced doom for an entire people and it blamed that doom upon
the liberation movement in government that was portrayed as an evil to be discarded without any regard for peaceful and constitutional means to get rid of
it. These media were in fact inviting the people to stage a *coup d'état* and MDC
leader Morgan Tsvangirai eventually said this out loud and clear, accompanied
by fanfare.

On 21 February 2001 *The Daily News* put a date to Morgan Tsvangirai's call
to oust the liberation movement in government by violent means. It announced
that this would happen by 1 July 2001.

The next month, March 2001, Norman Reynolds posted articles on the Internet and in South African papers which further sought to terrify and terrorise the people. He claimed that by July 2001 there would be no bread, no mealie meal, no fuel; nothing in Zimbabwe. This would lead to the collapse of the country unless people overthrew the government.

Reynolds continued his campaign into January 2002 when he suggested the means by which the liberation movement in government in Zimbabwe could be removed despite its popularity. His solution combined elements of an externally induced *coup d'état* and a rigged election. Reynolds argued that Southern African Development Community (SADC) armies should occupy Zimbabwe, or at least conduct war games on Zimbabwe's borders in order to influence the population to vote against ZANU(PF) and elect the MDC in the 2002 presidential elections.

The year 2003 was to be much worse than 2002. Amani Trust, the Zimbabwe Human Rights NGO Forum and Crisis Zimbabwe Coalition worked together to produce a substantial document entitled *Is genocide imminent in Zimbabwe?* They proceeded to answer their own question by saying there would be genocide in Zimbabwe by January 2003 and that this genocide would be far worse than the Rwandan genocide of 1994.

The Swedish journalist, Torbjorn Bjorkman, visiting Zimbabwe in 2006, confirmed that the terror documents predicting genocide in Zimbabwe by January 2003 were widely circulated in Europe where they generated many stories demonising Zimbabwe and its government.

But when the genocide failed to happen, the same groups and media who had predicted it started to agitate for a national uprising called *The Final Push* which would oust government from power unconstitutionally. The Final Push was organised in June 2003 and it failed dismally.

Other expressions of media terror in 2003 included the following:

- 'Zimbabwe edges toward a negotiated settlement as social explosion threatens ZANU(PF) and MDC' (*The Daily News*, 22 May)
- '100,000 may die: Starvation stalks Matabeleland South' (*Daily News*, 21 July)
- 'Army fails to pay soldiers' (*The Daily News*, 22 July)
- 'Resume talks or face more mass action, MDC warns Mugabe' (*Daily News*, 26 August).

Then on 5 September 2003 Catholic Bishop, Pius Ncube, used various media to claim that there was rampant rape and torture of citizens in Zimbabwe perpetrated by youth militias and by the ruling ZANU(PF). These media fabrications seemed intended to fill the embarrassing void created by the false predictions of massive genocide and a 'final push'.

On 9 September 2003 the South African paper *The Sunday Argus* extended Pius Ncube's terror lies to other bishops in South Africa who came out allegedly calling for a *coup d'état* to end the misery of the people of Zimbabwe. To encourage the imagined coup plotters, South African papers reported that

President Robert Mugabe and his Vice-President Simon Muzenda were both seriously ill and that a succession war was imminent in Zimbabwe.

By 23 October the lies had assumed a new dimension. It was alleged in South African and British media that the people of Zimbabwe were starving to death and Britain, which was waging an economic and propaganda war against the government of Zimbabwe, had nonetheless pledged enough funds to feed half of the whole population of that country! This was intended to kill two birds with one stone. To suggest that if Britain was going to spend more than US$9 million feeding half of Zimbabwe, then it must be true that there is real starvation; and to suggest that the British are after all not the cruel racists the Zimbabwean leaders accuse them of being. Otherwise, how could they pledge so much money to feed starving Zimbabweans? Yet all these were lies. They served to portray Zimbabwe as a failed state; just as the Tibaijuka report was to attempt the same in 2005.

Likewise, even if there were no corpses on the streets of Zimbabwean cities, if foreign parliaments moved motions to indict President Robert Mugabe for genocide, then the genocide would somehow become real. That is what happened on 9 October 2003 when both African People's Party (AFP) and South African Press Agency (SAPA) reported a motion in the Canadian Federal Parliament to indict the President of Zimbabwe for crimes against humanity and for genocide. The vilification campaign was extended to Paris, New York and Washington DC, with the *Daily News* faithfully following and reporting it, for instance, on 20 February and 21 July 2003.

By February 2004, the local and global media had failed to find any bodies in Zimbabwe anywhere close to those that littered Rwanda in 1994. So the liar's camera had to find an alternative object.

The BBC's Hilary Anderson made a very brave attempt in this regard when she staged a video in South Africa claiming to depict the insides of Zimbabwe's National Youth Training Programme. She called the video *Secrets of the camps*. While a little of the footage was borrowed from Zimbabwe, the bulk of it was staged in South Africa. Anderson augmented her video fiction with articles, including one on 28 February 2004 called *Zimbabwe's torture camps*.

The ZANU(PF) slogans that were supposedly coming from the training camps in Zimbabwe were uttered in Afrikaans and Cape coloured accents. Table Bay and Table Mountain could be seen through the window in one of the scenes this video.

Similar terror tapes were forged and smuggled to the UN Human Rights Commission and rejected because they seemed either to implicate the camera person as a participant in the violence or to suggest a total fake. These failures worsened the crisis of cognitive dissonance in the anti-Zimbabwe campaign.

Later in 2004 the MDC *Restart* document told Zimbabweans that there would be a coalition government in Zimbabwe by July 2004 and a fully-fledged MDC government by November 2004, without elections being held. The 2005 parliamentary elections in March showed how absurd the *Restart* predictions were when ZANU(PF)'s winning of a two-thirds majority in parliament in March eventually led to the split of the MDC into two factions in October.

Therefore, by the time of the Tibaijuka mission scepticism had mounted about the allegations of a failed state in Zimbabwe.

The report is a classic case of cognitive dissonance. Instead of dealing with the habitat requirements of Zimbabweans, it seeks to justify Zimbabwe's suspension from the Commonwealth in 2002 before Zimbabwe had left that body in 2003. It seeks to justify US, British and European Union (EU) decisions and statements on Zimbabwe. It raises all the issues that Britain, the EU and US had raised against Zimbabwe previously: compensation paid to war-veterans in 1997; involvement of Zimbabwe in the Democratic Republic of Congo (DRC) war; relations between ZANU(PF) and the opposition MDC.

The report does not attempt to address habitat issues until page 31; yet the entire main text is only 83 pages long. Even after briefly addressing habitat issues in Chapters 3 and 4, the conclusion is foregone: that the government must allow outsiders to fix its internal politics before the UN or any other donor agrees to assist the people.

The application of framing theory can best be illustrated by looking at the selectivity of the report's findings and recommendations. In this case, the Tibaijuka mission had already been framed by Zimbabwe's detractors and, therefore, could not create its own frame. As a result, the findings and recommendations could only be those acceptable to those detractors who had already imposed illegal sanctions against the country.

Instead of putting responsibility on those who opposed Zimbabwe's land reform and imposed illegal sanctions on the country, the report uses agent deletion as a tactic, saying, 'The 2000 and 2002 elections and the fast-track land reform programme *triggered* the deterioration of relations with the international donor community and the start of isolation of Zimbabwe from the wide international community. It also prompted the imposition of targeted sanctions' (Tibaijuka 2005, 19).

This sets the frame. From there, it is not surprising that the very first finding the report makes is not on housing people but on the donor-demanded 'political dialogue' between the government and its opponents. The second finding is again not about housing but about the need for law reform. The third finding is again the donor demand for 'unlimited access' by external forces to the people and communities of Zimbabwe. The fourth and last finding is on donor-demanded 'governance,' where already the United Nations Economic Commission for Africa had already been induced to publish a report claiming lack of 'good governance' in Zimbabwe which had to be withdrawn because of its defects.

In an attempt to arrive at recommendations, the same selectivity prevailed.

The first recommendation is what all the detractors of the state were already demanding before the appointment of the mission: Stop Operation Murambatsvina.

The second recommendation reveals what the government is already trying to do without specifying what UN Habitat and other agencies in the 'humanitarian community' would undertake to do.

The third recommendation is not about habitat, but law reform, without any proof that it is lack of law reform that prevents UN Habitat or the mission from helping people in co-operation with the state.

The fourth recommendation is again the same donor-demanded political dialogue between the government and its foreign-sponsored opponents.

The fifth recommendation is not a recommendation but an allegation of bad governance. It alleges that the various parts or departments of the Government did not consult one another and agree on the operation. It also alleges that crimes were committed as part of the operation, making it necessary to recommend the criminal prosecution of the officers involved. One is impressed by the highly political, and even subversive, nature of the supposed recommendation.

The fifth recommendation falls within the framework of the Commonwealth Judicial Workshops of the 1990s. It is on human rights and the rule of law, seeking to categorise urban slum clearance as a violation of human rights, if not a crime against humanity. Since there is no global agreement on these doctrines, it is not clear what the purpose of the recommendation is supposed to be. Recommendation 7 regrets Zimbabwe's abandonment of the economic structural adjustment programme and urges the government to return to it in the name of macroeconomic reform. Just why Zimbabwe needs a UN mission and UN Habitat to be told this is not made clear. Was it the mission of this visit to restore the Economic Structural Adjustment Programme?

The eighth recommendation is a propaganda line from the opponents of land reform: instead of admitting that the opponents of Zimbabwe's African land reclamation movement are, in fact, supporters of the Rhodesian racist land tenure system which had benefited the British, these opponents want the world to believe that the Zimbabweans who have taken their land now discriminate against the Malawian farm workers who used to work for white farmers before land reform. So, Anna Tibaijuka allows Recommendation 8 relating to rural farm workers to be included in a report on urban slum clearance. Tibaijuka urges the Government of Zimbabwe to grant full citizenship to former migrant workers and their descendant who have no such legal status.

The ninth recommendation is the only one directed at the UN, but it was not seriously intended or honoured. Recommendation 10 merely returns to the donor demand for political dialogue between the government and its foreign-sponsored opponents as a prerequisite for 'international' acceptance. In other words, Tibaijuka is admitting that part of her mission is to reinforce the illegal sanctions against Zimbabwe under the guise of UN Habitat.

Recommendation 11 is a return to the search for punitive measures using all the donor-sponsored and donor-funded schemes such as the African Peer Review Mechanism (APRM).

Linear perspective explains this type of communication perfectly. Despite the over-use of the word *dialogue* in the report, the mission is not about dialogue or consultation. It is about the linear privilege of both fact-finding and choosing the facts to find.

The voices of reporters, NGOs and donors mobilised by the mission have been so pre-selected and primed that they drown even the alleged victims to be rescued by the mission. This is clear not only from the findings and recommendations but also from the over-reliance on the foreign-sponsored media and foreign-sponsored NGOs as sources of 'facts'. The regular demands made by these same sources prior to the mission are the very same ones that found their way into the report.

To use Romanyshyn's language, Zimbabwe was observed through a window whose levers and padlocks are all on one side. Those on that side decided who could and who could not go through. This window and its frame had been in the making for more than a decade.

Anna Tibaijuka, back in New York, handed her report to the very same powers behind the judicial workshops called 'Judicial Colloquia on the Domestic Application of International Human Rights Norms'. These powers were the United Kingdom and the US, who attempted to force the Security Council of the United Nations to put the report on their agenda.

Conclusion

How should we understand the Tibaijuka report as linear communication?

In *War of the Worlds*, Mark Slouka takes Romanyshyn's analysis of linear perspective further by examining its ethical implications. He gives the example of a woman who refused to express any judgement on proven murder cases and other incidents of violence and conflict. She said she needed to wait for the film versions of the cases or stories in order to make up her mind. And she was serious. Slouka's reading was that to this woman, mediated experience had become superior to real-world experience. Mediated experience had become more reliable than direct experience. And scripted media judgements were now superior to people's own judgements about their world. (Slouka 1995, 1–3). In the short-term analysis, people can read the Tibaijuka Report and deduce that the report was 'occasioned' by the actual Operation Murambatsvina that saw the slum clearance in Zimbabwe. What people may not obviously realise is that in its capturing and reporting of Operation Murambatsvina, the Tibaijuka report selected events, ordered them, highlighted some and suppressed others in order to construct its version of the operation that would suit outside interests. By the time of the Tibaijuka mission, it is clear that what has been written and broadcast by Zimbabwe's detractors was taken as superior to what can be observed on the ground. Hence, one ends up with more displaced persons in the report and the media stories it is based on than can be located on the ground. This does not matter in terms of this linear view. What has been reported about Zimbabwe in the anti-Zimbabwe media is superior to what can be verified on the ground.

So, in seeking to understand the hidden dimensions of the Tibaijuka report on Operation Murambatsvina, one needs to address the international power discourses that frame the South to control knowledge on what can be said of the South. This desire to control the South through 'reports' can ultimately be viewed as imperialist discourse, which in another context, Edward Said (1977) described as Orientalism.

In short, a crucial aspect to understanding some hidden dimensions of the physical Operation Murambatsvina can be achieved when one critically re-reads the verbal, visual and symbolic processes by which the Anna Tibaijuka report, named and described, the actual Operation Murambatsvina, which is the report's object of study. This chapter has analysed the report not so much to dismiss it entirely, but to show readers of it that in its mode of describing Murambatsvina, the report has been ideologically prevented from saying certain things; the report has been silenced and ends up saying more about Murambatsvina from what it *does not say* than from what it is forced to authorise. In its failure to disclose the most important causes and dimensions of Murambatsvina, the Tibaijuka report participates in undermining the quest for democracy in Zimbabwe.

Bibliography

Commonwealth Secretariat, Human Rights Unit. 1988. *Developing Human Rights Jurisprudence : The Domestic Application of International Human Rights Norms.*

Jervis, R. 1976. *Perception and Misperception in International Politics.* Princeton, New Jersey: Princeton University Press.

Johnson, P. and D. Martin. 1989. *Apartheid terrorism.* Report for the Commonwealth Committee of Foreign Ministers on Southern Africa.

Morgenthau, H.J. and K. Thompson. 1985. *Politics among Nations: The Struggle for Power and Peace.* New York: Alfred Knopf.

Romanyshyn, R.D. 1989. *Technology as Symptom and Dream.* London: Routledge.

Said, E. 1978. *Orientalism.* London: Vintage Books.

Slouka, M. 1995. *War of Worlds: Cyberspace and the High-tech Assault on Reality.* New York: Basic Books.

Tibaijuka A K. 2005. Report on the Fact-finding Mission to Zimbabwe to Assess the Scope and Impact of Operation Murambatsvina by the UN Special Envoy on Human Settlements Issues in Zimbabwe. Harare: July 18.

Notes on Contributors

Maurice Vambe is Associate Professor in the Department of English Studies, at UNISA where he teaches African literature. Vambe is the author of *African Oral Story telling tradition and the Zimbabwean Novel in English* (2004), and co-edited *Charles Mungoshi: A Critical Reader* (2006) with Memory Chirere. Vambe has also published numerous articles on Zimbabwean and African literature in English and in African Languages.

Alois Mlambo is Professor of history in the Department of Historical and Heritage Studies of the University of Pretoria. He has published numerous articles on Zimbabwe's social and economic history in scholarly journals in addition to books, including: *The Economic Structural Adjustment Programme: The Case of Zimbabwe, 1990-1995* (UZ Publications, 1997); and *White Immigration Into Rhodesia: From Occupation to Federation* (UZ Publications, 2002). He has recently edited *African Scholarly Publishing: Essays.* (African Books Collective, 2007).

David Moore is a Canadian now teaching at the University of KwaZulu-Natal in Durban, South Africa. He began his Ph.D research examining the construction of hegemony within Zimbabwe's nationalist struggles. He has continued studying Zimbabwean politics and history, as well as development theory more broadly. His most recent edited book is *The World Bank: Development, Poverty, Hegemony* (University of KwaZulu-Natal Press, 2007), and his latest publication on Zimbabwe is '"Intellectuals" Interpreting Zimbabwe's Primitive Accumulation: Progress to Market Civilisation?', *Safundi*, 8, 2 (April 2007), pp. 199-222.

Ashleigh Harris holds a Ph.D from the University of the Witswatersrand, South Africa. She has published in the fields of Zimbabwean and South African literature, feminism and African-American writing. She is currently a lecturer in the Department of English at Uppsala University, where she is temporary chair in British Literature until December 2009. She is presently working on a monograph on contemporary Zimbabwean Literature, media and political rhetoric.

Deborah Potts is a Senior Lecturer in the Geography Department of King's College London, having previously lectured for over 20 years at the School of Oriental and African Studies. She works in the broad research field of urbanisation and migration in sub-Saharan Africa, particularly southern Africa. She also works on land and environmental issues in the region in the context of political ecology. She has worked on Harare since 1985 in collaboration with Dr Chris Mutambirwa of the Geography Department of the University of Zimbabwe. Relevant recent publications include '"Restoring Order"? The interrelationships between Operation Murambatsvina in Zimbabwe and Urban Poverty, Informal Housing and Employment', *Journal of Southern African Studies* 32, 2 (2006): 273-91 and 'City life in Zimbabwe at a time of Fear and Loathing: urban planning, urban poverty and Operation Murambatsvina', in Murray, M. and G. Myers (eds) 2007. *Cities in Contemporary Africa*, Basingstoke: Palgrave.

Mickias Musiyiwa is a lecturer in literary theory, oral literature and African culture in the Department of African Languages & Literature at the University of Zimbabwe. His research interests are in African music, children's literature, culture, gender, and the arts in general. He has published several articles in peer-reviewed journals and chapters in edited books in these fields.

Beauty Vambe graduated from Belvedere Teachers College with a certificate in education, in which she majored in English and physical education. She has published on censorship in popular music of Zimbabwe. At present, she is studying for an LLB degree with UNISA. Her main areas of academic interests are Indigenous Law, Intellectual property and Human Rights Law.

Tinashe Chimedza is a Zimbabwean currently working and residing in Australia. He studied Social Inquiry at the University of Technology, Sydney and is especially interested in issues of citizenship and governance in Zimbabwe. He has previously worked with a diverse group of civil society organisations in Zimbabwe including the Zimbabwe National Students Union, the National Constitutional Assembly and the Crisis in Zimbabwe Coalition.

Tendai Chari is a media analyst and lecturer in Media Studies in the Department of English and Media Studies, University of Zimbabwe. Currently, he is based at the University of Fort Hare in South Africa, where he is pursuing a Ph.D in Media and Communication Studies. He has published several articles and book chapters on Media Ethics, Media and Democracy, Development Communication, Political Communication and Visual Communication.

Richard Nyamanhindi graduated from the University of Zimbabwe with a BA (Hons) in Economic History. He holds a Post-graduate Certificate in Education, an MA in African Economic History, a Post-graduate Diploma in Media Studies and Communication, and an MA in Communication and Media Studies. Currently he is a Teaching Assistant at the University of Zimbabwe, in the Department of English and Media Studies. His interests are in research and writing, with a particular focus on the influence of the media on African society and political communication.

Nhamo Mhiripiri is a Senior Lecturer in the Media and Society Studies department at the Midlands State University in Zimbabwe, where he was also the founding Acting Dean of the then Faculty of Arts and Social Sciences. He has previously worked as a researcher and writer for ZANU(PF), and has also lectured at the University of KwaZulu-Natal and the Zimbabwe Open University. He is currently revising his doctoral thesis with the University of KwaZulu-Natal. He has published a book and journal articles on film, cultural tourism and music copyright, and is also an award-winning fiction writer. Research for the paper included in this book was partly funded through the Midlands State University's Research Board and it was also peer-reviewed in the CODESRIA-funded Faculty of Social Sciences Seminar Series at MSU.

Tafataona Mahoso is a social commentator and the Executive Chairman of the Media and Information Commission in Zimbabwe. He is also a columnist for the state-owned weekly *The Sunday Mail*.